MEDIEVAL AND POST-MEDIEVAL DEVELOPMENT WITHIN BRISTOL'S INNER SUBURBS

edited by Martin Watts

55–60 ST THOMAS STREET, REDCLIFFE, BRISTOL: EXCAVATIONS IN 2006

by Peter Davenport, Roger Leech and Mike Rowe

26–28 ST THOMAS STREET, REDCLIFFE, BRISTOL: EXCAVATIONS IN 2002

by Martin Watts

HARBOURSIDE, BRISTOL: INVESTIGATIONS FROM 2003–2008

by Mary Alexander and Chiz Harward

CABOT HOUSE, DEANERY ROAD, BRISTOL: INVESTIGATIONS IN 2008

by Ray Holt and Roger Leech

D1354571

Cotswold Archaeology

Bristol and Gloucestershire Archaeological Report No. 7

By agreement with Cotswold Archaeology this report is distributed free
to members of the Bristol and Gloucestershire Archaeological Society
To accompany Volume 129 of the Society's *Transactions* for 2011

Cotswold Archaeology Bristol and Gloucestershire Archaeological Report No. 7

Published by Cotswold Archaeology
© Authors and Cotswold Archaeological Trust Ltd, 2011
Building 11, Kemble Enterprise Park, Cirencester, Gloucestershire GL7 6BQ

ISSN 1479-2389
ISBN 978-0-9553534-4-4

Cotswold Archaeology BAGAR series

1   **A Romano-British and Medieval Settlement Site at Stoke Road, Bishop's Cleeve, Gloucestershire**, by Dawn Enright and Martin Watts, 2002

2   **Later Prehistoric and Romano-British Burial and Settlement at Hucclecote, Gloucestershire**, by Alan Thomas, Neil Holbrook and Clifford Bateman, 2003

3   **Twenty-Five Years of Archaeology in Gloucestershire: a review of new discoveries and new thinking in Gloucestershire, South Gloucestershire and Bristol, 1979– 2004**, edited by Neil Holbrook and John Juřica, 2006

4   **Two Cemeteries from Bristol's Northern Suburbs**, edited by Martin Watts, 2006

5   **Prehistoric and Medieval Occupation at Moreton-in-Marsh and Bishop's Cleeve, Gloucestershire**, edited by Martin Watts, 2007

6   **Iron Age and Romano-British Agriculture in the North Gloucestershire Severn Vale**, edited by Neil Holbrook, 2008

7   **Medieval and Post-Medieval Development within Bristol's Inner Suburbs**, edited by Martin Watts, 2011

Series Editor: Martin Watts

Cover image: extract from 'The way from Canon's Marsh to the Butts, looking east', watercolour by T.L. Rowbotham, 1826 (M2540) © Bristol's Museums, Galleries and Archives.

Produced by Past Historic, Kings Stanley, Gloucestershire, GL10 3HW
Printed in Great Britain by Henry Ling Limited, Dorchester, DT1 1HD

FOREWORD

In some respects the title of this volume is misleading. All four sites reported herein were indeed located within historic suburbs of Bristol: two in the planned 12th-century suburb of Redcliffe, to the southeast of the medieval city; the other two to the southwest in the medieval district of Billeswick and in the vicinity of St Augustine's Abbey, also established in the 12th century, the church of which is now Bristol Cathedral. However, with the exception of a small part of the former abbey/Cathedral precinct uncovered at Harbourside, it is the lack of evidence for any substantial development at these sites throughout the medieval and post-medieval periods (up to the beginning of the 18th century) that provides a common theme.

The scarcity of evidence for medieval and post-medieval development at some of these sites is unsurprising. Both of the Billeswick sites, Cabot House and Harbourside, were in the ownership of the abbey or cathedral throughout this period, and were clearly of value as undeveloped land, either as parkland (as at Cabot House) or meadow (i.e. Canon's Marsh, south of the precinct at Harbourside). The dearth of evidence from the St Thomas Street sites in Redcliffe has been more unexpected, though this appears to corroborate documentary evidence suggesting that this part of the suburb remained something of a backwater into late post-medieval times. At nos 55–60, there was no evidence for anything more substantial than a few simple timber structures, perhaps used for drying cloth, until the beginning of the 18th century. At nos 26–28 there was no evidence for tenements until late into the post-medieval period and the site may well have been a part of a medieval grange, noted in the documentary record for the adjacent site to the south. The development of the first substantial buildings at both St Thomas Street sites, of new streets and terraces at Cabot House, and of the ropewalks and later industrial development of Canon's Marsh at Harbourside, all reflected the rapid expansion and building boom Bristol enjoyed in the 18th century, largely a result of the city's involvement in the Atlantic trade.

It was Bristol's much more recent building boom of the 2000s that saw redevelopment of these four sites and the opportunity for their archaeological investigation. Unfortunately, funding was not available subsequently to complete post-excavation work on the records and finds from nos 26–28 St Thomas Street. The summary of results in this volume has been produced by Cotswold Archaeology to complement those from nos 55–60, the sites being directly opposite each other, but it should be made clear that this summary is based on preliminary work only, and that detailed analysis of the stratigraphic record and important assemblages of finds and biological material from this site remains outstanding.

Martin Watts
Head of Publications, Cotswold Archaeology
December 2011

CONTENTS

Foreword iii

Contents... v

Abstracts vii

55–60 St Thomas Street, Redcliffe, Bristol

Introduction 1

Excavation Results 5

The Documentary Evidence 24

The Finds 26

The Biological and Geoarchaeological Evidence 45

Discussion 54

Acknowledgements 66

Bibliography 67

26–28 St Thomas Street, Redcliffe, Bristol................................. 73

Harbourside, Bristol

Introduction 79

Results 82

The Finds 94

The Biological Evidence 107

Discussion 109

Acknowledgements 116

Bibliography 116

Cabot House, Deanery Road, Bristol

Introduction 121

Results 125

Finds Summary... 133

The Documentary Evidence 133

Discussion 140

Acknowledgements 142

Bibliography 143

ABSTRACTS

Nos 55–60 St Thomas Street, Redcliffe, Bristol: Excavations in 2006

Excavations in 2006 at the corner of St Thomas Street and Mitchell Lane in Redcliffe revealed evidence for six tenements of medieval origin, which survived through into the 20th century as nos 55–60 St Thomas Street. During excavation the tenements were recorded as four plots, reflecting episodes of amalgamation and subsequent subdivision. The earliest remains appeared to be of mid 13th-century date, a hundred years after the documented laying out of the planned suburbs of Redcliffe and Temple Fees, suggesting that this area was slow to develop compared to more northerly parts of the suburb closer to Bristol Bridge. One boundary between tenements was part of the boundary between Redcliffe and Temple parishes, and was marked by a substantial drain. The tenements seem to have remained largely open and unoccupied, with no evidence for any substantial streetside buildings until the later 17th century. However, the area was clearly in use during the late medieval and post-medieval periods, with numerous fencelines, pits and some timber structures, including parallel beam slots that may have been the remains of drying racks for cloth, a trade with documented historical associations with this part of the city. There was also some evidence for medieval ironworking and post-medieval copper-alloy casting in the vicinity. Phases of activity were separated by substantial horizons of dumped material, perhaps deposited to raise the ground level periodically in this area of former marsh.

Substantial archaeological remains survived from development that commenced in the late 17th or early 18th century, and intensified throughout the 18th and 19th centuries, reflecting Bristol's booming trade and growing wealth at that time. Stone-built streetside buildings were erected, respecting the tenement structure established several centuries earlier, and their rear gardens were rapidly filled in with extensions to houses, and outbuildings and yards. In the 18th century the properties were a mix of commercial and domestic use, including public houses at nos 55 and 60. The early 19th century saw the establishment of an iron foundry at nos 56–57, which by the mid 20th century had expanded across the whole site, reflecting the early 20th-century industrialisation of the suburb.

Nos 26–28 St Thomas Street, Redcliffe, Bristol: Excavations in 2002

Excavations in 2002 at the corner of St Thomas Street and Three Queen's Lane in Redcliffe found evidence of activity from the medieval period onwards, but with little evidence for any formal subdivision of the area until the late post-medieval period, when substantial streetside buildings were constructed within tenements fronting St Thomas Street, many with large stone-lined tanks to the rear. This report presents a summary of the preliminary results only from this excavation.

Harbourside, Bristol: Investigations from 2003–2008

A series of evaluation trenches and two open areas were excavated within the Harbourside redevelopment area between 2003 and 2008. These revealed evidence for medieval, post-medieval and later activity within part of the former precinct of St Augustine's Abbey (the church of which is now Bristol Cathedral), and within the western part of Canon's Marsh. Borehole investigations revealed little evidence for exploitation of the floodplain prior to establishment of the abbey in the 12th century. At the northern end of the site, the remains of several small medieval buildings and gardens were revealed next to a lane leading southwards to the precinct gate to Canon's Marsh, and to either side of a channel that was part of the abbey's water management system. In the post-medieval and later periods, houses were rebuilt to either side of the lane at its junction with Anchor Lane, which ran to the south of the former precinct boundary. These buildings were prebendal properties of the Cathedral's Dean and Chapter and included a shop, from the remains of which fragments of glass phials were retrieved.

Within Canon's Marsh, the remains of 17th-century sea banks protecting the marsh were recorded and the remains of 18th and 19th-century industrial buildings were observed, including those of a ropewalk. The arrival of the railway in the 20th century saw Canon's Marsh given over to transit sheds and sidings, and the demolition of all buildings along Anchor Lane, which was relocated to the present position of Anchor Road.

Cabot House, Deanery Road, Bristol: Investigations in 2008

Investigations in 2008 at Cabot House included the excavation of two areas of former 18th-century housing development. Borehole investigations of deposits within the infilled valley, over which the housing development had been constructed, revealed little evidence of exploitation of the area during the Neolithic period. There was also little evidence for any activity up to the 18th century either, the area having been parkland belonging to St Augustine's Abbey (and later Bristol Cathedral) during the medieval and post-medieval periods. However, the recorded remains of the former 18th and 19th-century properties that preceded Cabot House provide insights into the construction, use and changing status of the buildings in this part of the city, for which detailed documentary evidence also survives.

55–60 ST THOMAS STREET, REDCLIFFE, BRISTOL: EXCAVATIONS IN 2006

by Peter Davenport, Roger Leech and Mike Rowe

with contributions by
Angela Aggujaro, Edward Besly, Dana Challinor, Reg Jackson, Julie Jones,
E.R. McSloy, Elaine L. Morris, Hannah Russ, Sylvia Warman and Keith Wilkinson

INTRODUCTION

Between January and May 2006 Cotswold Archaeology (CA) carried out an archaeological excavation on land at the junction of St Thomas Street and Mitchell Lane, Redcliffe, Bristol (centred on NGR: ST 59237257; Fig. 1), on behalf of Blenheim House Construction Ltd for CB Richard Ellis Investors Ltd. The project was designed to mitigate the impact of the construction of a five-storey office building with associated basement car parking. The archaeological potential of the site had been previously investigated by desk-top study (BaRAS 2002a) and evaluation (BaRAS 2002b) and the combined results of these investigations suggested that there was good survival of a sequence of occupation dating from at least the 13th century AD. Given the archaeological potential of the site, the planning application was agreed subject to the condition that a programme of archaeological work took place, comprising excavation and a borehole survey (Fig. 2). This report describes the results of those investigations.

This site lies within the parish of Redcliffe on the floodplain of the River Avon. The upper geological deposits formed of estuarine alluvium were encountered at the base of the excavations. The underlying solid geology is recorded as Triassic Redcliffe Sandstone and Keuper Marl (BGS 1974), which current usage refers to as Mercia Mudstone. The ground surface before excavation was level and lay at a height of approximately 8.5m AOD.

Historical and archaeological background

Development of the Redcliff and Temple Fees in the 12th century is the earliest known use of this part of the Avon floodplain, and resulted in the formation of a suburb that was to rival in size the built-up area of the town. A fee was an area of lordship, which could be made profitable through rents. The Redcliff Fee was developed by Robert Fitzharding, being part of his manor of Bedminster (Cronne 1946, 32–3). The two main streets of this development were St Thomas Street and Redcliff Street; the latter was the principal route to the south, towards Fitzharding's manor of Bedminster. Each street was laid out with burgage plots to either side, those on the west of Redcliff Street stretching to the Avon. Dendrochronological dating of structural timbers from the excavations at Dundas Wharf (no.1, Fig. 1) has shown that the west side of Redcliff Street was being developed from c. 1123–33 and that quays were being built by 1147–8 (Nicholson and Hillam 1987, 141).

The Temple Fee was granted by Robert Earl of Gloucester to the Knights Templar between 1128 and 1148 (Taylor 1875, 27–78). The building of Temple church followed, together

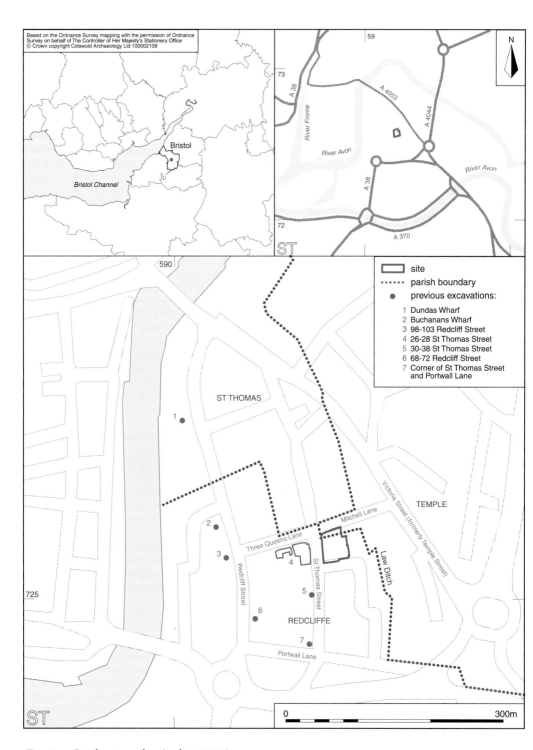

Fig. 1   Site location plan (scale 1:5000)

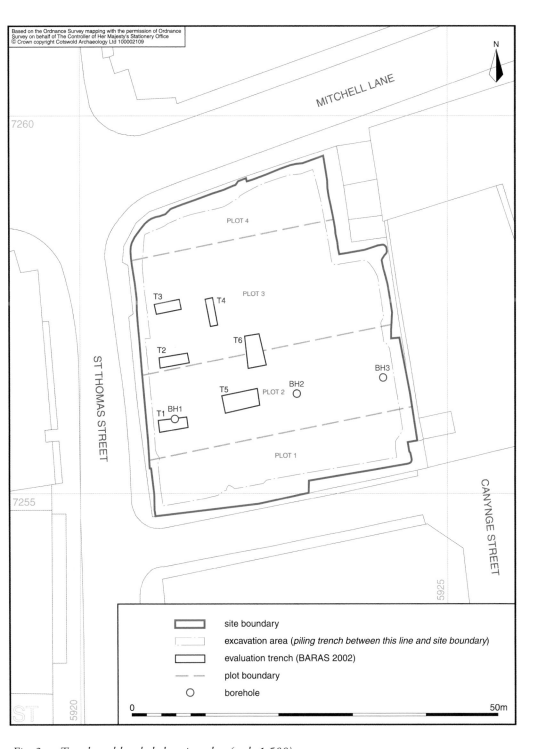

Fig. 2   Trench and borehole location plan (scale 1:500)

with the setting out of Temple Street and the subdivision of the land either side into burgage plots. The boundary between the two Fees was called the Law Ditch (a common name for the early boundary ditches in Bristol), which also served as a drain and open sewer for the tenements on both sides (Fig. 1). Each burgage plot from ditch to thoroughfare was about 10 to 12 'poles' in length (a 'pole' being approximately 5m). The majority of the site was in the former Redcliff Fee, however the northern end (Plot 4, Fig. 2) was formerly part of a western extension of Temple Fee that is known to have existed in the vicinity of Mitchell Lane (Fig. 1). The course of the Law Ditch therefore crossed the northern part of the site from east to west, between Plots 3 and 4. Like the Law Ditch, Mitchell Lane was probably part of a plan agreed between the lords of the two Fees.

The earliest map to depict this area in any detail is Smith's map of 1568, which shows this part of St Thomas Street as developed. Millerd's plan of 1673 shows St Thomas Street frontage fully developed and two buildings fronting Mitchell Lane (Fig. 3). Millerd's revised plan of *c.* 1715 shows no change, and neither do Rocque's map of 1743 and Donn's map of 1773 (BaRAS 2002a, 5). In the numbering system introduced by James Sketchley in the first Bristol Directory (Sketchley 1775), the house plots that fall within the excavated area are nos 54–60 St Thomas Street (house numbers are taken from BRO: Goad 1887 Fire Insurance Plan; Fig. 6). The widening of Mitchell Lane in 1905 (BRO: Building Plan Book 47, fo.68) truncated almost all of no. 54, and the remaining properties on St Thomas Street also lost their frontages to street widening in *c.* 1938. Later uses of the site included a garage fronting St Thomas Street. Prior to development the site had been

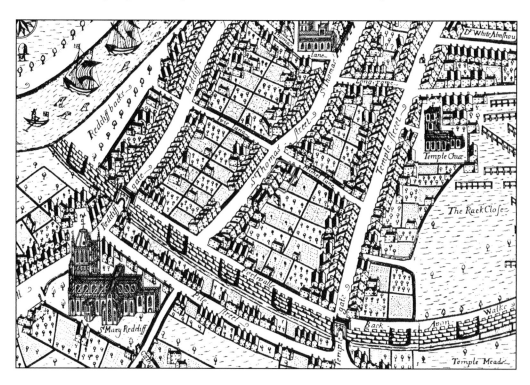

Fig. 3   Extract from Millerd's plan of 1673, with site in outline

levelled and was used as a car park. Detailed histories of excavated tenements appear below (*The documentary evidence*).

Excavation methodology

A 1m-wide trench was excavated around the perimeter of the site to a depth of *c.* 0.5m to insert sheet piling (Fig. 2). This was undertaken by a mechanical excavator with a toothless grading bucket, under archaeological supervision. Archaeological features exposed in the trench were excavated and recorded with the same methodology as the main excavations. Once the sheet piling had been installed, modern surface material and overburden were excavated mechanically from the main excavation area. The depth of overburden removed was up to 0.2m across the site, with some deeper areas where modern intrusions were removed. The archaeological features thus exposed were hand-excavated to the bottom of stratified archaeological deposits. Where widespread homogeneous deposits were identified, these were mechanically removed under archaeological supervision. Petrochemical contamination from the former garage prevented excavation in an area near to the St Thomas Street frontage. The presence of this contamination slowed the removal of spoil from the site, resulting in the excavation area being dug in two halves.

For the borehole survey, three boreholes were drilled (Fig. 2) to examine the Pleistocene and Holocene layers below the level of excavation. Drilling was abandoned at the depth that fluid sands were encountered (up to 7m). The cores were processed off-site and a detailed report is included (see *Borehole stratigraphy*, below).

Following excavation, the site data were assessed for their significance, and further analysis was undertaken in accordance with the work specified in the Post-Excavation Assessment and Updated Project Design. The results form the basis of this report.

EXCAVATION RESULTS

Archaeological remains were found across the whole of the excavated area. Three principal periods of activity, each subdivided into two, were identified through analysis of the stratigraphic sequence, dated by the artefactual evidence:

Period 1a: medieval (13th to early 14th centuries)
Period 1b: late medieval (14th to 15th centuries)
Period 2a: early post-medieval (15th to late 16th centuries)
Period 2b: post-medieval (late 16th to 17th centuries)
Period 3a: later 17th to early 19th centuries
Period 3b: 19th to mid 20th centuries

During excavation, the site was divided into four plots, numbered 1 to 4, south to north. These were based on substantial boundaries evident from the archaeological remains, and provide the framework used for describing the results as they could be recognised from all but the very earliest levels, although detailed analysis and historic mapping suggest that these plots had a complex history of division and amalgamation. The series of horizontal deposits that formed horizons between the principal periods are not shown on the site plans. Much of the ceramic dating is referenced to the Bristol Pottery Type (BPT) series (see *Pottery*, below).

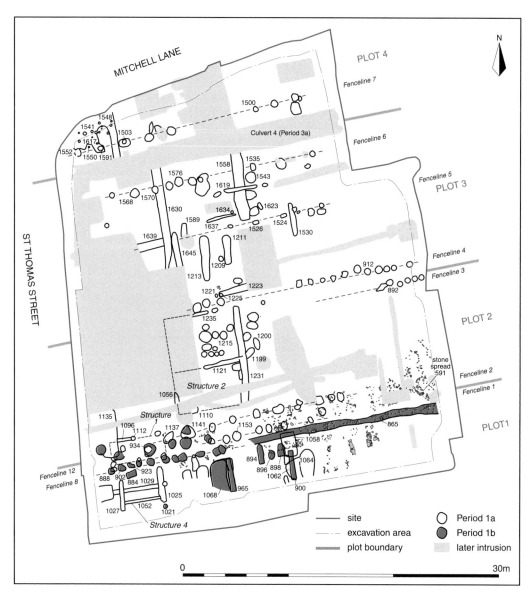

Fig. 4   Periods 1a and 1b (13th to 15th centuries) (scale 1:350)

Period 1a: medieval (13th to early 14th centuries) (Fig. 4)

Trampled alluvial clays pre-dated the earliest activity, which comprised a number of pits, postholes and gullies, some representing ephemeral buildings. The earliest plot boundaries were defined by post-built fences. With a very few exceptions, the pottery was of types current in the 12th and 13th centuries, including Ham Green 'A' wares (BPT 26), Minety wares (BPT 18, BPT 84) and coarseware types BPT 114, BPT 32 and BPT 46. Ham

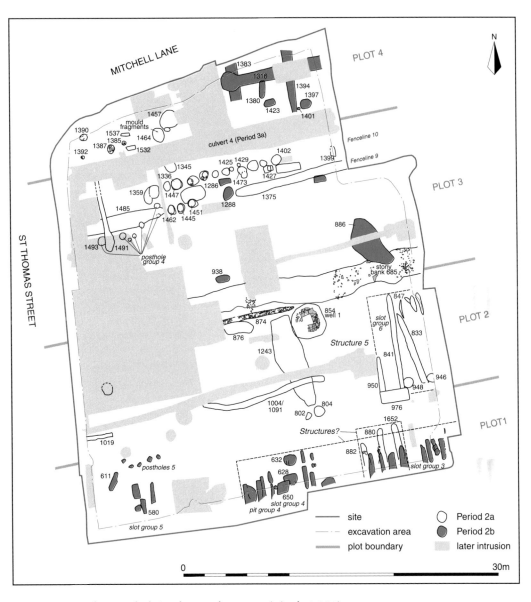

Fig. 5   Periods 2a and 2b (15th to 17th centuries) (scale 1:350)

Green 'B' type (BPT 27) in later jug styles, late forms of Bristol glazed ware (BPT 118) and occasional Bristol types BPT 121 and BPT 128, suggest the late 13th to early 14th centuries for the infilling of features. Some stratigraphic relationships between features suggest that not everything in this period was strictly contemporary, and some features may well be of earlier 13th-century date. The deposits that sealed activity from this period (Horizon 1) were of mid 14th-century date.

The alluvial clay silts at the base of the excavation lay at approximately 6.8m AOD. A

7

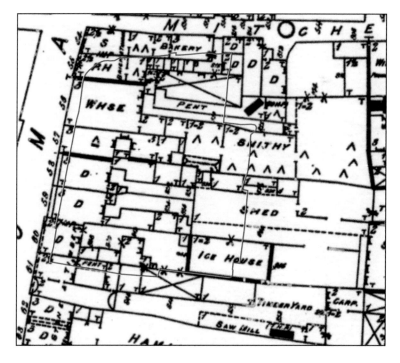

Fig. 6   Extract from the Goad 1887 Fire Insurance Plan (BRO)

series of trampled and disturbed alluvial clays above the alluvium, with an upper surface at between 6.8m and 7m AOD, pre-dated almost all of the features of Period 1a. Layer 1563, of red-brown silty clay, covered an area south of Fenceline 6 and either side of the drain gully 1630, which post-dated it. Also pre-dating the plot divisions was a shallow scoop 1582, cut by a posthole of Fenceline 6. Layer 1563 and scoop 1582 contained 12th to 13th-century pottery. Above this, silty clay 974 was recorded across most of the site. The equivalent layer 925 from the piling trench was cut by postholes of Fenceline 3. Both contained pottery of mid to late 13th-century date, animal bone and charcoal.

These layers were cut by a number of pits of various sizes, and gullies. The profile and generally shallow depth of these features strongly suggested that they had suffered truncation. Some grouping was apparent, the most obvious of which were the lines of postholes for timber fences, some of which showed signs of postpipes.

Two pits (686 and 688) and a scoop, only seen in section on the east side of Plot 1, could not be allocated to Period 1a or 1b specifically as, although they cut the earliest occupation layers, they were not sealed by any other contexts. However, 13th to 14th-century pottery collected from the fills exposed in section suggests the earlier period, as does a fragment of roof tile from pit 688.

Plot 1
Fenceline 1 ran east/west, 5–6m north of the southern edge of the excavation. It comprised postholes at varying distances and with variable depths, ranging from 0.06m to 0.45m. All but one contained substantial sandstone fragments or slabs at the base. The pottery

suggests abandonment in the 13th or early 14th century. Just to the north, Fenceline 2 extended further to both west and east, and contained 11 larger and more regularly spaced postholes. The fills were similar to Fenceline 1, as was the pottery dating. Postholes 1141 and 1137 contained post-impressions and possible packing.

A group of postholes and beam slot 1096 at the western end of Fencelines 1 and 2 appeared to comprise part of a rectangular structure (Structure 1), 5m east/west by 2m north/south, although the fills were very similar to the fencelines and may have been directly associated. The structure was cut to the west by north/south gully 1135.

In the south-west corner of Plot 1, Structure 4 was represented by a pair of gullies, 1029 and 1052, cut by parallel gullies 1025 and 1027, and posthole 1054. All were very shallow, less than 0.1m deep. The slots were mostly flat-bottomed with vertical sides and very straight, suggesting that they were beam slots. The north/south gullies were very similar to the 'slot groups' in this area in Period 1b (see below).

South of Fenceline 1 were several shallow pits and gullies. Most notable were pits 1058 (subrectangular, 1.2m x 2.2m) and two intercutting oval pits, 1062 and 1064, between 2.1m and 2.4m in width. All were 0.4m deep with gently sloping sides and flattish bases. These pits produced the majority of the animal bone from this period. The pottery suggests infilling in the mid 13th century.

Plot 2

Fenceline 3 consisted of a short east/west run of five small circular pits at the east side of the site. With Fenceline 4 (below) it marked the boundary between Plots 2 and 3 in this period. These pits were very close-set at only 0.55m centre to centre. Four of the pits were identical in diameter (0.4m) and depth (0.1m). The fifth (892), cutting a shallow scoop forming the western terminal of the eastern part of the row, was bigger and 0.33m deep.

A substantial north/south gully, 1231, *c.* 0.6m wide with vertical sides and a flat base, with smaller gullies 1121/1199, 1056, 1110 and 1235, suggested a rectangular enclosure measuring 6m x 8.5m (Structure 2). Nearly half of this structure had been truncated by modern disturbance. All the gullies had contained sandstone rubble in a yellowish-brown clay with chalky/limey patches and gravel, suggesting a timber-and-daub or a cob-type construction. Gully 1121 cut the fill of gully 1231, but if gully 1231 was a foundation for an earth wall, then gully 1121 could have been a drain passing through it, rather than post-dating it.

Occupying the northern half of Structure 2 was a close-packed group of pits forming a series of possible parallel alignments. It is unclear if these fulfilled a structural function; only pit 1215 had a profile and stone packing suggestive of a posthole, and was also by far the deepest pit. Five other pits, oval in plan, lay east of the supposed wall line of gully 1231. Dating evidence from most of these features was of the 13th-century, and was sealed by deposit 807, also of 13th-century date. Pit 1200 to the east of gully 1231 was not associated, as it was not sealed by deposit 807 and contained 14th-century pottery.

Plot 3

The southern boundary of Plot 3 was defined by Fenceline 4. Fenceline 6 may have been an early northern boundary (before it was moved to the line of Culvert 4). Fenceline 5 divided Plot 3 into two, a property boundary that reappeared in later periods.

The fills of the postholes of Fenceline 4 were similar to Fenceline 3, but with a high proportion of sandstone rubble. The greyer fills of two postholes (also noted in some Fenceline 3 postholes) may have derived from an overlying stony bank (685: see Period 2, below).

Finds were predominantly centred on the 13th century; one sherd of 16th or 17th-century pottery found in posthole 922 is assumed to be intrusive.

Fenceline 5, 6.5m north of Fenceline 4, was made up of six widely spaced postholes and a straight gully (1639), separated from the postholes by a gap of 5m. The two rectangular postholes in the centre (1524 and 1526) could have been gateposts. The range of pottery recovered from the fills suggests a 13th-century date for abandonment. The postholes and gully were overlain by layer 1404, the boundary of Periods 1a and 1b.

Fenceline 6 ran east/west, just south of the later Culvert 4. The postholes were irregularly spaced, close together at the west end and further apart at the east end, and with varied fills. Posthole 1568 had a large flat stone in the base, and posthole 1535 had two large possible packing stones. Pottery gives a date of the 13th century, apart from 14th to 15th-century pottery from posthole 1576, which may be intrusive from the overlying pit 1447 from Period 2a. A large gully, 1630, ran northwards across Plot 3 with a distinct fall to the north, where it was cut away by Culvert 4 (Period 3a). It was probably a drain that pre-dated Fenceline 6 and emptied into a predecessor of Culvert 4. To the east, parallel gully 1558 had vertical sides and a flat base, and at up to 0.54m this was probably a robbed masonry structure. Its slope down to the north, where it was also cut by Culvert 4, suggested it was a drain, like gully 1630.

To the south of Fenceline 6, a series of postholes and gullies, some of which crossed the alignment of Fenceline 5, may represent timber structures post-dating the abandonment of Fenceline 5, although they did not form any coherent plan.

Pit 1543, to the north of slot 1619, was flat-bottomed and vertical-sided, just under 1m across and 0.37m deep. Sitting neatly in the base of the pit was a wooden barrel base. This was buried by a 0.2m-thick layer of yellow, sandy mortar, topped by a dump of dark brown clay silt with much carbonised wood. No side timbers survived (Fig. 7). Pottery suggests a 13th-century date or later for the infilling. The fills of postholes 1634 and 1623 contained mortar, perhaps due to their proximity to pit 1543, suggesting that they were contemporary. The pottery from the postholes was of the early 14th century.

Fig. 7   Wooden barrel base in pit 1543, Plot 3, Period 1a (scale 0.3m)

Plot 4

As with Plot 3, there was a line of postholes (Fenceline 7) in Plot 4 running parallel to Culvert 4, with a central gap caused by later disturbance. Depths averaged 0.22m, and posthole 1546 showed evidence of a possible postpipe (1503) and contained large packing stones.

North of Fenceline 7 in the north-west corner of the site was a group of 15 small postholes. This group of postholes, and postholes 1552 and 1591 at the west end of Fenceline 7, were sealed by deposits 1540 and 1541, composed of successive lenses of clay, burnt clay and carbonised wood only 0.06m thick in total. One of the lenses contained a smithing hearth bottom, providing evidence of ironworking. The oak charcoal from here, unlike that from elsewhere, suggests that these deposits were the residue from iron smelting (*The wood charcoal*, below).

Horizon 1 (not shown on plan), composed of clayey silts, clays and loams, overlay all the features of this phase. The pottery from this horizon was all of 12th to 14th-century date, with some mid 14th-century wares. The horizon overall was 0.3m thick. The layers generally extended across the whole of each area of excavation, and where there was not a direct relationship, could be linked from area to area by a common level and character.

Period 1b: late medieval (14th to 15th centuries) (Fig. 4)

The datable material from this period was not significantly different from Period 1a, but the stratigraphic succession and depth of deposits suggest the later dating given here. Features assigned to this period were sparse, and were limited to Plots 1 and 2.

It seems that the northern boundary of Plot 1 was redefined as Fenceline 8, and a shorter parallel fence (Fenceline 12) immediately to the north, suggesting a slight shift of the principal boundary of about 1m to the south. Dating suggests these features are 14th-century or later.

Fenceline 8 consisted of eleven postholes to the west, with rectangular pit 884 possibly associated, and a stone-packed gully (865) to the east. Four of the postholes contained the remains of post-packing. The fill of posthole 902 contained a fragment of tap slag, indicative of iron smelting. Gully 865 was the foundation trench for a boundary wall, packed with unmortared flat and roughly coursed stones. To the east it extended beyond the edge of excavation.

Fenceline 12 was made up of seven postholes which superseded both Fencelines 1 and 2. Relatively large stone fragments for post-packing were common. It defined only a small section of the boundary, which may elsewhere have been linked to gully 865 or marked in some way that left no recognisable trace.

To the south of this boundary were four linear slots aligned north/south, and a posthole. The fills were similar grey silts with gravel, but slot 900 also contained rubble. The slots were similar in size and alignment to Period 1a slots 1025 and 1027 to the west. Slots 894 and 898, closer to the northern boundary and flanking posthole 896, were equally shallow and slightly wider than the other slots. Pottery was sparse but suggested a mid 13th to 14th-century date. The function of these slots was unclear, but they may have been structural.

Slot 965 was cut into the top of a large oval or subrectangular pit, 1068. Despite its size it was only 0.17m deep. Its fill was dark and contained oyster and mussel shell, animal bone and charcoal, suggesting domestic waste. There appears to have been a connection between these two features as the slot followed the outline and depth of the side of the pit. The only other feature of this period was isolated posthole 1021.

The demolition of the stone wall within gully 865 was indicated by stone scatter 591, which spread across Plot 1 and the southern part of Plot 2. It was not particularly dense, except for where it lay to either side of gully 865. This layer sealed slots 898 and 900 and was covered by Horizon 2, which divided features of this period from those of Period 2a.

Period 2a: early post-medieval (15th to late 16th centuries) (Fig. 5)

The beginning of this period was represented by the dumping of layers of silty clay up to 0.26m thick (Horizon 2) over the earlier layers and features. A high level of residuality was present in this period with over half the pottery of medieval date. Abundant Malvern Chase redwares (BPT 197) suggest that the main focus for activity was earlier than *c.* 1600, although the presence of Somerset glazed wares, including BPT 280 and BPT 96, extends the period to the mid or later 16th century.

Plot 1

At the south-east corner of the site, three slots (880, 882 and 1652) projected northwards from the edge of excavation. The slots were only 0.15m deep and filled with rubble and silt, suggesting that they were structural, perhaps for sill beams supporting a small structure about 4m across. A 16th-century date is indicated from pottery from two of the slots. No other features of this period were apparent.

Plot 2

The southern boundary of Plot 2 was inferred from the southern limit of a number of slots at the eastern edge of excavation and from two pits, 804 and 802. The northern edge was marked by a stony bank (685), built directly over Horizon 2, running more or less over former Fenceline 4. Stone-filled gully 874, along the southern edge of the bank, followed the alignment of the earlier Fenceline 3.

Bank 685 may have been a metalled path running from St Thomas Street towards the rear of the tenements. It was 2.5m wide at the east end, truncated to 1.5m at the west end. Its crown was over 0.5m above its base (Fig. 8) and it was formed with a clay core, 879. Stone and silt from the eroded bank (878) was cut by a straight gully (874), 0.15m deep in the side of the bank, which appeared to have been dug to redefine the boundary. Its fill contained a lot of sandstone rubble fragments and pink mortar. The gully was cut into by a kidney-shaped pit (876) of rounded profile and filled with clean yellow clay, possibly the remains of a clay storage pit.

At the east end of Plot 2 was a group of long straight gullies, with some pits, postholes and short, irregular gullies. These were probably the remains of the ground beams and posts of a timber building (Structure 5). The fills of all the gullies were similar silty clays, apart from gully 950, which was packed with stone. The two large round postholes (946 and 948) were 0.4m deep with very stony fills. Pottery was of the range 12th to 15th centuries. Cutting across the southern end of gullies 841 and 950 was a 1m-deep rectangular pit (976), packed with stone rubble.

Pit 1243, by far the largest feature from this period, ran across the full width of Plot 2. It was flat-bottomed and steep-sided, up to 0.89m deep, with a shallow shelf at the top, extending its width to the west by another metre or so. The feature cut eroded bank material (878) and was therefore dug some time after the bank construction. Its thin basal fill was a mix of a reddish brown clay, pink mortar and sandstone roof tiles, separated from a series of upper fills by a thin layer of stone-free reddish, silty clay. The upper fills were

Fig. 8   Longitudinal section though stony bank 685, Plot 2/3, Period 2a (scale 1m)

predominantly ceramic tile and brick, pink mortar and sandstone roof tiles in a reddish silty clay. Despite the presence of residual 13th to 14th-century pottery, a few sherds of 16th-century pottery and a piece of clay tobacco pipe of 16th or 17th-century date from the upper fills suggest a late Period 2a to 2b date for these fills, which is consistent with the stratigraphic sequence and with the type of mortar present. The purpose of such a large feature was unclear. Despite containing building debris, it did not appear to be structural and nothing in the character of its fill indicated its purpose.

Well 1 cut into the north-east side of pit 1243. It was built with walls of flat sandstone slabs (854) set in a pinkish mortar tightly lining the well cut and leaving a shaft of 0.9m^2 but of unknown depth. Following the infilling of the well shaft, the stone lining was robbed to a depth of *c.* 0.4m, leaving a cone that was filled with a series of dumps.

There was no dating evidence from the well or its infilling or robbing, but it post-dated the infilling of pit 1243. The very close similarity between the fills of pit 1243 and the construction materials of Well 1 suggest that both could be derived from the same source, with the pit being filled in to facilitate the construction of Well 1, which would therefore be dated to the late 16th or early 17th century. The eastern end of gully 874 was probably filled in at the same time, as the fills were nearly identical. The gully was clearly a boundary feature but it was not obvious whether there was any functional relationship with pit 1243.

A sinuous gully (1004/1091) running east/west just north of the Plot 1/2 boundary, cut across infilled pit 1243. However, it was not sealed by anything earlier than late Period 3 layers. It most closely resembled a drainage gully but was not clearly related to any other feature. It contained pottery of the 13th and 14th centuries but its relationship to pit 1243 means this pottery must have been residual.

Plot 3
There was no evidence for subdivision of Plot 3 in this period. Fenceline 10 seemed to be a replacement for Fenceline 6, following it exactly but stopping a few metres short at either end.

The 11 postholes in Fenceline 10 were quite large but relatively shallow; the exception was posthole 1402, at the east end, at 0.45m deep. A small, squarish pit, 1399, near the eastern edge of excavation may have been a part of this fence. The main fenceline was augmented by two smaller postholes, 1425 and 1429, and postholes 1359, 1427 and 1473 had been replaced or reinforced at some point. The pottery suggests a 16th-century date for backfilling of these posts, and their lack of post-pipes and homogeneous character indicate that this would refer to demolition rather than construction. The common occurrence of 13th to 15th-century pottery might indicate a 15th-century construction date.

Fenceline 9 formed the south side of a double boundary with Fenceline 10, with a 2m gap between. Fenceline 9 was defined by two slots, 1375 and 1485, both slightly V-shaped in profile with a steeper south side. The profiles suggest post-trenches, with the posts set against the more vertical south edges. The distance between their terminals was *c.* 6m. The western half of the gap between featured three postholes (1445, 1451 and 1462). The datable material recovered from the trenches and postholes is of 16th-century date, while much residual material suggests construction in the 15th century. Post-dating the infilling of gully 1485 were three of seven postholes of unknown function (Posthole Group 4).

One of the latest features in Period 2a (if not actually later) was gully 1491. This feature, with a bulbous southern end, ran northwards to the later Culvert 4. It cut through the infilled gully 1485 and posthole 1493. It is presumed to run into a drain replaced by Culvert 4 of Period 3a. It was sealed by deposits containing 18th-century and modern pottery.

Plot 4

In the north-west corner of Plot 4 was a scatter of postholes or similar features. Posthole 1387 had large flat stones in the base and many large fragments of stone rubble in its fill, suggesting packing and a post-pad. Close by were postholes 1392 and 1385, and two rectangular postholes, 1537 and 1532. These features may have related to the pits described below, and were infilled in the 16th century.

Two notable pits lay to the east of these features. Pit 1457 was roughly circular and flat-bottomed, only 0.1m deep but 1.75m across. Its fill was a dark, orangey brown, friable sandy clay with much charcoal, suggestive of soil that had been subject to a lot of heat, perhaps the rake-out from a hearth or oven. It is not clear whether the pit edges and base were affected by heating, but this might have been an oven or hearth base. There was no evidence for any associated structure but the area immediately north and east was truncated by later activity, which may have destroyed such evidence. Next to it was pit 1464, bowl-shaped in profile and 0.43m deep. Its fill contained some stones that had been reddened by heat and showed carbon staining but it had no evidence of *in situ* heating, and it may have been associated with the same activity as pit 1457. A total of 176 clay mould fragments for casting metal cauldrons was retrieved from pit 1464 (a few fragments from layer 1410 into which the pit was cut are considered intrusive). Dating, both by typology of the cauldron and the associated pottery, suggests a 15th-century date for the pit fill. A similar-sized and shaped pit (1345) occurred just south of these features in Plot 3, partly removed by the later Culvert 4, but showed no evidence of heating.

Period 2b: post-medieval (late 16th to 17th centuries) (Fig. 5)

A discontinuous layer of silty clay (Horizon 3) sealed Period 2a features in Plots 1, 3 and 4, and most features ascribed to Period 2b were cut into this. It was not present in the central area of Plot 2 and the southern half of Plot 3, but very few Period 2b features were found in those areas. Where present, Horizon 3 was 0.2m to 0.3m thick. Pottery from this horizon was of 16th to 17th-century date, including cups in the Cistercian ware tradition (BPT 93 and BPT 275). Some residual 14th and 15th-century material came from the layers beneath, and this horizon may represent deposits reworked by gardening activity.

Plot 1

In the centre of the plot, two rounded pits (628 and 632) cut into the soils of Horizon 3 and shared a fill of pale yellow sandy silt similar to those of some of Slot Group 3 (see below). Pit 628 was cut by pit 650 associated with Slot Group 4. Pottery from these pits has a fairly wide date range of 15th to 17th century.

This area was otherwise dominated by a row of straight north/south gullies, mostly running off under the southern edge of the excavation and therefore of unknown length. They fell into three groups in plan, although the gap between the central and western ones was partly due to later disturbance.

Slot Group 3 contained eight slots, all aligned north/south (a ninth was seen as a fragment in the eastern edge of excavation). Three at the east end were complete, being 1.5m to 2m long. The others continued into the southern section. The northern ends of the slots were all *c.* 2.5m from the southern edge of excavation. Slot Group 4 was similar, and contained five slots. Aligned with them was pit 650, 0.15m deep with a very flat V-shaped profile with a vertical face at each end and a narrow, flat base. Its fill was dark brown with a large proportion of carbonised wood fragments. Three of the slots were segmented. Further west, Slot Group 5 may have been associated. The majority of the slots were very shallow. The four complete slots at the east end of Slot Group 3 and the two interrupted slots at the east end of Slot Group 4 had the same yellow-brown sandy silt fill but the other fills varied. The few sherds of pottery from these features suggest a 17th-century date.

The function of these slots was unclear. It they were garden features, the silty fills and rounded profiles suggest open features such as drainage between raised beds, rather than the loamy and humic fills of bedding trenches. As with the short gullies in Period 1, these might have been slots for sill beams, with edges eroded following the removal of the timbers, but no other features representing such structure were apparent. A further slot-type feature 611, seen just north-west of Slot Group 5, is not considered to be associated with the others as it lay at an oblique angle and was filled with a dark brown clayey silt similar to the fills of a row of small postholes just north of Slot Group 5.

Plot 3

Evidence for activity in this period was limited to a scatter of pits. On the south, close to the stony bank, was oval pit 938. A larger irregular pit, 886, was dug across the edge of bank 685 but contained no dating evidence. Further north, in the gap in Fenceline 9, was a round pit, 1288, possibly an addition to the boundary. Close by was rectangular pit 1286, with vertical sides and a flat base. Its top was packed with stone rubble but this did not continue at depth. Another rectangular pit was recorded south of gully 1375, cutting into its fill. Evidence from pits 938 and pit 1286 indicated a 17th-century date.

Plot 4

Evidence to the north of Culvert 4 was limited to the northeast corner, where a few pits, probable drains and a ditch were found. Gullies 1383 and 1394 were presumably drains

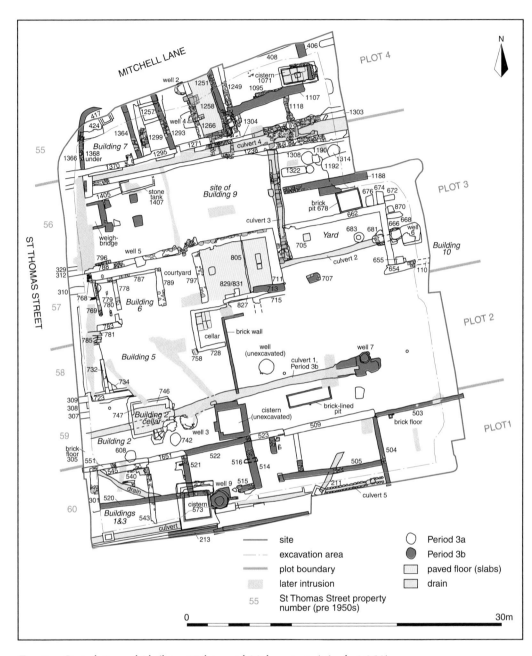

Fig. 9   Periods 3a and 3b (later 17th to mid 20th centuries) (scale 1:350)

leading into the predecessor of Culvert 4. The fill of gully 1394 included sandstone rubble and 16th to early 17th-century pottery. Both gullies were cut through by a substantial east/west gully (1316) with a bulbous, pit-like western end. It was 1m wide and 0.74m deep, and its western end was 1.8m in diameter. It contained no debris to suggest it had a structural function and presumably was a drain leading from a sump at the west end. It seemed to have been filled in by the early 17th century.

To the south of gully 1316 were four pits. Pit 1401 had 16th to early 17th-century pottery in its fill, pit 1397 only had residual medieval pottery. Pit 1380 contained charcoal and charred seeds, including the greatest concentration of charred wheat grains from the site (*Charred and waterlogged plant remains*, below). The fills of these pits and the later drain were covered by layer 1072 and other related layers (Horizon 4), which served as garden soils until later building in Period 3.

Period 3a: later 17th to early 19th centuries (Fig. 9)

The period was defined by post-dating the widespread layers of Horizon 4 which covered the earlier features. There was evidence for early pits, gullies and other construction work prior to the construction of masonry buildings and the associated drains and culverts. The buildings were mostly represented by sandstone footings, with the remains largely being of basements (Fig. 10). Four cellars were recorded, one largely complete, and several cisterns, two brick-vaulted. Brick was increasingly used.

The large amount of pottery in Horizon 4 showed that this period post-dated the late 17th century. Apart from a little residual medieval pottery, the pottery was of mid/later 17th and earlier 18th centuries in date, featuring quantities of yellow slipware (BPT 100), tin-glazed earthenwares (BPT 99) and Somerset earthenwares (BPT 280). Finds of mid/late 17th to 18th-century date included two Royal farthing tokens (see *Coins/jettons catalogue*, below) dating to 1614–34 and 1625–34, and a Nuremburg jetton of 1586–1635. A large assemblage of clay pipes confirmed this date range, with many pipe bowls identified to Bristol pipemakers (*The clay tobacco pipes*, below). The dating from cut features in Period 3a is also late 17th to 18th century, but it is probable that the period lasted into the early 19th century and some buildings certainly survived into the 20th century.

Fig. 10   Structural remains in the western halves of Plots 1–3, looking west

Horizon 4, 0.3m thick, comprised layers of dark silts and soils with building rubble. These were probably the Period 2b garden soils mixed up by the building of Periods 3a and even 3b. Deposit 547 in this group contained pieces of hearth or furnace lining, but nothing *in situ*.

The street numbering current in St Thomas Street during this period, and into the 20th century, is used to describe the buildings. The concordance of archaeological plots with street numbers is as follows:

Plot 1:   no. 60 St Thomas Street
Plot 2 (south):   no. 59 St Thomas Street
Plot 2 (north):   no. 58 St Thomas Street
Plot 3 (south):   no. 57 St Thomas Street
Plot 3 (north):   no. 56 St Thomas Street
Plot 4:   no. 55 St Thomas Street

Plot 1: no. 60 St Thomas Street

Building 1 was represented by fragments of wall and stone surfaces representing a rear room of the main building, an external subterranean cistern, a yard surface with integral drain, and a fragment of wall from a rear outbuilding. No separate footings existed, the walls of rubble sandstone rising directly off earlier deposits to about 0.5m above the base. Wall 301 was a wide north/south wall that lay on the line of the 20th-century street frontage at the west of the excavation, but seems to have been a major internal wall pre-dating the road widening. Wall 545 represented the northern side wall running back from wall 301. Its external wall was rendered, indicating that the area to the north was not built on when it was erected. Its junction with wall 301 was truncated by a later drain trench. With wall 543 (the return wall to the south), these defined three sides of a room, presumably the rear room of a small house, whose southern side fell beyond the edge of excavation. In the internal angle of the walls was a fragmentary paved surface of sandstone slabs (540); pottery from the make-up layer below this surface suggested a late 17th or early 18th-century date for construction.

A couple of metres to the rear of the building was a stone-built cistern, 573, of two phases. The original build was 2.8m x 3.6m internally. Further east, a wall (516) under a later (Period 3b) wall was truncated at each end by later disturbance, but it may have been part of outbuildings.

A stone and brick drain (Culvert 5), capped with large sandstone slabs, ran towards cistern 573, but the intersection had been truncated by Period 3b Well 9, and any internal evidence was obscured by a later lining within the cistern. Culvert 5 was built in a grey cinder mortar, similar to the cistern. A contemporary pitched stone surface, 211, was recorded along most of the northern side of the culvert, adjacent to and at the same level as the capping stones. Another culvert ran westwards from the cistern. Another drain, leading northwestwards, cut wall 545, indicating it was of a later period.

Plot 2 (south): no. 59 St Thomas Street

Before the masonry buildings were constructed in this plot, three postholes were dug that formed three corners of a rectangle (postholes 608, 734 and 742). The sides of this notional structure would have been 6.5m x 4.5m. The pits were all round in plan and vertical-sided, and pit 734 had a clear postpipe. The fills all showed evidence of burning, with ashy layers, abundant carbonised wood and very dark stained silts. Pottery from all three suggested a late 17th-century date. Also belonging to this preliminary phase was a substantial masonry wall, 307, seen in the piling trench (this was not investigated further due to contamination). It was stratigraphically earlier than the Period 3a walls of Building 2 (see below), being under the bedding for a brick floor of that building.

The surviving elements of Building 2 consisted of a cellar with a stone stair, and the southern boundary wall of the tenement. The boundary wall was built up against north wall 545 of Building 1, cut across its west wall 301 of Building 1, and extended most of the way to the eastern limit of excavation. The wall was built in several sections (walls 551, 1651, 523 and 509), which suggests it was extended eastwards over time. The walls were rubble in a grey cinder mortar, surviving to between 0.6m and 0.7m above their foundation-less bases.

The Building 2 cellar was of sandstone rubble set in a white lime mortar, smoothly plastered internally. The cellar, 3.3m x 3m and surviving 1m above its flagstone floor, was reached by a stone winder stair, of which three steps survived. The cellar had been altered by the addition of a flagstone floor laid on a bed of clay (747). This same clay was used to line up to 0.4m of the northern wall and parts of the east and west walls. The clay lining featured pink plaster where it had been trapped behind a later stone structure (746), built against it. The rendered clay lining must have been an attempt at damp-proofing, and wall 746 was probably a stone bench built against it.

The cellar was approximately 3m north of the south wall of Building 2, and the position of the winder staircase left space for a corridor (or external passage) between. The north side of the cellar was in line with the boundary with no. 58 St Thomas Street (Plot 2, north). Wall 308 marked the position of this boundary in the piling trench. It was associated with a brick floor (305) on its southern side, on a mortar bedding which ran down to abut wall 551. This floor was 0.8m above the cellar floor and was probably a half-basement of the front of Building 2. No dating evidence was retrieved from this building, but the style of construction would not be amiss in the early to mid 18th century. The bricks in the floor 305 were less than 2½" (62.5mm) thick, which, unless they were special paviours, would also suggest an earlier 18th-century date or before.

Next to the cellar, just by its southeast corner, was stone-lined Well 3. Its construction could not be clearly dated, but it was backfilled in the 19th century.

Plot 2 (north): no. 58 St Thomas Street

Building 5 survived as a few fragments: a boundary wall and cross wall at the southwest corner of Plot 2 (north), a fragment of the northern boundary wall with Plot 3 and part of a cellar to the north. The south boundary wall (309/723) was of coursed sandstone in white mortar, of which only the footings survive. Wall 732 ran north from it, forming an internal cross wall. It came to an end 3.1m to the north. Also to the north, a short length of east/west wall, 781, marked the northern boundary.

No Building 5 remains survived further to the east, except for the western end of a stone-flagged cellar (728) and a further fragment of the northern boundary wall, 715. The cellar walls stood to 1.25m above its floor on the north side and retained the seating for a vault, which probably crowned at about 2m above floor level, given the width of 3.1m. A stub of wall 715 gave an east-to-west length of 5.9m for the cellar. The floor of the cellar was at 7.21m AOD, a little higher than the cellar floor of Building 2. The northern boundary of this property was also represented by wall 654 at the eastern end of excavation.

Two fragments of stone drain (758 and 785) appeared contemporary with Building 5. Drain 785 ran east/west against the south side of wall 781, and drain 758 clipped the southwest corner of the cellar. A well was noted at this level southeast of the cellar along the southern plot boundary. This was not examined due to oil contamination but it was probably contemporary, within an external yard of the building.

A lease plan of no. 61 St Thomas Street survives from 1816/17 (Fig. 20), which closely matched the surviving fragments of Building 5 at no. 58, suggesting a similar construction. An elevation was also drawn, allowing the age of the building to be gauged both on stylistic grounds as well as the plan type: a late 17th-century date seems likely.

Plot 3 (south): no. 57 St Thomas Street

Floor 768 was a patch of pitched stones pre-dating the construction of Building 6, recorded in the piling trench as floor 310. This was very similar to cobbles of this phase in Plot 4 (below).

The foundations and lower walls of Building 6 survived more completely than the others of this period. As with the other tenement boundaries, the southern wall of this building was independent of the northern boundary wall of no. 58. Two wall fragments, 783 and 827, survived, both of similar character to the other walls of this period described above. The northern wall of Building 6 (788) and its east end wall (711) were integral. A full width rear room was partitioned off by cross wall 797, and further subdivided by a thin stone partition (805) near the east end. The room was stone flagged and vaulted in brick. A structure on the south side, walls 829 and 831, may have been a chimney breast. This room was clearly a vaulted cellar under the rear of the building, although at 8.2m AOD, the floor was considerably higher than the cellars in Buildings 2 and 5.

Three rooms towards the street were separated from the north boundary wall by a passage, which opened into a courtyard between cellar wall 797 and cross wall 789. The eastern room was just under 4m². West of wall 778 was a smaller rectangular room with two post-pads along the centre line (779 and 780), which may have supported part of a staircase. Another room west of wall 769 was probably of a similar size to the eastern room (to the original frontage), but only a small part was within the excavation.

Well 5 was integral with the north tenement wall, 788. Its cap was of the same construction as its lining and the wall was built over the cap. It was presumably a shared well, as was sometimes found on property boundaries, but its position is rather unusual, apparently being reached from an internal corridor. There was no artefactual dating, but the plan and construction details suggest a later 17th or early 18th-century date for Building 6. The building can be identified on a survey of 1914, incorporated within the rebuilding of a foundry in Period 3b (Fig. 22), so it survived well in to the 20th century.

Wall 662 was L-shaped and formed the north and east sides of what was probably a yard or garden to the rear of Building 6. The southern side was presumably wall 654, which it abutted, and while the junction of walls 662 and 711 had been truncated when Culvert 3 was demolished, the lack of any scars on wall 711 shows that wall 662 must have been an addition. A single square sandstone paving slab, 705, may have been the sole surviving floor slab of this yard.

Two culverts crossed the yard enclosed by wall 662. Culvert 3 ran from immediately east of the centre of wall 711 northwards to Culvert 4. Like Culvert 4, its sides were of rubble stone and brick, and its base and capping were of sandstone slabs. Two silt traps were incorporated into the drain at the south end, suggesting that sinks or similar drained into the culvert. These may have been housed in small outbuildings which have left no trace, or the drain was for lead downpipes from the room above the vaulted cellar (there were no signs of pipes or drains through wall 711). Culvert 2 originated under a masonry structure (666) against the east face of wall 662, and then passed westwards under the wall and across the yard, past the south end of Culvert 3, and dived under the floor of the cellar of Building 6. It was not traced beyond this point. Structure 666 seems to have been the top of a drain for excess water, pumped or spilt from Well 6, to which it was adjacent. At the east end of the yard, against the western face of wall 662, was a rectangular brick structure over a circular brick shaft (681) that led down into Culvert 2. This was some kind of water feature, designed to handle flowing water and send the excess back into the drain. Nearby, a ring of radially arranged bricks (683), only 0.4m in diameter, may have been the remains of a hollow plinth for a garden feature or planter. Well 6 appeared to sit within an enclosure or building east of wall 662 (Building 10). This was indicated by the continuation of boundary wall 654 eastwards and the existence of stubs of similar walls (668 and 870) north of the well. It may have been a well house.

Plot 3 (north): no. 56 St. Thomas Street

At the western end of Plot 3 north was a linear spread of sandstone rubble (1405), 1m wide, possibly a path. It was truncated by later structures to the west (below), and to the east by a stone tank 1407. The latter was a rectangular pit with walls of sandstone blocks and the underlying alluvium as its base. It was filled with a series of irregular tips and lenses of red and orangey mortar, ashy clinker and dark brown soil layers (1408). These two features appear to have been domestic structures such as might have been expected in a rear yard, i.e. a garden path and cess pit.

At the eastern end of Plot 3 north were a number of pits. One of these was an elongated rectangular pit (1322) which contained dark brown silt with animal bone and pottery of a late 17th-century date. Two large round post-pits (1308 and 1314), 1.1m in diameter and up to 0.5m deep, contained clear evidence of post-sockets constructed from sandstone set vertically. These two pits could have completed the line of Fenceline 10 of the previous period; however, finds and stratigraphy make it clear that they belong in this period.

No coherent structural remains from this period survived in this plot, but some elements of a building were recorded. To the west, wall 329/796 was a fragment of a boundary wall between nos 56 and 57 St Thomas Street, and was earlier than Building 6, suggesting that the building here went up before Building 6. To the east, stub walls 672, 674 and 676 were later than wall 662 of Building 6, and were therefore clearly not the same phase as wall 329/796. Close to the stub walls, a mortared pitched cobble spread (1192) was probably the remains of a yard surface. Just adjacent was a squared, stone structure, 1190, that may have been the footings or base of a brick pier. These features post-dated pits 1308 and 1314.

Culvert 4 formed the north side of Plot 3 in this period. The culvert was 1m wide internally and 1.98m deep. The side walls (1238 and 1303) were mortared rubble and brick, up to 0.6m thick. It was roofed by the corbelling of the side walls inwards at the top, and bridging the gap with sandstone slabs. Its northern wall supported the southern boundary wall of Building 7 (no. 55 St Thomas Street, below). Halfway along the culvert was a manhole, built through the corbelled capping.

Plot 4: no. 55 St Thomas Street

Wall 408, just visible in the northern side of the piling trench, may have been the northern boundary wall to Plot 4. Cobbles 424 and 1368 at the north-western corner of the plot were very similar to cobbles 310/768 in Plot 3. Such surfaces were generally external or in workshops, being very hard wearing. It is not clear what they were here, as no associated structural evidence survived. Pottery associated suggests a late 17th-century date.

Building 7 lay north of Culvert 4, its northern side beyond the edge of excavation, and was of several phases of construction. Walls 1370, 1295 and 1271 formed the southern wall running partly over and partly alongside the north wall of Culvert 4. Wall 1370 had the remains of a return to the north at its eastern end where it was butted by wall 1295. Wall 1295 was contiguous with wall 1271 and its return north, wall 1249, which formed the eastern end of the building. Two cross walls (1299 and 1266) were recorded, the latter with back-to-back fireplaces. A flagged floor had been laid between this wall and the end wall 1249. A stone tank (1257) was recorded against the east side of wall 1299, but with no sign of a vaulted roof. It may have been a cess pit. Walls 1095 and 1118 were the east and north walls of a rear extension or outshot to Building 7 on the south side of the plot, and only half its width. The plan form of Building 7 suggests a single tenement running back from St Thomas Street rather than a series of smaller ones fronting Mitchell Lane.

A certain amount of rebuilding and alterations can be inferred in this building. Wall 1299 was only 2m east of the northwards return of 1370, and seems to have been a replacement. It butted wall 1295, suggesting it was secondary. It is possible that wall 1266 and its fireplaces were also added subsequently to the south boundary wall. The construction of wall 1295 extended the property to the rear, and wall 1266 created a further two rooms in what was probably originally a yard. This interpretation is supported by the way that wall 1266 cut across both Well 2 and Well 4. The wells are likely to have occupied originally the open yard, with the cess pit against the rear wall of the house.

Cistern 1071, a brick-built tank with a stone-flagged floor, was built against the outer corner of the outshot (wall 1095). The cistern was vaulted in brick with a central access hole. It was rendered internally in pale grey cinder mortar, whereas the brick had been laid in a white mortar, together indicative of an 18th-century date. The flagstone flooring was not watertight suggesting that the tank was more likely to have been a cess pit than a water storage tank. It had no direct relationship to Building 7, but was truncated by structures of Period 3b, so was probably contemporary with Building 7.

Period 3b: 19th to mid 20th centuries (Fig. 9)

During the later 19th century the buildings on the site were replaced or extended and modified piecemeal. Final major changes followed street widening in 1938. Most of the replacement walls were laid in a dark cement mortar and there was an increased use of brick. Further development and recent demolition left little in place of these changes but wall footings and drains. A small assemblage of pottery from this period was consistently of the (mid/later) 19th century and later, with 19th-century Bristol stoneware (BPT 277) and refined whitewares dating to 1840/50 found with more broadly dated 19th-century transfer-printed (BPT 278) and Mocha wares (BPT 223). This dating is supported by associated clay pipes (*The clay tobacco pipes*, below).

Plot 1: no. 60 St Thomas Street

Building 3 was a rebuild of Building 1. This involved alterations to and partial rebuilding of the south wall of Building 2 in brick (walls 522 and 503), extending the wall to beyond the eastern edge of excavation, which henceforth acted as a party wall rather than part of a double wall arrangement typical of the earlier periods. A new wall was laid along the centre of the plot (505, 545 and 520) with cross walls 514 and 521 linking it to the northern boundary wall. Wall 301 from Period 3a was retained, as wall 520 butted it. At the east end, wall 504 ran the full width of the plot, and wall 505 ended against it. Walls 503 and 504 enclosed a brick-floored yard or room. A brick wall with a kink (seen in the piling trench, 213) marked the southern boundary. Cistern 573 was relined with rubble and given a brick vault, reducing its size to 2.2m x 2.5m internally and *c.* 2.3m deep. Next to the cistern was stone-lined Well 9, the construction of which had truncated the cistern wall, which seems to have been the occasion for the relining of the cistern. The well presumably pre-dates 1882 as a pump is shown in this position on the 1882 Ordnance Survey map (Fig. 21). The rebuild does not match the plan of the property given in 1882 (Fig. 21) or 1887 (Fig. 6) but does match the rebuild shown in a plan of *c.* 1939 (Fig. 24).

Plot 2: nos 58–59 St Thomas Street

Culvert 1 was a brick-built and vaulted culvert that ran most of the length of Plot 2 (south) at no. 59 St Thomas Street. It was tunnelled under the cellar of Building 2, clipped the north side of Well 3 and continued beyond the western edge of excavation. At its east end was brick-lined Well 7, with the base of a cast iron pump still *in situ*. Immediately south of it was a square brick shaft forming the head of the culvert. A vertical stone baffle, acting as a U-bend or trap, was still in place. Together, these features constituted a pumped well and adjacent overflow. To the south of the culvert was a brick-lined rectangular pit, probably relating to the workshops of the Bristol Foundry Company, which extended its premises to nos 58–60 after the Second World War. To the west of this was a cistern, shuttered in asbestos and not excavated.

Plots 3 and 4: nos 55–57 St Thomas Street

The boundary wall over the north edge of Culvert 4 was retained as a footing along most of its length. To the north, wall 417/1366 was the front wall onto St Thomas Street and Mitchell Lane, curving around the corner of the new street line that resulted from the widening of Mitchell Lane in 1905. Three new north/south walls 1364, 1293 and 1251, butted the re-used south wall of Building 7 of Period 3a; the rest of the walls were not reused. The brick vault of cistern 1071 was removed to allow the construction of a back room, comprising a wall (1107), which ran eastwards from wall 1251, and wall 406, a remnant of the northern return wall recorded in the piling trench.

Building 9 occupied the northern half of Plot 3. It incorporated Building 6, but the buildings on the rest of the plots were completely replaced. Further south, only a few scattered structures could be allocated to this period. Near the present street frontage were the remains of a weighbridge pit, accompanied by four concrete stanchion foundations shown on the 1914 plan inside the main entrance from St Thomas Street (Fig. 22). The four foundations supported posts that held up the upper floors to either side of a hauling way that led from the weighbridge to the yard at the rear. At the east end of the site east/west wall 1188 bisected the space between wall 662 and Culvert 4. On plans of 1904 (Fig.

23) and 1914 (Fig. 21) this wall divided a yard area to the north from store rooms and foundries to the south. Brick pit 678 also belongs to this period. The southern wall of these rooms was represented by wall 713, a short length of sandstone wall, built over the cellar of Building 6. Wall 707 may have been more of this wall.

THE DOCUMENTARY EVIDENCE
by Roger Leech

This section supplements an earlier desktop study (BaRAS 2002a) that consulted published and unpublished sources at the Bristol Record Office and the National Archives, including Building Plan Books, Corporation Plan Books, Land Tax returns, Poor Rate assessments and Parish Deeds. The previous work was supplemented by research of individual tenement histories through early leases and rentals, derived partly from conveyances relating to acquisitions by the City Council for street widening, and the examination of the title deeds held by Electricity Supplies Nominees Ltd (the present owners of the site).

The origins of the name of Mitchell Lane are obscure. It may be equivalent to the 'Boketeslane' referred to in a will of 1416/17 (Wadley 1886, 98; BaRAS 2002a), and is first mentioned as 'Hundon Lane' in 1496 (BRO: P/StT/D/139). It is also variously known in leases as 'Howne Lane', 'Hownden Lane' or 'Houndenlane' up to the 18th century: a name it appears to have shared with the equivalent lane on the west side of St Thomas Street, now Three Queens' Lane (BaRAS 2002a, 5).

Detailed tenement histories

Nos 54–55 St Thomas Street (Plot 4)
These two properties formed part of the lands or endowment of Foster's Almshouse on St Michael's Hill. No property in St Thomas Street is mentioned in the will of John Foster of 1492 (TNA: PROB11/9 Dogett 9), and the site probably formed part of lands said to be 'in Bristol' more generally. The earliest mention of the properties in St Thomas Street belonging to Foster's Almshouse is in a deed of 1505 between the Mayor of Bristol and the Master of St Mark's Priory, declaring that John Estefield, a merchant, had lately been empowered by John Foster to endow the newly founded almshouse with various lands including 'a garden lying in [St] Thomas Street' (Manchee 1831, 1, 82). As shown below, nos 54–55 were part of a larger block of land, nos 54–57 all belonging to Foster's Almshouse.

In 1617, nos 54 and 55 were the tenement, garden, lodge and a rack called 'Parke Corner', formerly of Thomas Dale, apothecary, and now in the holding of the widow Ledman, leased as part of the lands of Foster's Almshouse to Julian, Alice and Mary Godman (BRO: 04041 fol.298; 04335(5) fol.98), between 'Howne Lane' (which later plans show to be the same as Mitchell Lane) on the north and the Law Ditch on the south, extending from the street on the west to the land of John Priddy, merchant, on the east. From 1694 the property was divided into nos 54 and 55, and a property fronting 'Hounden Lane'; the latter was probably to the east beyond the limit of excavation. The mention of the Law Ditch on the south refers to a ditch which was also at this point the boundary between the parishes of Temple and St Mary Redcliffe. In the laying out of the new suburbs in the 1120s to c. 1150, for reasons unknown, the parish of Temple extended westward at this point to include nos 54 and 55 St Thomas Street.

From 1694, nos 54 and 55 were the tenement at the corner of Hownden Lane and St Thomas Street leased to Isaac Partridge, his lease renewed in 1710 (BRO: 04335(7) fol.162; 04335(9) fol.102). In *c*. 1740, this was also the tenement leased for a rent of £1 to Mary Greenfield, spinster, late of Isaac Partridge, now in the possession of Thomas Goldsmith, cordwainer, held by a lease of 1717, and from 1750 leased to Thomas North (BRO: 04044(1) fol.222; 04479(2) fol.114, showing location). By 1775, no. 54 was occupied by William Crisp, baker; the bakehouse is shown on a plan of 1802 (BRO: 04479(2) fol.114). In 1775, no. 55 was the Ring of Bells, held by Samuel Speir, victualler; by 1802 it was held by Philip Tanswell, victualler (BRO: 04479(2) fol.114), and is shown as a public house on the 1802 plan. It was still the Ring of Bells in 1837 and was also listed as such in the 1877 survey of properties of the Bristol Municipal Charities (Manchee 1831).

It is quite possible that by the early 15th century a property fronting St Thomas Street could have been entirely garden. It was a part of the city in which there were scattered gardens with garden houses, the lodges or second residences of wealthier citizens (for which see Leech 2003), and where gardens and open spaces were places in which to site racks for the drying of cloths. Close to nos 54 and 55 was no. 61, described as a garden and lodge in 1566 and 1602 (BRO: P/StT/D/15–16). This lodge was possibly the single-cell structure set back from the street and shown on a plan of 1816–17 (BRO: P/StT/Ch/3/31 fol.4) (Fig. 20). Further south in St Thomas Street, nos 64–66 were in 1572 described as 'two lodges under one roof and gardens to either of them belonging', one with two racks for the drying of cloths (BRO: P/STMR/D/4/1). On the north side of Mitchell Lane a garden fronting Hownden Lane in 1496 (BRO: P/StT/D/139–40) was, by 1636, described as the site of 'a lodge and a stable with a garden adjoining' (BRO: P/StT/D/4). With a garden, lodge and rack in 1617, nos 54 and 55 St Thomas Street were therefore typical of this part of the urban landscape of Bristol south of the Avon.

The plan of 1904 (Fig. 23), drawn up in the year before the widening of Mitchell Lane, shows that nos 54 and 55 continued as a pub and bakehouse respectively. Following road widening, a very detailed plan of the site of nos 55–57 in 1914 (BRO: 38041/BMC/12/PL3 fol.71) shows the corner of Mitchell Lane and St Thomas Street cut back, and a property, a single room in width, at the front end of the tenements (Fig. 22). These boundaries are the same as those shown on a plan of 1953 (BRO: 24529(5)).

Nos 56–57 St Thomas Street (Plot 3: north and south)

Early tax returns do not list a full complement of properties for nos 56–57 St Thomas Street (or for nos 58–60, see below), and named occupants cannot be ascribed to specific properties within the site with any confidence. Post-1700 Land Tax returns for Redcliffe list three entries running north from no. 60, and it is unclear whether no. 56 is omitted or included with no. 57. The house and yard which are described as the northernmost Redcliffe property in 1730 can be traced through occupancy to 1775 when it is numbered 57 St Thomas Street. It is notable that the 1870 Matthews Directory skips no. 56 altogether, as does the Redcliffe Parish first rate assessment. The property at no. 57 was occupied by a wheelwright from 1755. In.1810, John Geves, an iron founder, is listed here and the property continued as an iron foundry through the rest of the 19th century; the Goad 1887 Fire Insurance Plan (BRO) shows a warehouse with a foundry to the rear. By 1939, the property had been absorbed into the Bristol Iron Foundry which had taken over most of the area within the limits of excavation (BRO: 24529; Fig. 24). Nos 56–57 formed part of Foster's lands when conveyed by the trustees of the almshouse to Weston's Estates Ltd in 1904, the properties being shown in detail on the plan of that date (Fig. 23). Nos 56 and 57 clearly formed one property by 1914, when shown on the plan of that date (Fig. 22) as the foundry of Messrs Weston's Ltd. The plan within an Abstract of Title of *c.* 1939 shows nos 55–56 and no. 57 as the same holding (Fig. 24). At an earlier date, no. 57 was probably a separate property, having on the street frontage a house of two rooms in depth with a central staircase, a plan typical of the 17th century.

Nos 58–59 St Thomas Street (Plot 2: north and south)

Early tax returns do not list a full complement of properties for nos 58–59 St Thomas Street, and as a consequence, it is difficult to establish the occupation or occupier at no. 58 until John Merewether was named in the Redcliffe Land Tax for 1745, later listed as 'gent' (Sketchley 1775). By 1800, Charles Powell was resident and the 1810 tax returns list him as 'seedsman', although William Dibben at no. 59 was the proprietor of both premises. The 1820 Land Tax lists a cooper at no. 58, a cab proprietor in 1870, and in 1875 a smith, but the property continued to be listed as a dwelling house throughout with no shop or workshop attached, and it may be that these trades were practised elsewhere. The 1882 Ordnance Survey (OS) map shows a shared yard with no. 57 occupied by Campbell Foundry (Iron), although the property at the street front continued as a dwelling house (BRO: Goad 1887 Fire Insurance Plan).

   At no. 59, Mary Gee, grocer, succeeded Captain Brackinridg in the 1760s tax returns and in Sketchley's Directory of 1775. In 1790, William Dibben, the proprietor of both nos 58 and 59, was in residence, replaced by James Bartlett, corn factor (corn dealer), in 1820. By 1841, Mary Parker ran a seminary here, and in the remaining years of the 19th century the property housed a tailor, sign-painter, bellows-maker and basket-maker. Nos 58–60 were rebuilt in 1938 (Winstone 1987, pl.134; BRO: Building Plan book 174, fo.28). The plan within an Abstract of Title of *c.* 1939 shows nos 58–59 as one holding (Fig. 24).

No. 60 St Thomas Street (Plot 1)

Deeds for no. 61 dated from 1409, 1438 and 1446 record land to the north as a garden of the Abbot and Convent of Keynsham (BRO: P/StT/D/133–35). In 1456 and 1457 the abuttals record John Benett, tucker (woolworker), at no. 60 (BRO: P/StT/D/1; P/StT/D/137); in 1468 the abuttals refer to the garden 'of Richard Earle' (BRO: P/StT/D/136). No further information was available until 1681 when no. 60 was in the tenure of Joseph Ivy, a weaver (BRO: P/StT/D/154). By the mid 18th century the Redcliffe Land Tax included tenements that may have lain behind the main property at the street frontage. By 1764 the tax payer at this property was the licensee of the Artichoke public house, and the 1775 Sketchley Directory lists Joseph Jenkins as 'victualler', although his profession in 1784 was a house carpenter. Tax assessments of the mid 19th century continue to list a house and tenement for this property (BaRAS 2002a). The plan within an Abstract of Title of *c.* 1939 shows no. 60 as one holding (Fig. 24).

THE FINDS

Pottery, by E.R. McSloy

A total of 3327 sherds of medieval and later pottery, weighing 49.07kg, was recovered from

356 separate deposits. Of these, 2668 sherds, weighing 27.25kg, were from the medieval period and 659 sherds, weighing 21.82kg, were post-medieval and modern. The pottery was sorted by fabric type, using as a basis the Bristol Pottery Type (BPT) series (Ponsford 1988; 1991). Sherd count and weight were recorded for each context and, where these could be determined, vessel form and rim EVEs (Estimated Vessel Equivalents). A system of form classification was utilised, adapted from the Medieval Pottery Research Group's scheme (MPRG 1998) and incorporating recording of rim, base or handle morphology.

The bulk of the assemblage was recovered from hand excavation, with further material (167 sherds weighing 461g) retrieved from bulk soil samples. Mean sherd weight values, excepting sherds extracted from soil samples, are 10.4g for the medieval component and 33g for post-medieval/later material. This difference reflects both the greater robustness of the later wares and the moderately high levels of fragmentation noted for the medieval component.

Assemblage composition: medieval

The assemblage is broadly reflective of medieval groups recovered from excavations across the city, with types produced in or near Bristol making up the majority (58.2% by sherd count). Of the remainder, most comprised regional 'imports' from the neighbouring areas, primarily north Wiltshire. Among this material, the major production centres at Minety and also (probably) Nash Hill, Lacock (Wiltshire), are moderately well represented. The largest element comprised the so-called 'Bath A' type coarseware (BPT 46) which is thought to originate in west Wiltshire or north-east Somerset. Continental imports are present as a small group of north French wares (seven sherds or 0.3%; BPT 366) and, reflecting the later medieval emphasis in the assemblage, south-west French wares (60 sherds or 2.3% by count; BPT 156 and 157).

Assemblage composition: post-medieval and modern

The later part of the assemblage, although much smaller, follows broad trends of supply established from city assemblages for the post-medieval period, with the shifting of production away from the city after *c.* 1450 (below). The composition of most groups reflects the limited evidence for activity after *c.* 1700. The range of continental types present supports this chronological emphasis, the most common types being Rhenish stonewares of the 16th and earlier 17th centuries. Of similar dating are Iberian types (BPT 81 and BPT 282); their presence also reflects increased trade with Portugal from the 15th century onwards.

Chronology: c. 1120 to c. 1200

The earliest identifiable pottery comprised small quantities of BPT 6, a type first identified in association with the filling of the castle motte ditch, and thought to date before *c.* 1120 on this basis (Ponsford 1991, 136–7). This occurs as small bodysherds, for the most part from Period 1a deposits (posthole fill 1154, layer 1563 and fill 1588 of gully 1558) and all in association with later material. A slightly larger volume of material conforms to types typically datable to *c.* 1120/1150 to *c.* 1200. Most characteristic of this period are Ham Green 'A' jugs (BPT 26), identifiable from sherds with 'stepped' shoulders and/or sherds with lines of diamond-patterned roller-stamping, and pitchers in a pale-firing gritty south-east Wiltshire fabric (BPT 18c) from Period 2a layer 848 (Horizon 2). In addition a proportion of the Minety ware (BPT 18) pitchers (Fig. 11, nos 2–3) and coarseware types BPT 114,

BPT 32 and BPT 46 very probably relate to this period. The quantity of types certainly datable to before *c.* 1200 is small and a portion of this group appears to be residual.

Chronology: c. 1180/1200 to c. 1250/1270

The earliest substantive activity contained within Period 1a took place within this date range and probably after *c.* 1200. The most characteristic pottery types of this date range are Ham Green wares, principally the Ham Green 'B' jug style (BPT 27), the classification and dating for which has been discussed by Ponsford (1991). Ham Green 'B' vessels at nos 55–60 St Thomas Street are four times more common compared to the earlier type 'A' vessels, and it might be expected that a similar balance is the case among the undifferentiated material (BPT 26/27). The 'B' vessels identified are the typical handmade, round-bodied jugs and feature collared rims, bridge spouts, applied frilled bases and applied (self-coloured) strip decoration. In a small number of instances is it possible to apply Ponsford's proposed dating scheme based on aspects of form and decoration (Ponsford 1991): sherds from three vessels (Period 1a layer 1563; Period 2b layer 850, Horizon 3) feature stabbed 'deer hoof' motifs, of the kind thought to occur with early styles intermediate between 'A' and 'B' styles (Mike Ponsford, pers. comm.) and therefore probably of later 12th century. Three vessels are of Ponsford's plainer, late style where decoration is confined to close-set grooves, concentric or spiralled up from the girth (Fig. 11, nos 4–5). The dating for the late-style vessels is in the range *c.* 1225–1275 (Ponsford 1991). Significantly this matches the proposed dating for Period 1a pits 1062, fill 1063, posthole 1500, and fill 1499 of Fenceline 7, based on associations with Bristol Redcliffe glazed wares (below).

Handmade Minety wares (BPT 18) are contemporary with Ham Green and occur moderately commonly in Period 1a. Represented forms consist of tripod pitchers, usually identifiable from sherds with high, flaring rims or from feet and globular jars with short, simple everted rims. Bodysherds with combed wavy decoration probably come from pitchers. A pitcher from Period 1a layer 1563 (Fig. 11, no. 3) features a strap handle with applied pads, which is distinct from the 12th-century composite rod handles described by Vince (forthcoming), and may be a later style.

Ham Green coarsewares (BPT 32) occur most characteristically as sandy, red-firing fabric, distinct from that used for jugs (BPT 26/27), although the occasional presence of spots of glaze indicates the two products could have been fired together. Forms consist mainly of jars, typically with rounded bodies, simple everted rims and sagging bases and a decoration of combed wavy lines to the shoulder and/or rim. A more unusual vessel form is a lamp or small bowl from Period 1a Fenceline 1 (Fig. 11, no. 1). It is unclear whether the manufacture of Ham Green coarsewares is contemporaneous with the glazed wares (i.e. from *c.* 1120), though Vince (1984) favoured a later *floruit*, between *c.* 1180 and *c.* 1250. A variant ('proto-Ham Green' BPT 114), distinguished by the presence of mixed inclusions of larger quartz, sandstone and some calcareous inclusions, may be earlier or of equivalent date and made at an adjoining manufacturing site at Pill (Mike Ponsford, pers. comm.). A second variant, BPT 305, is characterised by larger jar vessels; it is a type known most commonly from waterfront sites and dates to the late 12th or early 13th centuries.

Bath A type coarsewares (BPT 46) are more common compared to the equivalent Ham Green products, although this may reflect a lengthier period of production. Forms comprise mainly jars with developed/moulded everted rims differing in detail. There is frequent evidence for use as cooking vessels in the form of carbonised residues. In addition

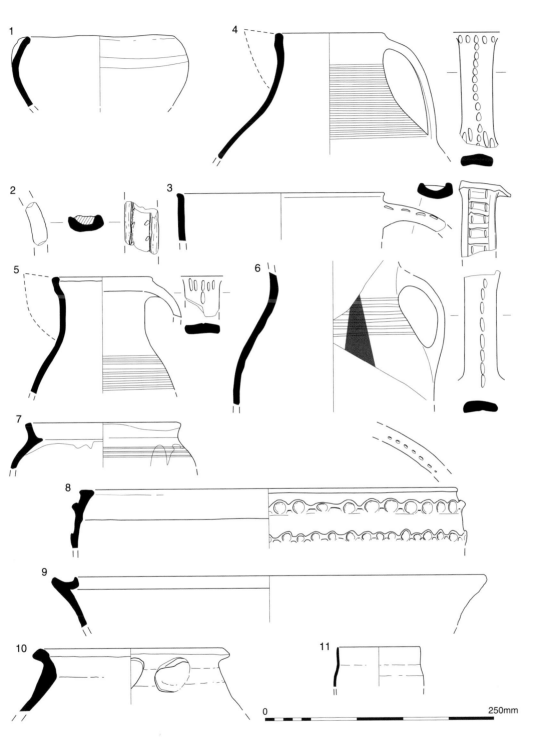

Fig. 11   Medieval and post-medieval pottery, nos 1–11 (scale 1:4)

to the jars there are rare instances of inturned dishes or 'West Country' vessels (from Period 1a layer 1563 and pit 1524, fill 1525). The three recorded vessels of this type, which are sometimes interpreted as the bases for bee hives (Jope 1952, 65), are identified from the distinctive base sherds. It is possible that some rims from such vessels are also present in the assemblage, these being indistinguishable from those of the more common jars.

Chronology: c. 1250/1270 to c. 1350/1400

The outline model for later medieval pottery supply in Bristol is defined by the demise of the Ham Green 'industry' probably by the third quarter of the 13th century, the appearance at broadly the same time of the production of Bristol glazed wares within the city's suburbs, and a little later on (after *c.* 1300), by marked shifts in the supply of pottery coarsewares.

Bristol glazed wares ('standard' jug type BPT 118 and its variants) were routinely present across the medieval Periods 1a and 1b, and overall are twice as common as Ham Green jug fabrics BPT 26/27 (796 sherds compared to 365). The majority of identifiable forms are jugs and these more commonly exhibit 'early' features not dissimilar to the Ham Green series including collared rims, bridge spouts and applied frilled bases. Other than wheel manufacture another distinguishing feature is the decoration, which includes applied strips or iron-rich slips contrasting with the body colour of the vessel (Fig. 11, no. 6). Some vessels feature decoration as applied strips or 'blackberry' motifs and these 'highly decorated' style vessels probably date before *c.* 1300/25 (Ponsford 1998). French influence is apparent in jug styles from the start of the 14th century and this is seen in vessels with splayed-out bases in the manner of some southwest French jug forms. It is likely that Bristol glazed wares continue in production well into the 15th century, before the increased availability of Malvern Chase wares brought about a halt (Ponsford 1998). There are very few of the plainer and smaller late-series jugs represented as type BPT 118L. Two sherds with French-style splayed bases are rare examples. Of non-jug forms, only jars (BPT 85; Fig. 11, no. 7) are reasonably well represented (18 vessels).

Among the more distinctive glazed wares from non-Bristol sources is a sandy fabric with 'sandwich' pale orange/grey firing which is tentatively identified as Nash Hill ware (BPT 368), and one sherd in a fine buff fabric (Period 1a layer 925) which is probably a Laverstock product from southeast Wiltshire. Other less distinctive glazed wares or sherds which are burnt or otherwise 'altered' (catch-all group BPT 252) may include material from Bristol, south Somerset or south Wales.

Wheelthrown Minety ware (BPT 84) is moderately well represented in Periods 1 and 2, occurring primarily as jars with fewer jugs and a bung-hole cistern from Period 2b gully 1394, fill 1395. The adoption of wheel-throwing at Minety occurs at some point in the 13th century, and thereafter an increasing range of vessels is produced (Musty 1973) and the ware is a constant presence in 14th/15th-century groups from Bristol (Ponsford 1988, 125). An elaborately decorated vessel from Period 1a gully 1056, fill 1057 (Fig. 11, no. 8) is probably an example of this later repertoire.

Continental wares are rare in the Period 1a/b assemblage. The majority comprised south-western French mottled-glazed wares (BPT 156 and 157), which are expected to date after *c.* 1250, continuing to *c.* 1350 (Ponsford 1991, 137). Most are unfeatured jug sherds, although a vessel from deposit 806 (Horizon 1, Period 1b) features a wide, splayed base and probably dates after *c.* 1300. A thick-walled sherd in sandier variant BPT 157 is probably from a mortar (from Period 1b, bank 685). Jugs which are unglazed or have a sparse glaze 'bib' (BPT 160) represent a late variant, dating after *c.* 1350 and continuing into the post-medieval period. This variant is less common overall, although, significantly, the majority of sherds occur from deposits dated to later medieval phases (Periods 1b and Period 2b).

Chronology: c. 1400/50 to c. 1600/50

A small number of types define pottery supply in the period *c.* 1400 to *c.* 1600 and are moderately prominent at nos 55–60 St Thomas Street in Periods 2a and 2b. Most common are Malvern Chase redwares (BPT 197), which are noted in a wide range of forms including jars (Fig. 11, no. 10), pipkins, skillets, bowls (Fig. 11, no. 9), jugs and a cistern. No distinction was made at the time of recording between the reportedly earlier fabric (Vince, forthcoming) and the later finer and pink-firing variants; however, it would appear that the large majority conforms to the later type and probably dates after *c.* 1500. As noted by Vince (ibid.), Malvernian wares are not thought to continue much beyond *c.* 1600.

'Tudor Green' type wares are moderately sparsely represented: 22 sherds, predominantly from Period 2a/b. Cups in this tradition from the Hampshire/Surrey borders (Pearce and Vince 1988) occur in Bristol from *c.* 1420, probably continuing into the 16th century. Forms consist of thin-walled bodysherds or handle fragments from cups, including a lobed cup from Period 2a pit 1464, fill 1465. Cups in the Cistercian ware tradition, consisting of hard redwares with a dark brown glaze (BPT 93 and 275), overlap in date with the Tudor Green vessels, the main period of use being the 16th and 17th centuries. An emphasis in the later end of this range is suggested by the phasing: three sherds occur from Period 2a and 11 sherds from Period 2b (below). The illustrated example from Period 2a posthole 1411 (Fig. 11, no. 11) compares with 16th-century examples from Acton Court (Vince and England 2004, fig. 9.4, no. 110).

The middle to late 16th century is marked in Bristol by further changes in the supply of pottery coarsewares and a shift southwards from Malvern Chase to sources in Somerset (principally Nether Stowey type BPT 280 and Wanstrow type BPT 96). This shift is demonstrated most clearly in Bristol from the well dated Narrow Quay assemblage (Good 1987). At nos 55–60 St Thomas Street the range of forms differs between the main types: the Wanstrow group comprised small jars comparing to those from Narrow Quay (Good 1987, fig. 33); pipkins (ibid., figs 24–25); deep bowls (ibid., fig. 20); chafing dishes (ibid., fig. 38) and jugs. The Nether Stowey group typically comprised more decorative forms, mostly large plates/chargers with *sgraffito* or over-slipped decoration (Fig. 12, no. 16) and fewer deep bowls (Fig. 12, no. 14), jars and a chafing bowl (Fig. 12, no. 15). The Somerset wares, including the unattributable type BPT 285, are scarce until Period 2b, where they represent 50% of the total sherd count (excluding the residual medieval element).

Continental imports attributable to this period occur only sparsely and include Rhenish stonewares (Raeren type BPT 287 and Frechen BPT 286), the latter type continuing into the 17th century, and Iberian types ('olive jar' type BPT 81 and micaceous redware BPT 282). Some of late south-west French wares (BPT 160; above) may also extend into the 15th and 16th centuries and this type is significantly better represented in Period 2a than in earlier phases (16 sherds). Continental imports are present sporadically across Periods 2a/2b, mostly as unfeatured sherds. Large and joining sherds of a Frechen drinking jug/mug (Fig. 12, no. 12) are among a group of material which appears incongruously early within Period 3a gully 1316 (fill 1317) and it is likely that this vessel dates to the 16th century. A notable 'import' (Fig. 12, no. 13) unfortunately redeposited within modern

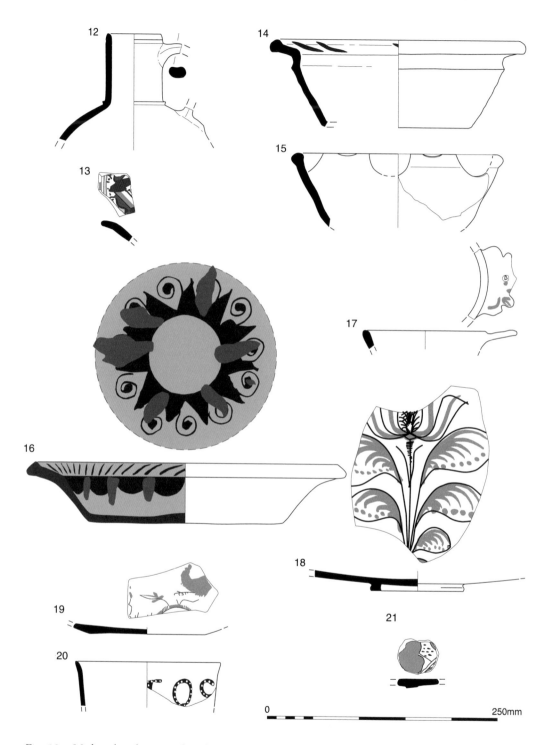

Fig. 12   Medieval and post-medieval pottery, nos 12–21 (scale 1:4)

deposit 529, is a sherd from north Italian Montelupo tin-glazed earthenware (BPT 107). The form is a large plate or charger with painted polychrome decoration identifiable as of the 'nastri' (stars) design sometimes referred to as ribbon pattern (John Allan, pers. comm.). Dating for this vessel is probably in the range *c.* 1525–1625.

Chronology: c. 1650 to c. 1780

Pottery attributable to this period (within Period 3a), is under-represented at nos 55–60 St Thomas Street compared to earlier material, although the general trends in supply are still reflected. The Somerset glazed earthenwares remain in production well into the later 18th century and this is reflected in their continued presence into Period 3a. By 1650 coarse 'gravel-tempered' wares (BPT 112) and a finer, commonly *sgraffito*-decorated type, appear and during the 18th century are a common element of coarsewares. Production of tin-glazed earthenwares (BPT 99) began in Brislington in the 1640s and in Bristol soon after. Early (17th-century) English tin-glazed wares are present in the assemblage as porringers (Fig. 12, no. 17) and as plates possessing footrings, where the undersides are of clear lead-only glaze (Fig. 12, nos 18 and 21). Later flatwares with plain bases also occur and include examples with 'chinoiserie' designs (Fig. 12, no. 19) and, after *c.* 1750, with powdered manganese decoration (Period 3a, Culvert 5). By 1690/1700, yellow slipwares (BPT 100) made either in Staffordshire or in Bristol itself appear and are abundant in 18th-century groups. An example with slipped motto is illustrated (Fig. 12, no. 20).

Catalogue of illustrated sherds

No. 1   BPT 32. ?lamp or bowl with pouring lip. Period 1a Fenceline 1 posthole 1153 (fill 1154).
No. 2   BPT 18. Composite pitcher handle. Period 1a Horizon 1 (layer 1501).
No. 3   BPT 18/84. Pitcher or jug. Period 1a early occupation (layer 1563).
No. 4   BPT 27. Ham Green B late-style jug. Period 1a Fenceline 7 posthole 1500 (fill 1499).
No. 5   BPT 27. Ham Green B late-style jug. Period 1a pit 1062 (fill 1063).
No. 6   BPT 118. Jug with slip decoration. Period 1a early occupation (layer 1563).
No. 7   BPT 85. Jar (or pipkin?). Period 2a Fenceline 9 slot 1375 (fill 1376).
No. 8   BPT 84. Large jar or bowl with applied, thumb-impressed strip decoration. Period 1a gully 1056 (fill 1057).
No. 9   BPT 97. Bowl(?). Period 2b Well 1 (fill 857).
No. 10 BPT 97. Jar. Period 2b Horizon 3 (layer 411).
No. 11 BPT 275. Cup. Period 2b, posthole 1411 (fill 1412).
No. 12 BPT 286. Mug/drinking jug. Period 2b gully 1316 (fill 1317).
No. 13 BPT 107. Large plate with 'nastri' design. Modern deposit 529.
No. 14 BPT 280sg. Bowl with *sgraffito* decoration to rim. Period 3a Horizon 4 (layer 737).
No. 15 BPT 28. Chafing bowl. Period 2b Well 1 (fill 860).
No. 16 BPT 280sg. Plate. Period 3a Horizon 4 (layer 507).
No. 17 BPT 99. Porringer. Period 3a Horizon 4 (layer 737).
No. 18 BPT 99. Footring dish with clear glazed underside and tulip design. Period 3a Horizon 4 (layer 737).
No. 19 BPT 99. Plate. With 'Chinoiserie' design featuring cockerel. Period 3b Building 9 (fill of Culvert 3).
No. 20 BPT 100. Bowl with motto or personal name in pelleted characters. Period 2b Posthole Group 3, posthole 1322 (fill 1323).
No. 21 BPT 99. Counter cut-down from footring plate with clear glazed underside. Period 3a stone tank 1407 fill (1408).

Discussion

The pottery assemblage from nos 55–60 St Thomas Street reflects the patterns of supply established for Bristol across the medieval and subsequent periods. In common with many Bristol sites, this assemblage lacks the larger discrete feature groups which permit intra-site comparisons and can often provide the best insights into contemporary pottery supply and use. The bulk of pottery derives from extensive layers where the potential for accumulation and 'reworking' over a extended periods is high.

Evidence for activity before *c*. 1150/1200 is sparse, but would appear to be continuous thereafter. The medieval wares occur in the narrow range of vessel forms which are typical for the period up to *c*. 1325/1350. Such forms may have performed a variety of uses, although cooking and storage were undoubtedly primary. Most common are jars with rim forms and body profiles which may differ in detail but where such differences are unlikely to relate to specific function. A broad distinction in the assemblage can be made between tablewares, made up of glazed serving vessels (pitchers and jugs) and kitchen/utilitarian classes, made up of the unglazed types, mostly comprising jars with a very few bowls/dishes and possible lamps. Using this broad-based distinction, the 'utilitarian' component makes up 48% by count of the Period 1a assemblage. This figure is somewhat higher compared to equivalently dated/sized assemblages from 1–2 Redcliff Street (37% by count; McSloy, forthcoming[a]) and Cabot Circus (43% by count; McSloy, forthcoming[b]). All of the sites referred to, as well as St Bartholomew's (Ponsford 1998, 144), demonstrate a fall-off in kitchen wares into the late medieval period (14th to 15th centuries), almost certainly the result of increased use of metal cooking vessels.

It is possible that the proportionally larger kitchen/utilitarian component recorded for Period 1a might reflect lower status for this location. Determining status using an essentially low-status commodity, widely available in the setting of a major port city, has proven frustratingly difficult and there are as yet too few published comparanda to permit comparisons. On the available evidence, French imports, initially mainly from Normandy and then from the south-west, were widely available and occurred at most Bristol sites in moderate quantities. There is some variability in representation, however the figure of 2.2% for south-west French wares at nos 55–60 St Thomas Street (by count as a proportion of the total medieval assemblage) is very closely matched at 1–2 Redcliff Street (2.1%; McSloy, forthcoming[a]) and Cabot Circus (2.6%; McSloy, forthcoming[b]). Higher representation at St Bartholomew's Hospital (8.1% by count) might in part be a result of a bias to deposits of *c*. 1250 to 1350, but also hints that the institution, or possibly its master's lodging, was well appointed (Ponsford 1998, 145). For all sites, the majority of the south-west French wares comprise jugs with mottled green glazes (BPT 156/160). Perhaps significantly, the more decorous Saintonge polychrome products (BPT 39) are best represented at St Bartholomew's Hospital (34 sherds or 0.5%) and are very scarce or wholly absent at the other sites described.

The later medieval period (Period 1b) continues to reflect the major patterns of supply established for the city, albeit viewed through the confusion of earlier, redeposited material. There are no clear indicators of higher status of the kind recorded from some Bristol groups in the form of south Mediterranean imports dating as early as the later 15th century (Gutiérrez 2008, 61–2). The post-medieval/earlier modern assemblage (Periods 2/3) is relatively small, although it reflects the patterns in supply usual for the period. As with earlier periods, 'status' remains difficult to assess. The presence of Spanish olive jars (BPT 81) and of the Montelupo sherd (Fig. 11; no. 13) are hints of higher status in the 16th/17th centuries, although this material is highly fragmented and the possibility that it originated off-site must be considered.

The clay tobacco pipes, by Reg Jackson

Introduction and methodology

The excavation produced 336 clay pipe fragments from 34 contexts plus some unstratified material. Of these, 209 were pipe bowls or bowl fragments, of which 13 bowl fragments were too small to be dated. There were five decorated or marked pipe stems.

The pipes have been dated by the use of the general bowl typology developed by Oswald (1975), and refined by Jackson and Price (1974) for pipe production in Bristol. A relatively close date for a pipe can be achieved unless a large part of the bowl is missing or its typology cannot be determined, then only a wide date range can be given. The position, type and style of a maker's mark can be used to refine dating and identify the place of manufacture. The pipemakers working in Bristol have been extensively researched using documentary sources (Price *et al.* 1979). Bristol was a major centre for the manufacture of clay tobacco pipes and most of the pipes found at nos 55–60 St Thomas Street were made in the city. The marked clay pipes are described below in order of their likely production dates. The names of the Bristol pipemakers whose pipes appear in the assemblage, and their known working dates, are taken from Price *et al.* (ibid.) and descriptions of their pipes are given below.

Early to late 17th century

Pipe bowls marked with a symbol rather than a maker's name or initials cannot be assigned to a particular maker, although the bowl forms suggest that they were made in Bristol or the immediate vicinity in the mid 17th century. These symbols, all on the heels of the pipes, are a flower in a heart from deposit 507 (Fig. 13, no. 1), a *fleur de lys* from deposits

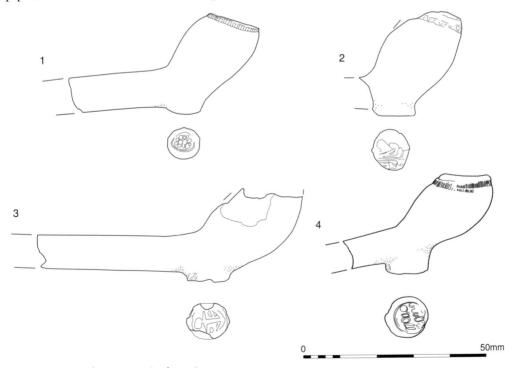

Fig. 13   Clay tobacco pipes (scale 1:1)

35

507 and 1247 (Fig. 13, no. 2) and an anchor from deposit 530 (Fig. 13, no. 3). These deposits all form part of Horizon 4 (Period 3a).

A previously unrecorded and unusual mark occurred on two pipes from deposits 530 and 547, Horizon 4 (Fig. 13, no. 4). It is a two-line mark incuse on the heel but in cursive script rather than the more usual capital letters. The first line is illegible but the second line appears to read 'ovell', perhaps the surname Lovell. Both bowls are forward projecting, burnished, and in the so-called West Country style commonly found in Somerset and Wiltshire but also produced by the Hunt family of pipemakers in Bristol. No pipemaker with the name Lovell has so far been recorded working in Bristol or the surrounding area during the mid 17th century when this bowl type was produced. Pipes with marks in cursive script are rare in southwest England although examples are known to have been made by Thomas Hunt (Atkinson 1965, fig. 1.7) and by Jeffry Hunt (T. Wilcox 1980, fig. 9.10).

Bristol Manufacture

Thomas Monkes. A heeled bowl, with the initials 'TM' (the T above and joining the centre of the M) incuse on the heel, from deposit 530, Horizon 4, Period 3a. Thomas Monkes obtained his freedom to work as a pipemaker in the city (hereafter 'was free') in 1626 and was still working in 1670.

John or Jane Wall. A heeled bowl with the initials 'IW' with decoration above and below, all incuse on the heel, from Well 7, fill 652, Period 3b. John Wall was free in 1639, last recorded working in 1647 and was dead by 1650. His wife Jane carried on the business after his death until she died in 1661.

Philip Edwards I. Heeled bowls with the initials 'PE' incuse on the heel from Well 7, fill 652, Period 3b, and Horizon 4, Period 3a deposits 507, 546, and 730. Philip Edwards I was free in 1650, last recorded working in 1681 and was dead by 1683.

Humphrey Partridge. Two heeled bowls with the joined initials 'HP' incuse on the heel, from deposit 773, Horizon 4, Period 3a, and unstratified. Humphrey Partridge was free in 1650 and had died or left Bristol by 1654.

James Fox. A heeled bowl with the initials 'IF' with a dot between within a dotted circle, all incuse on the heel, from deposit 507, Horizon 4, Period 3a, and a heeled bowl fragment with the initials 'IF' with a single dot above and below, all in relief in a circle on the heel, from Well 7, fill 652, Period 3b. James Fox was working from at least 1651 and died in 1682.

Flower Hunt. A forward projecting bowl with a burnished finish, with the initials 'FH' with dotted decoration above and below, all in a circle incuse on the heel, from deposit 507, Horizon 4, Period 3a; a forward projecting bowl with the initials 'FH' in a circle, incuse on the heel, from Well 7, fill 652, Period 3b, and a forward projecting bowl with a burnished finish, with the three-line mark 'FLO/WER.H/VNT' incuse on the heel (unstratified). Flower Hunt was free in 1651 and died in 1672.

Thomas Smith I. A heeled bowl with the initials 'IS' incuse on the heel, from deposit 1072, Horizon 4, Period 3a. Thomas Smith was free in 1651 and dead by 1667.

Richard Nunney. A heeled bowl with the initials 'RN' with decoration above and below incuse on the heel; a heeled bowl with the initials 'RN' with a dot between, all within a circle incuse on the heel; a heeled bowl with the initials 'RN' with a dot between and decoration above and below, all within a circle incuse on the heel, all from Horizon 4, Period 3a; a heeled bowl with the initials 'RN' incuse on the heel (unstratified). Richard Nunney was free in 1655, was last recorded working in 1696 and was dead by 1713.

William Evans I or II. A spurred bowl with the initials 'WE' below a crescent of triangles, all incuse on the back of the bowl from Culvert 2, Period 3a. William Evans I was free in 1660, William Evans II was free in 1667, and one of them was working until at least 1713.

Timothy Ricketts. A heeled bowl with the initials 'TR' incuse on the heel from deposit 730, Horizon 4, Period 3a. Timothy Ricketts was free in 1660.

Llewellin Evans. A heeled bowl with the initials 'LE' incuse on the heel from deposit 547, Horizon 4, Period 3a; five spurred bowls with the initials 'LE' incuse on the rear of the bowl from Culvert 1, Period 3b, fill 1408 of stone tank 1407, Period 3a, and unstratified; a stem fragment with rouletted decoration in the form of one band of interlocking diamonds containing the initials 'LE' between two lines of milling (unstratified). Llewellin Evans was free in 1661 and died in 1688.

John Sinderling. A spurred bowl with the initials 'IS' in relief in a circle on the side of the bowl from deposit 530; a spurred bowl with the initials 'IS' incuse on the back of the bowl from deposit 1247; a spurred bowl with the initials 'IS' with a dot between, all in relief in a circle on the side of the bowl, both from deposit 1247, all from Horizon 4, Period 3a, and a bowl with an oval heel and the initials 'IS' incuse on the rear of the bowl, deposit from the fill of posthole 1322, Period 2b. John Sinderling was free in 1668, last recorded working in 1696 and was dead by 1699.

Somerset manufacture

Jeffry Hunt I or II. A single pipe bowl from deposit 799, Horizon 4, Period 3a, made by either Jeffry Hunt I or II, father and son, who were working in Norton St Philip, Somerset, from 1625 to the late 17th century (Lewcun 2004, 356).

Late 17th and 18th centuries

Bristol manufacture

Robert Tippet II. A spurred bowl with the initials 'RT' incuse on the back of the bowl and the three-line mark 'R/TIPP/ET' in a circle in relief on the side of the bowl, from deposit 530, Horizon 4, Period 3a. Robert Tippet II was free in 1678 and died in 1722.

William Tippet I. A bowl fragment with the initials 'WT' incuse on the back of the bowl, from deposit 730, Horizon 4, Period 3a. William Tippet I was free in 1690 and still recorded working in 1728.

Thomas Owen. Three spurred bowls with the initials 'TO' incuse on the back of the bowl from deposits 684 and 730, Horizon 4, Period 3a. Thomas Owen was free in 1698 and dead by 1725.

John Macey I. A spurred bowl with the two-line mark 'IOHN/MASE' in relief in a circle on the side of the bowl, from deposit 530, Horizon 4, Period 3a. John Macey I was free in 1700, last recorded working in 1727 and was dead by 1739.

John Ricketts I. A spurred bowl with the initials 'IR' incuse on the back of the bowl, from deposit 684, Horizon 4, Period 3a. John Ricketts I was free in 1707 and last recorded working in 1715.

John Wickham. A spurred bowl with the initials 'IW' incuse on the back of the bowl from deposit 1247, Horizon 4, Period 3a. John Wickham was free in 1723 and died in 1754.

Chester(?) manufacture

Chester origin. A single stem fragment with elaborate moulded decoration in the form of repeating spiral bands of grape vines and flowers (unstratified) is not typical of Bristol-made pipes, although a similarly decorated stem was found during excavations at Union Street in the city (Jackson 2010). However, stem decoration of this type is common on pipes made in Chester during the mid 18th century and that seems the likely origin of this example (Rutter and Davey 1980, e.g. fig. 62).

19th century

The assemblage contained a number of 19th-century pipes with decorated bowls, quite often comprising paired leaves on either side of the front and rear mould lines. More elaborate decoration included a bowl with footballers in relief, a bowl in the form of a lady's boot and a pipe where four large leaves in relief cup the bowl. These bowl forms and types of decoration commonly occur on pipes made throughout the United Kingdom during the 19th and early 20th centuries, and Bristol pipemakers are known to have been making similar examples (Insole and Jackson 2000, fig. 5. 19; Price *et al.* 1984, e.g. fig. 6).

One pipe stem is marked with the name 'Fiolet' and was made by that company in St Omer, northern France in the late 19th century (deposit 117, part of demolition of Culvert 4, Plot 4, Period 3b). Fiolet pipes were high-quality products, often with elaborately decorated or figural bowls, that were popular throughout northern Europe, so its occurrence in Bristol is not unexpected.

The majority of the stratified material derived from deposits grouped together as Horizon 4, Period 3a. The date range of the pipe bowls with pipemaker's marks supports the late 17th to 18th-century date suggested by the pottery. Within the assemblage were a small number of pipe bowls with previously unrecorded and unusual marks, illustrated here for the first time.

Medieval ceramic roof tile, by Angela Aggujaro

A total of 137 fragments of ceramic roofing material, weighing 7394g, was recovered. A total of 47 fragments (1914g) from Periods 1 and 2 was selected for detailed recording of fragment count and weight per fabric, and where present such attributes as crest form and decoration. The fragments from the medieval phases mainly comprise glazed crested ridge tiles of the type familiar from excavations in Bristol (Williams and Ponsford 1988, 145–9). Two fragments of louvre (a decorative roof vent), are also described, although both are residual pieces from post-medieval deposits.

Composition

Fabric classification is adapted from Williams and Ponsford's scheme (1988):

Type 1: Bristol type with common non-homogenised clay lumps (ibid.).
Type 4: Bristol type with abundant white quartz inclusions (ibid.).
Type 4a: variation of Type 4 with black organic inclusions.
Type 7: red-firing Malvernian fabric with sparse igneous rock inclusions (Vince 1977, 274)
Type Minety: Minety tile fabric. Characterised by fine oolitic limestone inclusions (Ireland 1998, 141).

Roof tile

The majority of the Period 1 group consists of ridge-tile fragments conforming to Types 1 and 4. These are commonly considered to date to the later 13th and 14th centuries, and were produced in Bristol alongside Bristol Redcliffe glazed pottery. Three fragments are attributed to Type 4a, a variation distinguished by the presence of black organic inclusions.

One fragment, from Period 1 pit 688 (fill 689), is identifiable as of Minety-type and probably dates to the late 13th century or 14th centuries (Ireland 1998, 141). Only one tile fragment, from Period 1a posthole 1209 (fill 1210), may date to after c. 1400. This is a fragment in Type 7, and is representative of material most commonly seen in 15th to 16th centuries (Vince 1977, 274). As such this fragment may be intrusive.

Decoration

Five fragments feature a knife-cut crest, probably of triangular form. Two examples, in Type 1 from Period 1b posthole 923 (fill 924) and posthole 888 (fill 889), both feature low triangular crests (under 20mm). The remaining examples in Type 4 all feature higher crests (25 to 40mm). Stabbed decoration was noted to the base of each triangle crest. Nine tiles feature an applied strip that is either thumb-impressed or pinched in 'pie-crust' fashion.

Louvres

Two fragments of roof furniture thought to derive from louvres were recovered from Period 2a posthole 1427, fill 1428 and posthole 1471, fill 1472. Both occur in a fabric comparable with roof tile Type 4 and were probably Bristol products. That from deposit

1428 consists of a flattened finial knob, with thick lead glaze, and is similar to examples known from Bristol (McSloy forthcoming[c]) and also from Nash Hill (McCarthy 1974, fig. 23). The fragment from deposit 1472 is glazed internally and externally and is possibly part of a vent aperture.

Coins/Jettons catalogue, by Edward Besly

No. 1 Copper 4-maravedis. Spanish America, Juana and Carlos I (1516-55); Santo Domingo, 1542–55. From fill 1261 of Culvert 3.

No. 2 Copper-alloy jetton. Rose/orb type Nuremberg jetton. Obv. Legend: HANNS KRAUWINCKEL IN NUR; Rev. legend: GOTT ALLEIN DIE EERE SEI; Hans Krauwinckel II 1586–1635. From layer 730, Horizon 4, Period 3a.

No. 3 Copper-alloy Royal farthing token; contemporary counterfeit of James I Lennox/Charles I Richmond types, 1614–34. Nonsense legend on obverse. From layer 519, Horizon 4, Period 3a.

No. 4 Four Royal farthing token; Charles I Richmond type 1625–34, probably counterfeit. From levelling layer 1292 within Building 7, Period 3a.

Metal and worked bone objects, by E.R. McSloy

The full assemblage of 241 objects of metal, and 9 of worked bone, was recorded. With the exception of items clearly identifiable as iron nails, and some clearly modern items, the metal artefacts were x-rayed to assist in object identification and constructional details. The majority of items comprised iron nails and fragmentary iron objects for which no function could be ascribed. Selected items of individual interest or which are datable by form are catalogued below including five illustrated items (Fig. 14, nos 1–5). Object dimensions are included with each item; measurements in millimetres (L. = length; W. = width; T. = thickness; D = diameter); (n.i.) = not illustrated.

Iron or composite (Fig. 14)

No. 1 Key with hollow stem and elaborate bit. Identifiable as Goodall's type B, likely to be of 13th century date (Goodall 1980, 148). L (overall). 73mm; W (bow). 21mm; W (shank). 8mm; W (bit). 23mm. From Horizon 4 deposit 547, Period 3a.

No. 2 Iron strip with two small and two large hollow copper-alloy rivets. Although parallels for this object have yet to be identified, use as a scale-tang knife handle is suggested due to similarities noted on examples recorded by Goodall (1980, 83).Scale-tang knives are dated to 13th–15th centuries. L. 66mm; W. 20mm; D. 4mm. From pit 886, fill 887, Period 2b.

(n.i.) Horseshoe. Almost complete horseshoe probably of Clark's type 4 of later medieval date, (Clark 1995, 88-9). Broad 'web' with rectangular holes in 3/3 arrangement. Nails are still present in two of the holes. Residual due to the 16th–17th century date of the associated pottery. L. 118mm W. (web max) 35mm. From backfill 860 of Well 1, Period 2b.

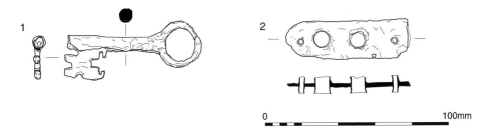

Fig. 14 Metal artefacts (scale 1:2)

(n.i.)   Fragmented iron horseshoe. Probably Clark's type 3 or 4 of later medieval date (ibid.). Broad 'web' with rectangular holes in 3/4 arrangement. Possible calkin or thickening of one heel visible on x-ray. L. 124mm; W (max web) 40mm. From gully 1213, fill 1214, Period 1a.

(n.i.)   Blade from whittle-tang knife or shears, broadly medieval in date. Straight-backed. The tang is at the centre line, suggesting a more probable use as a knife blade. L. 135mm; W. 25mm; T. 2mm. From fill of pit 1208, Period 1a.

(n.i.)   Iron horseshoe fragment. Elongated countersinking is visible on the two rectangular holes present. This feature is characteristic of Clark's type 2 shoes, which typically date to the 12th and 13th centuries (Clark 1995, 95). L (remaining) 80 mm; W. (web) 30mm. From layer 1563, Period 1a.

Copper Alloy

(n.i.)   Domed thimble of post-medieval type. Thick band of dot decoration in spiral form near the crown. Two separate bands of very small dots are visible lower down the thimble. A band of very small dots also covers the area near the open end. L. 25mm; W. (open end) 16mm; T. 0.5mm. Unstratified.

(n.i.)   Cast sub-rectangular buckle with drilled frame for separate spindles. Similar in style to Georgian-style shoe buckles in Whitehead (1996. 104), which date from 1720 to 1790. L. 37mm; W. 25mm; T. 2mm. From Horizon 4 deposit 547, Period 3a.

(n.i.)   Asymmetrical buckle with one large oval and one small rectangular loop. Likely to be post-medieval in date. L. 29mm; W (max). 25mm; T. 2mm. From deposit 547, Period 3a.

(n.i.)   Shaped strip. Shaped into two arcs formed from folded sheet with flattened, bent ends. This is likely to have been used as a purse suspender as it is similar in style to examples from Meols of medieval date (Griffiths *et al.* 2007. 126). L. 6.5; W. 4mm. From Horizon 4 deposit 547, Period 3a.

(n.i.)   Pin. The head appears (from the x-ray) to be solid rather than wound and of late medieval or post-medieval type. Similar examples are known e.g. from Colchester (Crummy 1988, 6–9). L. 46mm; W. (shaft) 1mm. From layer 684, Period 3a.

(n.i.)   'Loop fastener', a common type of clothes fastener frequently encountered in archaeological contexts of the 16th and 17th centuries. Similar examples from St Bartholomew's Hospital, Bristol (Good 1998, 168). Diameter (external) 10mm. From layer 850, Period 2b.

(n.i.)   'Loop fastener' as above. Diameter (external) 12mm. From layer 850, Period 2b.

(n.i.)   Lace tag formed from rolled sheet with overlapping seam. Metal lace ends tipped the leather 'points'. They were used to secure the doublet and hose in the late 14th and 15th centuries and were put to other uses in the 16th and 17th centuries (Crummy 1988, 13). L. 31mm; W. 3mm; T. 1mm. From fill 1317 of gully 1316, Period 2b.

Worked bone (Fig. 15)

No. 3   Die. Of regular type (the scores of opposing faces totalling seven), identifiable as Potter variant 5 (Potter 1992, 79–91) of late medieval to post-medieval date. Scores depicted as circles with central dots. Slight damage to one face (score two). L. 70mm; W 70mm; D 70mm. From Horizon 4 deposit 547, Period 3a.

No. 4   'Pinner's bone.' Adapted from a sub-adult cattle metapodial. Diagonal file marks visible on flattened proximal end. Such items were used in the manufacture/finishing of wire pins before the end of the 18th century when the process was mechanised (MacGregor 1985, 171). L. 127mm; W. (max.) 53mm (min.) 12mm. From fill of gully 1316, Period 2b.

No. 5   Spoon with plain, sub-rounded bowl with handle, 'twisted' midsection and scallop-shell handle terminal. Post-medieval dating is suggested on the basis of its association with pottery dating between the late 17th and 19th centuries. Parallels for this object are not forthcoming. It is likely that the design follows that of metal spoons. L. 88mm; W. (bowl) 20mm (max handle) 13mm. From fill 1261 of Culvert 3, Period 3b.

(n.i.)   Domino, 18th-century or later date. Double ring and dot in 6/9 arrangement. L. 25mm; W. 14mm; T. 4mm. Unstratified.

(n.i.)   Shaft and point from pin or needle, undiagnostic. Crudely formed though 'polished' from use. L. (surviving) 60mm; W. (max) 4mm (min) 1mm. From Horizon 4 deposit 547, Period 3a.

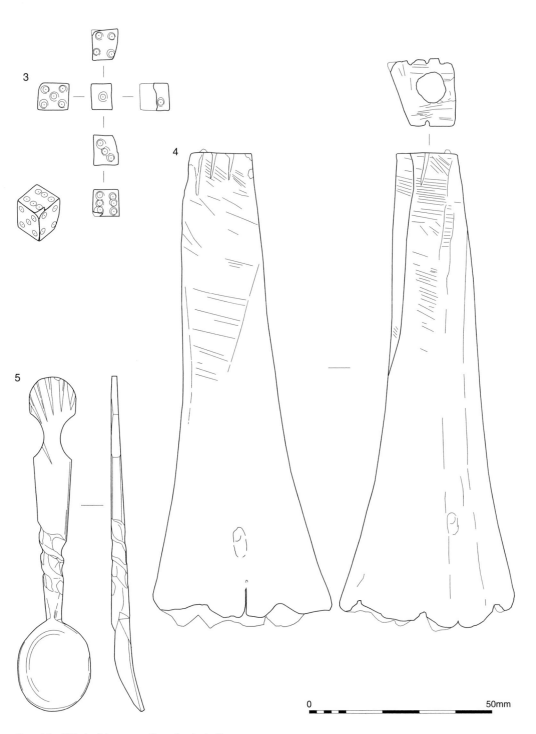

Fig. 15   Worked bone artefacts (scale 1:1)

Glass and glass waste, by E. R. McSloy

A total of 38 fragments, including vessel and window glass, was excavated in addition to a small quantity of waste material (900g) relating to glass manufacture. A descriptive catalogue for all fragments is included in the archive.

Vessel glass
A total of 21 fragments derived from post-medieval or later contexts, primarily from Periods 3a and 3b. Amongst these were a small number of tableware fragments. Stemmed drinking glass fragments derive from 18th or 19th-century dated deposits, but are insufficiently complete for close dating or further comment. A plain rim fragment from Period 3b deposit 518 (Fig. 16, no. 1) occurs in poor yellowish green glass (forest glass?) and may be an example of an earlier post-medieval (16th or 17th centuries) beaker or tumbler of English manufacture.

Examples of glass pharmaceutical phials were recovered from Period 3 and unstratified contexts. A complete phial from Period 3 deposit 1072 is of unusual form (Fig. 16, no. 2). Dating for this vessel in the 17th or early 18th centuries is likely (John Shepherd, pers. comm.) and there is a similar ribbed flask of comparable date from Canterbury (Charleston 1987, fig. 94, no. 20). That the form occurs somewhat later is however suggested by a bottle of similar size and form (though of 'silvered glass') displayed as a 'witch bottle' in the Pitt Rivers Museum, Oxford (PRM accession no. 1926.6.1), which is thought to date to the 1850s. Fragmented examples of phials from other deposits are of more typical cylindrical form and likely date to the 18th century (Noël Hume 1969, 73, fig. 17).

The majority of vessel glass comprised bottle glass fragments datable to between the later 17th and 19th/early 20th centuries. A fragment from the fill of posthole 1322, Period 2b, is from a short-necked bottle with string rim, datable to between the later 17th or early 18th centuries. Substantially complete cordial bottles from Period 3b cellar fill 1281, and an ink bottle from the fill of drain 1260, Period 3, date to the late 19th or early 20th centuries. Two cordial bottles from cellar fill 1281 feature embossed legends of later 19th-century type (see catalogue).

Catalogue (Fig. 16)
No. 1   Plain rim fragment from beaker or tumbler, thickening towards rim. Yellowish green glass with common bubbles. Diameter 60mm. From Horizon 3 (layer 518), Period 3b.

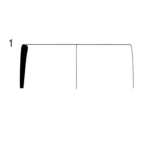

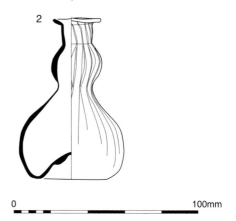

Fig. 16   Vessel glass (scale 1:2)

No. 2   Complete phial of ribbed, double-bellied form. Bulbous body, smaller neck expansion and out-curved rim. Clear glass with greenish tint. Height 84mm; diameter at maximum girth 56mm. From Horizon 4 (layer 1072), Period 3a.

(n.i.)   Moulded clear/natural green-coloured bottle with embossed legend 'H.L. WILLIAMS XXL NEWPORT MON and E. BREFFIT & Co. MAKERS LONDON'. The Breffit bottle manufacturer operated from *c.* 1880 to 1913. From Building 7 cellar fill, deposit 1281, Period 3b.

(n.i.)   Moulded clear/natural green-coloured 'Codd' bottle with embossed legend 'BATEY & Co. KINGSLAND RD'. The Batey ginger beer makers company was established *c.* 1853 and operated as a limited company from 1887 until 1952. This bottle was manufactured by Turner and Co. and probably dates to the 1880s or 1890s. From Building 7 cellar fill, deposit 1281, Period 3b.

Window glass

Window glass (17 fragments) was recovered from ten Period 2 and 3 deposits. The earliest material, including fragments from Period 2 deposits, consists of dark green forest glass panels deriving from diamond-leaded windows of 16th or 17th-century type. A complete 'quarry' which features grozed edges, was recovered from Period 3 deposit 507. The remainder of the window glass, mostly from Period 3, consists of fragments in natural green or colourless glass and probably dates to the 18th or 19th century.

Glass waste

Small quantities of glassworking waste (900g), comprising dark green-coloured blocky lumps and elongated 'runs/pulls', were recovered from Period 2 and 3 deposits. The material is typical of the glasshouses in Bristol and other areas, associated with bottle manufacture between the later 17th and early 19th centuries. The quantities of waste material are insufficient to imply close proximity of glassworking activity and it is probably residual.

Metallurgical residues, by E.R. McSloy

A smithing hearth bottom weighing 466g from the Period 1a charcoal-rich layer 1541 (*Wood charcoal,* below) in Plot 4 is the only direct evidence for smithing activity. More plentiful are residues including hearth/furnace lining (136g), vitrified clay/cinder (162g) and 'miscellaneous' ironworking slag (467g) which are unspecific of a particular process. A small quantity (23g) of 'tap' slag, characterised by low vesicularity and 'ropey' structure, was noted from Period 1 deposits, and was the sole evidence for iron smelting. In all instances the quantities recorded are much too low to imply ironworking in the immediate area.

Clay moulds, by E.R. McSloy

A total of 176 fragments of clay mould weighing 3429g was recovered, providing evidence for the casting of copper-alloy vessels. The bulk of the material derived from fill 1465 of Period 2a pit 1464, associated with pottery dating to the 15th or 16th centuries. A small quantity derived from Period 1 layer 1410, into which this feature was cut, is almost certainly intrusive. The system of recording and classification was adapted from that used for the clay mould material from Cowick Street, Exeter (Blaylock 2000). Thin-section analysis was undertaken on two samples from pit 1464 for the purposes of characterising and confirming the use of local clays (below).

Description

Fragments were identified from each of the two main components of the mould: an inner 'core' and an outer 'cope', which was probably made in two halves and luted together.

Cope and core fragments were fairly readily distinguishable with either a concave or convex casting surface. Some cope fragments exhibit the longitudinal 'wire' moulding which is a common feature of cauldrons and skillets of mid 14th to 17th-century date. In addition to the cope/core rim and body fragments, there are a small number of fragments identifiable as ribbed leg moulds (Fig. 17, no. 2). A small fragment with one curving surface surviving with a diameter of approximately 80mm may represent part of the sprue cup (the funnel-shaped 'in-gate' for the pouring of the molten metal).

Discussion and dating by form

Leaded-bronze cooking vessels, cast in clay moulds, are known from the late 12th century in England, becoming progressively more common throughout the medieval and early post-medieval periods. Casting in clay moulds continued to *c.* 1670/1700, with sand-casting dominant thereafter. No certain examples of handle moulds were recorded, making identification of the vessel forms produced problematical. The size of the vessels, indicated by the few larger surviving fragments of rim and leg mouldings (Fig. 17, nos 1 and 2), is most appropriate for cauldron vessels; the common form for which was with an everted rim and globular (medieval) or bag-shaped (post-medieval) body, with two round-sectioned L-shaped handles and three legs. This basic vessel form has its origins in the medieval period and continued into the 16th and 17th centuries. The few lower body mould fragments from nos 55–60 St Thomas Street suggest that at least some of the vessels produced were of low-bellied or 'bag-shaped' body profile, most typical of earlier post-medieval vessels (Butler and Green 2003, 8).

No structural evidence associated with metal casting was recorded and the mould fragments might represent a dump of material from activities located elsewhere. The assemblage is similar in character to material from 1–2 Redcliff Street dated *c.* 1400–1580, which was associated with well preserved reverbatory furnace structures (Hart, forthcoming), of the kind required for the melting of copper alloys.

Illustrated fragments (Fig. 17)

No. 1   'Core mould rim fragment' from vessel with diameter of *c.* 350mm, from pit fill 1465, Period 3a.
No. 2   Ribbed leg mould fragment, from pit fill 1465, Period 3a.

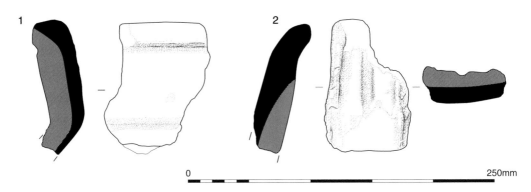

Fig. 17   Clay mould fragments (Scale 1:3)

Clay mould fabric, by Elaine L. Morris

Examination of five fragments of mould using a binocular microscope suggested potentially two different fabrics used in casting, but thin-section analysis showed composition to be uniform. The fabric is porous in texture and lightweight in nature with a low density, comprising abundant (35–40%) temper of carbonised vegetal matter or vesicles, and moderate (15–20%) naturally occurring inclusions of quartz, iron oxides, calcite and recrystallised limestone in calcareous clay with a scatter of limestone dispersed throughout. The inclusions in the clay matrix suggest that the clay source was alluvial, derived from degraded Triassic geological strata (Kellaway and Welch 1948) that can be found in the Bristol area, although no extraction of clays was evident in the excavated area. The preparation of richly organic-tempered fabrics to make metalworking moulds that were light and porous in nature and suitable for use in the casting process was a recognised production technique during the post-medieval period (Blaylock 2000, 38–41).

THE BIOLOGICAL AND GEOARCHAEOLOGICAL EVIDENCE

Animal bone, by Sylvia Warman

The animal bone assemblage comprised 9250 fragments from 9117 bones weighing 47kg. Animal bone was recovered from 251 of the 1256 deposits excavated, and dated to all Periods from medieval to modern. Deposits from features and early layers from Periods 1 and 2 were selected for detailed analysis, with a focus on those features where low residuality of pottery suggested securely dated assemblages. The animal bone from these 134 deposits totalled 846 fragments from 772 bones, and weighed 22.6kg.

Methods
For each specimen the following information was recorded: element, species, size, sex, weight and parts present (zones recorded following Dobney and Reilly 1988). Fusion of long bones, tooth wear, pathology, burning and butchery were also noted. Preservation was recorded using Behrensmeyer's (1978) weathering stages. The total numbers of bones identified for each species were presented as NISP. The number of animals represented was estimated using MNI (minimum number of individuals), calculated by the recording of the recurring presence of specific parts (following Dobney and Reilly 1988). Sheep and goat were distinguished wherever possible using reference specimens and the criteria of Boessneck (1969). Age estimates were calculated from tooth wear, following Grant (1982), and from long bone fusion, following Silver (1969) and using the approach of O'Connor (2000).

Results
The animal bone was generally in a moderate state of preservation with a high degree of fragmentation. The presence of reworked soil horizons between each identified period of activity resulted in a degree of residuality in all deposits, including cut features. The majority of the assemblage could not be related to specific activities on site, and may have derived from a mixture of sources, reflecting both domestic and industrial activities. There was no significant differentiation in the proportions of species present across the plots in either period. The number of features where primary disposal of animal bone could be assumed were few, and confined to a group of possibly domestic rubbish pits in Period 1.

Period 1: medieval

The animal bone selected for detailed analysis came from 80 deposits. The assemblage totalled 535 fragments from 493 bones, weighing 13kg. The species identified were horse, cattle, sheep, sheep/goat (undistinguished), pig, dog, cat, rabbit, goose, chicken and two duck species (mallard and teal). The assemblage was dominated by cattle and sheep/goat; the latter more numerous by MNI. Pig was also present in most deposits, and other domestic species, including horse, dog, cat and chicken, were present in very small numbers. Fragments of rabbit bone were also present in small quantities. There were no clear differences between plots in terms of the species present.

The disturbed alluvium at the base of the Period 1a sequence (layers 974 and 1563) produced a large assemblage of animal bone from cattle, sheep/goat, chicken, sheep, pig, cat and goose. The assemblage from the pits and cut features included cattle, sheep/goat, sheep, chicken, pig, dog, goose, rabbit, and duck (teal). The bulk of the material came from pits 1058, 1062 and 1064 within Plot 1. The animal bone assemblages from pits 1062 and 1064 were composed entirely of cattle and sheep/goat bones. The assemblage from pit 1058, whilst largely composed of cattle and sheep/goat bones, also contained single specimens of pig and goose.

The age at death estimated for cattle indicates that most of the animals were older than 18 months, and well over half were over 3.5 years old. For sheep/goat, almost all the specimens were older than 16 months, and three-quarters were older than 2.5 years. Over two-thirds of the sheep/goat had been slaughtered by the age of 3.5 years. The number of ageable pig bones was much smaller than for cattle and sheep/goat, but estimates indicate that two-thirds were less than one year old at death and that the assemblage did not contain any pigs over 3.5 years old. The other species represented were all from fully adult specimens.

The material must have been deposited quite rapidly as there is little evidence of weathering or gnawing by dogs. Evidence for butchery was noted on 14% of the assemblage, and comprised long-bone shafts either chopped through mid-shaft or occasionally split vertically, probably for the extraction of marrow. A handful of burnt bones (1.6%) was predominantly white in colour with some distortion, suggesting they had been burnt at a higher temperature than would generally be reached in a domestic fire. The burnt specimens come predominantly from pit 1543 and comprised sheep/goat foot bones. No long bones from domestic stock were sufficiently complete for measurements to be taken.

Period 2: post-medieval

The animal bone came from 54 deposits and totalled 311 fragments from 279 bones, weighing 9.7kg. The species identified were: horse, cattle, sheep, sheep/goat, pig, dog, cat, rabbit, goose and chicken. The proportion of the main domestic species was very similar to that seen in Period 1, with cattle and sheep/goat dominating and with sheep/goat the most numerous by MNI. Horse was represented by a single bone from the backfill of Well 1. Cattle and sheep/goat included a wide range of body parts including meat-bearing bones.

Most of the cattle present were older than 18 months; two-thirds were older than 2.5 years and just over a third were older than 3.5 years at death. This pattern contrasts with Period 1, where nearly two-thirds were over 3.5 years. Most sheep/goat specimens were older than 16 months, but only half of them exceeded 3.5 years old at death. When compared with Period 1, this indicates that more sheep were killed at a greater age, the opposite trend to that seen for cattle. Age at death was also calculated on a small percentage of the pig bones, of which half were killed before they reached one year of age. Pig, like cattle, shows a trend towards slaughter at an earlier age than was seen in Period 1. The other species represented by a handful of bones were all from fully fused adult specimens.

Here too, deposition must have been rapid as very few bones show signs of weathering or gnawing by dogs. Evidence for butchery was seen in 18% of the assemblage and comprised of long bones chopped through mid-shaft, with some specimens split vertically. Evidence of cess deposits on the bone surface was noted in 2% of the assemblage. No long bones from domestic stock were sufficiently complete for measurements to be taken.

Discussion

The animal bone assemblages from Periods 1 and 2 were very similar in the range of species present and the range of body parts from particular species. Cattle and sheep/goat were most numerous in both periods, with sheep/goat in the majority. A greater proportion of cattle and pigs were killed at younger ages in Period 2 than in Period 1. This may have been due to an increased demand for beef and pork. The lack of substantial numbers of cattle over 3.5 years old indicates that this was likely to be butchery and domestic waste, rather than the dispatch of older individuals exploited for secondary products such as milk or traction. Conversely, sheep/goat showed a shift towards slaughter of individuals of a greater age, which was also supported by mandible wear, which may indicate animals from wool-producing flocks.

The small number of goose and chicken bones is likely to represent food waste. There was very little evidence for the use of wild species apart from the two duck bones present in the assemblage from Period 1, and the rabbit bones may have been from wild specimens. The relatively narrow range of species present was not unusual for smaller medieval assemblages in this area, as at Temple Street, Bristol (Levitan 1988). There is an absence of evidence for high-status food consumption, such as deer bone.

The assemblages from Period 1 pits 1058, 1062 and 1064 within Plot 1 were almost entirely composed of cattle and sheep/goat. These were deep, well stratified deposits, in contrast to the shallower features which produced more mixed assemblages, and therefore are likely to reflect primary deposition, probably from a domestic context. A similar pattern of medieval-period deposition was noted at nos 30–38 Thomas Street (Higbee 2004).

For cattle and sheep/goat, and to a lesser extent pig, the range of body parts was wide, including both meat-bearing and non-meat-bearing elements. The presence of frequent butchery damage and large numbers of meat-bearing bones indicates that the cattle and sheep/goat assemblage includes waste derived from food consumption. The small assemblage from 3 Redcliff Street (Higbee, forthcoming) includes material of comparable date to the Period 1 and 2 assemblages, and has a similar range of species with a similar frequency of the main meat-bearing bones. Thus there was no clear evidence for primary butchery or tanning and associated industries except for some burnt sheep/goat toes bones from Period 1 pit 1543, which may represent whittawing waste but is perhaps more likely to represent the preparation of lime plaster.

Of the worked bone objects (*Metal and worked bone objects,* above), the Period 2 'pinner's bone' made from a cattle metapodial would have been used for weaving cloth, and it may be that small-scale 'cleaner' industries and crafts were carried out in these tenements, in contrast to the heavier and smellier industries identified elsewhere in the suburb, such as 1–2 Redcliff Street (Warman, forthcoming).

Fish bone, by Hannah Russ

Abundant fish remains were recovered through hand collection and environmental sampling. A wide range of edible fish species is represented, including those from deep and shallow marine and estuarine environments. The more diverse range of species and abundant remains were recovered from Period 1 and included European eel, thornback ray, cod and probable herring. Evidence for preparation and consumption is present in the form of fragments with cut-marks and burnt remains. The species representation from Period 2 is similar to that of Period 1, with herring and eel dominant, but thornback ray and cod reduced. Evidence for food preparation is absent in this period, and only one sample contained burnt remains. The similarity in species may reflect either continuing consumption in Period 2, or a high degree of residuality from Period 1. The small size of the Period 2 assemblage could be due either to reduced consumption or more off-site disposal of domestic waste. The presence of large deep-sea fish indicates net-fishing by boat, while smaller species mostly associated with coastal and estuarine environments suggest coastal and near-shore fishing. Cranial elements of smaller species were almost entirely absent, which may indicate that only processed fish (gutted, with head and possibly tail removed) were present, but may also result from taphonomic processes due to the reduced robustness of cranial elements compared to vertebrae in many fish species.

Charred and waterlogged plant remains, by Julie Jones

A total of 24 samples was processed from a variety of features, including pits, postholes, ditches and soil layers. The plant macrofossil concentration in the flots was low, with mostly single examples of charred cereal grain and weed taxa. A few examples of free-threshing wheat grains were well preserved, but other grains were very fragmented, with degrees of surface damage from the charring process. Small quantities of the main cereal crops of wheat, barley, rye and oat that were cultivated during the medieval and post-medieval periods were represented, often as individual grains. Many of the wheat grains were well preserved but barley and oat were often fragmented or eroded.

Samples from features such as rubbish pits and areas of burning from Period 1 (13th to 15th centuries) produced a small assemblage. The species identified include wheat, barley, oat, rye and Celtic bean, which are possible food remains. Charred hazelnut fragments may also represent food debris, but may equally be associated with the charcoal present in the majority of the samples. There was only one example of cereal chaff from the whole site, which was from rivet/macaroni wheat. Although this is very sparse evidence, it does suggest that two types of wheat, bread and rivet wheat, were cultivated and brought to the site in the medieval period. Other species identified were grass, brome, goosefoot, pea/vetch, common chickweed, common nettle, rush, hemlock, hawthorn, clover/medick, stinking chamomile and sedge.

The samples from Period 2 (15th to 17th centuries) were obtained from soil layers, pits and ditches. The species identified include wheat, oat, barley, Celtic bean, hazelnut and fig, which may all be food remains. Pit 1380 produced the greatest concentration of charred wheat grains from the site, in fair to good condition. Other species identified include oak, common nettle, elder and bramble, and are likely to represent the local flora of the site. Some non-charred elder and sedge seeds were also identified.

Such restricted assemblages limit the interpretation of domestic and economic activities associated with the site, apart from indicating the availability of these cereal crops, whether for purposes of human consumption or animal feed and bedding. However, such a sparse distribution of cereal remains is common to many of the other sites previously investigated in Bristol, such as at Union Street (Jones 2010) and Finzel's Reach (Jones, forthcoming); where greater concentrations of charred remains do occur, these are often primarily of cereal grain alone, suggesting that cereals were brought into the medieval city already processed, for use in the city mills or for general domestic use.

The only waterlogged preservation of seeds came from the basal fill of drain 1558 from Period 1a, which lay close to the water table. These include elder, bramble and nettle, which could easily have thrived in unkempt areas of the site, particularly where organic waste may have been discarded, as elder and nettle in particular thrive in nitrogen and phosphate-enriched soils. Similar non-charred assemblages have been found elsewhere in Bristol, particularly associated with later deposits such as garden soils, where they were frequently mixed with both organic and inorganic domestic waste, including bone, shellfish and eggshell. The site at 30–38 St Thomas Street produced similar assemblages associated with 16th to 17th-century garden soils (Jones 2004, 41–5). The mineralised preservation in rubbish pit 1062 may indicate localised deposition of cess in features such as these.

The wood charcoal, by Dana Challinor

Introduction

Charcoal from eight samples from Period 1 (13th to 15th centuries) and Period 2 (15th to 17th centuries) deposits was selected for detailed examination. The samples came from pits and burnt deposits, some of which were associated with domestic waste, and some which might have derived from activities associated with metalworking. The analysis focussed on differences between the context types and any changes over time.

Full analysis was undertaken of four samples, and broad characterisation of the remaining four samples. The latter group of samples was largely dominated by a single taxon and the aim of the analysis was to confirm identifications, check for additional species and record maturity data. For the full analysis, 100 fragments of the >2mm fraction were identified and for the broad characterisation, a selection of 20 fragments was identified. The charcoal was fractured and examined by microscope at up to X400 magnification. A full methodology is available in the archive.

Results

The results for the Periods 1 and 2 charcoal analyses are presented in Tables 1 and 2 respectively. Fragment count has been used as a method for broad discussion of quantification, although it is acknowledged that there are inherent limitations. Twelve taxa were positively identified: field maple, alder, birch, hazel, beech, ash, holly, hawthorn group, oak, willow/poplar, elder and elm. All were consistent with native species and no exotic species were recorded. The results indicated the use of both wide (>20mm diameter) and narrow (<20mm diameter) roundwood, with some oak and ash heartwood observed in several contexts.

Discussion

Given that the feature types examined were pits and burnt deposits, it is assumed that the charcoal for all assemblages was from dumps of spent fuelwood. With a couple of minor

Table 1: Charcoal from Period 1 features (by fragment count)
r=roundwood; s=sapwood, h=heartwood

	Feature type	burnt deposit	burnt deposit	pit	pit
	Feature number			1543	1068
	Context number	1541	1540	1544	1069
	Sample number	20	19	21	3
Ulmus sp.	elm			4	
Fagus sylvatica L.	beech	3	1	37r	
Quercus sp.	oak	17rsh	19sh	33rsh	50rs
Corylus avellana L.	hazel			18r	27r
Populus/Salix	poplar/willow				2r
Maloideae	hawthorn group			1	2r
Ilex aquifolium L.	holly				2
Acer campestre L.	field maple				6r
Fraxinus excelsior L.	ash			4	11r
Sambucus nigra L.	elder			3	
Total		**20**	**20**	**100**	**100**

Table 2: Charcoal from Period 2 features (by fragment count)
r=roundwood; s=sapwood, h=heartwood

	Feature type	pit	pit	pit	pit
	Feature number	1380	1457	1464	1467
	Context number	1381	1458	1465	1468
	Sample number	11	13	12	15
Ulmus sp.	elm	3h	13r		
Fagus sylvatica L.	beech	13r	13r	4	6
Quercus sp.	oak	28rh	68rh	16rh	9h
Betula sp.	birch	5			
Alnus glutinosa Gaertn.	alder	8r	1		
Corylus avellana L.	hazel		1r		
Betulaceae	birch family	3	3r		
Populus/Salix	poplar/willow	8			
Maloideae	hawthorn group	3			2
Acer campestre L.	field maple				2
Fraxinus excelsior L.	ash	29hr	1r		1
Total		**100**	**100**	**20**	**20**

exceptions, the use of fuelwood appears to have been consistent between Period 1 and Period 2. Oak and beech were the main fuelwoods, with more or less similar frequencies of ash and other taxa. The chief difference lies in the significance of hazel, which was well represented in the samples of Period 1, but apparently supplanted in Period 2 with a range of other taxa such as alder and birch. Whether this reflects a change in the local resources or a bias in the nature of the assemblages is difficult to ascertain.

Charcoal assemblages can usually be ascribed to two main activities, metalworking and domestic, on the basis of their association with artefacts and other ecofacts. The former category includes pit 1464, Period 2a, which also contained fired-clay mould fragments, and burnt deposit 1541, Period 1a, which also contained a smithing hearth bottom. Some of these 'metalworking' contexts also contained animal bone, cereal remains and other domestic-type rubbish, which suggests that there may have been mixing of waste material.

Metalworking activities commonly required the use of charcoal as fuel, until it was replaced with coke in the 18th century (Bayley *et al.* 2001). Oak, which makes a good calorific charcoal fuel but can be easily fragmented, was apparently used for metalworking at nos 55–60 St Thomas Street in both the medieval and late medieval periods. The metallurgical analyses suggest that any metalworking at the site was small-scale and it is likely that the oak was not transported over any great distance. The presence of oak in every sample, including those not associated with metalworking, suggests that this taxon was used for general fires, albeit with a range of supplementary fuelwood. Interestingly, there was one other oak-dominated sample from pit 1068 (Period 1a), which produced large quantities of mineralised material of possible cess derivation, and it is possible that the oak had been deposited as charcoal to minimise odours, a practice suggested at St James Priory, Bristol (Challinor, forthcoming).

The assemblages are generally consistent with results from comparable sites in Bristol (Gale 2006) and those from other urban medieval and post-medieval sites such as Oxford (Challinor 2009a) and Southampton (Challinor 2009b). The medieval period saw a rise in the use of beech as a wood fuel (which continued into the post-medieval period), supplemented by a range of other taxa. Although there is no direct evidence for coppicing/pollarding in the charcoal residues, most fuelwood throughout the early and later medieval periods was provided from the underwood of local, managed woodlands (Rackham 2006).

The analysis of charcoal from fuel residues of industrial and domestic-type deposits dating to the medieval and post-medieval periods indicates the use of similar fuels in both periods. The predominant use of oak and beech, supplemented with a range of other taxa, is comparable to fuelwood residues recovered from other medieval and post-medieval sites.

Borehole stratigraphy, by Keith Wilkinson

Three boreholes (BH1-3) were drilled within the excavation area (Fig. 2), with the objective of examining Quaternary stratigraphic layers buried at depths below which it was possible to excavate conventional archaeological trenches. Strata were not described in the field but sampled as a series of 1m-long and 50mm-diameter cores. Boreholes were drilled towards the end of the fieldwork, and hence archaeological strata were not sampled in the cores. Drilling continued until fluid sands were encountered, at which point the boreholes were abandoned. Thus BH1 was drilled to 7m below ground surface, but BH2 and BH3 could only be drilled to a depth of 5m. The borehole cores were prepared and cleaned in the laboratory and the exposed sediment strata were described using standard geological criteria (Tucker 1982; Jones *et al*. 1999; Munsell Color 2000). Stratigraphic and positional data were subsequently combined with prior geotechnical information as a database with the RockWorks geological utilities program (RockWare 2008), and that software was then used to plot the cross section shown in Fig. 18 and the deposit model shown in Fig. 19.

As a result of many geoarchaeological borehole investigations carried out in central Bristol since the late 1990s, the Holocene stratigraphy is broadly understood. Fluvial gravels of the Pleistocene Avon Formation (Campbell *et al*. 1999) are overlain by alluvial deposits of the informally defined Wentlooge formation (Allen and Rae 2007), with both units topped by 'made ground' (including archaeological deposits) of medieval and later date. The thickness of the Wentlooge formation and made-ground deposits depends on topographic location, but the broad trend is for sites in the centre of the valley and in westerly locations to have thicker Holocene stratigraphies than those on the valley sides and in easterly positions. A geotechnical study of the site carried out by WSP Environmental (WSP BH6 and WSP BH7) prior to the drilling of the geoarchaeological boreholes confirmed this basic sequence. Approximately 3m of made ground and 9.5m of Wentlooge formation sands, silts and clays overlay 2m of Pleistocene gravels (Avon Formation), which in turn lay above the Triassic Mercia Mudstone bedrock (Fig. 18).

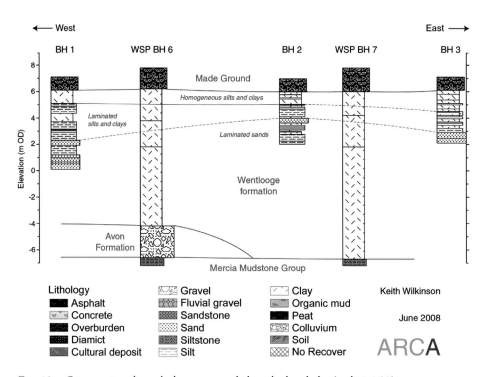

Fig. 18   Cross-section through deposits revealed in the boreholes (scale 1:350)

The deposit model (Fig. 19) demonstrates that the contact between the Wentlooge formation and the Avon Formation drops from *c.* -4m AOD in the west to *c.* -5.3m AOD in the east of the site. The data therefore suggest that a broadly north/south channel passes through the site in which the lowermost deposits of the Wentlooge formation lie. These basal Wentlooge formation deposits were only sampled in the geotechnical boreholes and have not been described in great enough detail to provide a firm indication of their genesis. However, it is likely, based on geoarchaeological data from elsewhere in Redcliffe where the entire Holocene sequence could be penetrated (e.g. Wilkinson 2008a, 2008b), that laminated silt/sand strata noted in the geoarchaeological boreholes below 3m AOD extend down to the Avon Formation gravels. The sand/silt sediments comprise 200mm thick sets of laminated reddish brown fine silts/clay and fine sands, with occasional thin beds of fine sand. Within each of the beds, wavy, parallel, continuous laminae of alternating silt/clay and fine sand are clustered in 20-50mm thick bundles. The sedimentary characteristics of the laminated sediments suggest that they formed in a deep-water channel environment.

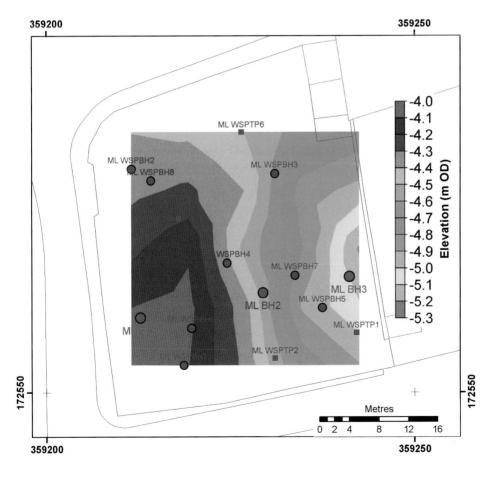

Fig. 19 Surface model showing the lower contact of the Wentlooge formation (1:500)

Similar laminated silt and sand strata have been found in the majority of geoarchaeological borehole surveys undertaken in Redcliffe, where a fluvial mode of deposition has been inferred. Although the nos 55–60 St Thomas Street laminated silt/sand strata could not be dated, radiocarbon dating has been possible on other sites and these demonstrate that the lower contact with the Avon Formation dates to between 5320–5070 cal. BC (6280±40 BP, Beta 245646) at 32–36 Victoria Street (Wilkinson 2008a), and 3630–3360 cal. BC (4720±40 BP, Beta 245645) at 1–2 Redcliff Street (Wilkinson 2008b).

The laminated silts/sands at nos 55–60 St Thomas Street, and indeed at other sites in the Redcliffe area, are conformably overlain by first laminated, then homogeneous silts and clays, the latter containing frequent iron and manganese oxide precipitates. The former silt/clays have a lamina structure that is predominantly straight, while occurrence is in regular-sized bundles. These structural and morphological properties suggest regular and pulsed deposition, most likely on mud flats or on channel margin depositional environments. The iron-stained homogeneous silts and clays probably formed in the same way as the laminated silts and clays previously discussed, but post-depositional processes resulting from water table fluctuation, bioturbation and exposure to sub-aerial processes have removed primary structural features. It has not been possible to date these silt/clay strata, either at nos 55–60 St Thomas Street or elsewhere in Redcliffe.

Archaeological and organic material is entirely absent from the Wentlooge formation deposits at nos 55–60 St Thomas Street, although charcoal layers have been found within the Wentlooge formation at other sites in Redcliffe (Wilkinson 2008a, 2008b; Wilkinson and Head 2008), demonstrating that people were active on the Avon floodplain in the Neolithic and Bronze Age periods. The value of the sediments recovered from the boreholes at nos 55–60 St Thomas Street is therefore not in their archaeological inclusions, but rather the information they provide on Middle Holocene landscapes in what is now central Bristol. The sediments track the change from a large, fast flowing river that passed across the site, to a channel-side location that was heavily influenced by tidal processes.

DISCUSSION

The excavations at nos 55–60 St Thomas Street covered the sites of six historic properties, the origin of whose boundaries are traceable to the 13th century. Over time these boundaries varied slightly in alignment, and various plots were combined and subdivided. The history of the site is in large part that of the plots which formed the framework of the fieldwork results. However, from the archaeological evidence alone it has not been possible to reconstruct individual plot or tenement histories that are chronologically distinct from their neighbours' until the late 17th century onwards (Periods 3a and 3b). The most puzzling aspect of the archaeological sequence is the episodes of dumping or aggradation between each major phase of structural activity and occupation. Most, if not all, of the features of each period showed evidence of truncation prior to burial by horizons of horizontal deposits. While it is possible that this truncation was the result of accidental machine excavation of the uppermost occupation layers of each Period, too homogeneous to be properly differentiated from subsequent mass deposits, the recognition of subtle stratigraphic relationships on many other levels of the site makes this seem unlikely. In the earlier period, if not later, the ground conditions in this area of former marsh may have been improved by periodically raising the ground level, and it is possible that some of these deposits derived from levelling and excavation at the street frontage when the principal buildings were altered or rebuilt. Similar deposits have been recognised at other sites in the Redcliffe suburb, where they have been principally assigned to horticultural activity, and examples of this are discussed below.

Periods 1a and 1b: 13th to 15th centuries

The earliest activity pre-dated the property boundaries. Deposits of trampled silty clay were clearly earlier than any boundaries and seem to represent casual activity rather than permanent settlement. The intention may have been to level up the irregular surface of the alluvium and these deposits contained the earliest pottery, of mid 12th to mid 13th-century date. The Redcliff and Temple Fees were laid out in the 1120s to 1140s, but there is no substantive evidence for occupation of these southern tenements as early as that. Animal bone was common in these deposits and it is clear that processing of animal carcasses must have been going on nearby, with this area used as a rubbish dump. The preponderance of head parts of cattle, and head and feet from sheep/goat, hints at hide processing, but cattle vertebrae probably indicate meat cuts as well. Similar mixed deposits lying above the natural alluvium were noted during investigations at sites at Portwall Lane (Good 1989, 22), and at nos 26–28 St Thomas Street (Watts 2011 [this volume]), at the latter site containing 11th to 13th-century pottery.

At nos 55–60 St Thomas Street, the upper layer (974) of the trampled silty clay deposits had pottery with a date range extending to the mid to late 13th century, and may have incorporated disturbance from the earliest construction activity. Therefore, the earliest date suggested for the laying out of tenements in Period 1a is the mid 13th century, which compares with the earliest occupation at nos 26–28 St Thomas Street (Watts 2011 [this volume]), and is a little earlier than the 14th-century pits at Portwall Lane (Good 1989, 22). In general the development of St Thomas Street would appear to be slightly later than the first occupation in the north and west of the Redcliffe suburb, notably at nos 68–72 Redcliff Street (Jones 1983) and nos 1–2 Redcliff Street (Hart, forthcoming), where occupation also followed on from some less identifiable exploitation of the area.

Most of the pottery from the first substantive occupation period in the 13th to 14th centuries was regional, but medieval Bristol's foreign contacts are reflected in a few sherds of Saintonge, Norman and other French wares. This range of pottery is typical of both rich and poor medieval households, and as such is not a reliable indicator of status, although a comparison of the percentages of utilitarian and imported wares with other published assemblages from Bristol would suggest that the occupation in this period was at the lower end of the economic scale. This is supported by the absence of evidence for consumption of high-status meat (such as venison) and a lack of artefacts that might reflect wealth.

The site was divided up into at least four plots or tenements by rows of posts and/or gullies in this period (Fencelines 1–7). The only two complete plots (2 and 3) were 10m wide, which probably represents two 'poles' (a 'pole' equalling just over 5m), although Plot 3 was subdivided into two unequally.

The two double rows of posts (Fencelines 1 and 2, and 3 and 4) appear to represent alleyways between the plots, giving access to the rear of the plots or the areas behind them to the east. The eastern boundary of these plots was beyond the limit of excavation, but was probably the Law Ditch, the parish boundary between the Temple and Redcliff Fees. Where this kinked westwards it formed the boundary between Plots 3 and 4. Fencelines 6 and 7 would have provided a level of security to the plots on either side of the Law Ditch, if it was open at this time. Fenceline 5, which was stratigraphically one of the earliest fencelines and pre-dated Fenceline 6, subdivided Plot 3 into two unequal parts, but was superseded by possible structural evidence which appeared to cross the sub-division.

Structural evidence from Period 1 was fragmentary and difficult to interpret. Two pairs of slots parallel and at right angles to each other in Plot 1 must be assumed to represent a temporary and insubstantial structure (Structure 4), probably to the rear of a more substantial building beyond the limit of excavation on the medieval St Thomas Street frontage, and Structure 1, comprised of postholes and the short slot 1096, suggests another insubstantial structure to the north. The evidence for Structure 2 in Plot 2 suggests a square or rectangular timber-and-daub building, occupying much of the width of the plot, but the full extent of this building was lost to later intrusions and the unexcavated area of contamination. A number of smaller pits and possible postholes were concentrated around this structure but no clear pattern or function could be identified.

The smaller, shallower gullies in Plot 3 may have been fragmentary beam slots for timber buildings, but while they were parallel or at right angles to each other, no clear plan could be determined, though they appear to define a rectangular area which is assumed to have been the extent of the Period 1 buildings. The robbed masonry drain 1558 was of a large enough scale to indicate more than merely domestic arrangements. This, and drain 1630 to the west, seemed to discharge into the Law Ditch where it ran between Plots 3 and 4. These features produced a large proportion of the animal bone from this period. Apart from this drain, there was no evidence for masonry structures on the site in this period. Small pit 1543, with a dump of mortar in a wooden tub, suggests the preparation of render for the walls of timber structures, or internal plastering. Lime-filled tubs in pits found elsewhere in Bristol have been suggested as lime stores for hide processing (Ridgeway and Watts (eds), forthcoming) but here the admixture of sand seems to indicate a dump of building mortar. A number of glazed crested roof tiles present in these early deposits suggest that fairly substantial domestic properties may have occupied the street frontage.

There was little to indicate any activity other than domestic occupation in Plot 1, 2 or 3. In Plot 4 there is some evidence for ironworking from relatively large quantities of oak charcoal and a smithing hearth bottom in the very thin layers of clay that sealed a cluster of small postholes. The layers also contained fragments of hearth waste and lining, and small amounts of non-specific slag, and tap slag; however, the amounts of slag were not enough to confirm smelting on site. Whether the waste was related to the posthole structures they sealed could not be demonstrated. The northern side of this plot lay beyond the site, precluding a fuller picture of the activity within it, but despite the poor quality of the evidence, it does seem to suggest a different use for this plot than for the others.

It may well be that the soil layers of Horizon 1 represent a horticultural phase of activity, following the construction of early buildings, and this might account for both truncation and the development of soils over the site. The development of Horizon 1 seems to have taken place in the early or mid 14th century. It may indicate the end of the 13th-century boom and the beginning of what appears to be a later medieval reduction in activity, at least at the back of the main buildings on the street frontage (beyond the limit of excavation).

Dry-stone wall 865 at the east end of Fenceline 8 was the earliest evidence for a masonry wall. The trench-built footing of this wall was flanked by its demolition debris spread across the top of Horizon 1. The slots to the south of this boundary are the earliest of this type of features, which were also recorded in Plot 1 in Period 2a, with additional and more extensive groups of these features in Period 2b. There are two possible interpretations: their rounded profiles suggest horticultural features, but the silty fills are indicative of open drainage trenches rather than bedding trenches, and in Period 2b the slots appear too closely spaced to represent raised beds. A series of shallow parallel slots was excavated at the site at Portwall Lane, but these were regularly spaced, approximately 2m apart, and were interpreted as for drainage or horticultural trenches (Good 1989, 23). The second possibility is that they were structural, either floor joists or possibly the ground beams of drying racks for cloth after dyeing or fulling. Millerd's plan shows drying racks at Rack Close in 1673, but these look as if they would leave rows of postholes as evidence, and for the medieval period, no examples are known. Nonetheless, the documents for no. 61 St Thomas Street refer to a woolworker next door at no. 60 (Plot 1) in 1456 and 1457 (BRO: P/StT/D/1; P/StT/D/137), so it is possible that these features relate to the processing of cloth; if not racks then some structural evidence for a drying room, such as that listed in a will of 1441, which may refer to a piece of land on the corner of Mitchell Lane and St Thomas Street (Wadley 1886).

Compared to the activity in Period 1a, the evidence from the 14th to 15th centuries suggests that most of the plots were open and therefore less developed than in the 13th century. Documentary evidence seems to confirm or at least strengthen this impression. Plot 1 (no. 60 St Thomas Street) was a garden throughout the 15th century (BRO: P/StT/D/134–35), and leases and wills of this period suggest that Plots 2, 3 and 4 were also largely open ground ('void ground' and 'garden'), although this remains a little uncertain because the exact site of the properties involved is arguable (Wadley 1886). However, Leech (*The documentary evidence*, above) argues that nos 54–57 St Thomas Street (Plots 3 and 4) were part of Foster's Charity land, described in the 15th century as garden.

If the laying-out of tenements in the later 13th century was intended to lead to a dense urban environment, the archaeological evidence suggests that this aim was not realised in Period 1. The cross-plot activity represented by Horizon 1 at the end of Period 1a is less puzzling when the relatively low level of activity seen in Period 1b is considered. Only the fencelines between Plots 1 and 2 were renewed in this phase, and there seems to have been little activity apart from the excavation of slots in Plot 1. The homogeneous layers defined as Horizon 2 can be interpreted as a silty soil developing over largely abandoned (or at least not actively developed) plots.

The lack of urban occupation here in the late medieval period is very different from the northern and eastern end of the suburb. Property boundaries were established from the 12th century at nos 98–103 Redcliff Street (BaRAS 1999). At nos 68–72 Redcliff Street the tenements appear to have been laid out in a single operation in the late 12th or early 13th century and the area was heavily occupied by the end of the 13th century (Jones 1983). At nos 110–112 Redcliff Street (Buchanans Wharf), the earliest stone footings date to the 12th century (Burchill 1987). Nos 1–2 Redcliff Street show occupation beginning at much the same time, developing into continuous activity with masonry buildings in the 13th and 14th centuries (Hart, forthcoming). In contrast, development at St Thomas Street appears to be later and less intense, as indicated by the excavations almost opposite the site at nos 26–28 St Thomas Street (Watts 2011 [this volume]) and nos 30–38 Thomas Street (Jackson 2004, 60), where dumping and pit digging in the 11th to 13th centuries was followed by construction of stone walls in the late medieval to post-medieval period, but there was no clear evidence of tenement creation. At the corner of St Thomas Street and Portwall Lane a brief period of gardening is described (Good 1989, 26) between the earlier pit digging and the late 14th or early 15th-century building, which echoes the separation of activity in Periods 1a and 1b by Horizon 1. It has been suggested that there was no substantive occupation of this part of the suburb until after the creation of the Portwall in 1240 (Hebditch 1968) and the archaeological evidence from nos 55–60 St Thomas Street certainly fits that model.

Periods 2a and 2b: 15th to 17th centuries

There was no evidence for a boundary between Plots 1 and 2 in Period 2, but the layout of features indicated that one continued into the post-medieval period. A metalled track formed the boundary between Plots 2 and 3, supporting the interpretation that the earlier fencelines flanked access lanes to the back of the plots. Another access lane is represented by double rows of postholes and gullies (Fencelines 9 and 10) on the north side of Plot 3. The large trench filled with building debris that ran north to south bisecting Plot 2 (1243) may have been some kind of internal boundary, although it is remarkably massive for such a purpose.

There was no evidence for a masonry building from which the debris in gully 1243 could have come, as Structure 5 at the east end of the plot appears to have been timber-built. This structure lacked a coherent plan and may represent several phases of activity. There was little else in the early part of this period to indicate major structural activity.

Well 1 in Plot 2 was the earliest identified. It was abandoned and robbed in Period 2b. The apparent lack of wells in Periods 1 and 2 may again suggest limited or no permanent occupation of these plots.

The mould fragments for casting of metal cauldrons found in pit 1464 in Plot 4 are redeposited, but provide evidence of fairly heavy industry in the vicinity. A scatter of post-pits to the west of pit 1464, including two sub-rectangular ones, may have been some kind of shelter associated with the cauldron casting. No plan was obvious but the stone packing in several of these postholes does indicate a structural function. The debris of metalworking in the preceding Period 1 suggests a continuity of industrial activity either on or near Plot 4. A similar sequence of ironworking followed by evidence for a copper-alloy foundry was found at nos 68–72 Redcliff Street (Jones 1983). Large quantities of clay mould fragments from copper-alloy casting were also found in late 14th to early 15th-century deposits at the corner of St Thomas Street and Portwall Lane, possibly from a bell foundry (Good 1989, 26).

Horizon 3 represented another probable episode of horticulture, which sealed the earlier Period 2 evidence in Plots 1, 3 and 4. Across the middle of the site in Plots 2 and 3 almost no archaeological evidence survived to suggest activity in Period 2b, other than a few scattered pits in Plot 3, and the absence of silty clay layers (Horizon 3) in Plot 2 suggests little use of the backplot even for horticultural purposes. Two stone-packed pits with 17th-century dating in the area of the alleyway on the north side of Plot 3 might be taken to suggest that the alleyway was blocked towards the end of this period.

The series of drains in Plot 4 suggests a sequence of activity in Period 2b, but cannot be ascribed to any clear purpose above that of drainage. Gully 1394 may have run into the precursor to Culvert 4 (Period 3a). The bulbous west end of ditch 1316 may have been a sump drained by the ditch. The fills suggested deliberate backfill rather than silting, so added little to understanding the function of these features.

The slots that extended across Plot 1 in Period 2b, dating to the late 16th or 17th century, have been discussed with similar features from the earlier periods. If these represent a structure, its full width could not be established as the slots extended south beyond the edge of the site. No other features apart from a few pits appeared to be associated with them.

The animal bone evidence shows that there was a change in meat consumption patterns in Period 2. While general patterns of food and other species were similar, if slightly more wide-ranging in the later period, the slaughter of younger cattle and pigs suggests a more specialised market for meat consumption, and possibly a rise in status. The pottery assemblage is too small to reliably contribute to this debate, although there are hints of higher status in the small assemblage of imported wares. The evidence for small-scale structural activity and open spaces across the site is consonant with the 15th-century documentary evidence, and the inference is that the tenements here in the later medieval and early post-medieval periods were often held as garden ground and lodges used for housing cloth racks, or as recreational retreats from the centre of town (*The documentary evidence*, above). The period of horticultural activity represented by Horizon 3 at nos 55–60 St Thomas Street has possible parallels with the 16th-century garden soils noted at the corner of St Thomas Street and Portwall Lane (Good 1989, 26) and at nos 30–38 St Thomas Street (Jackson 2004, 60); at both these sites this was preceded by the demolition of 14th or 15th-century masonry structures, that lay towards the street frontages. A similar sequence noted at nos 68–72 Redcliff Street (Jones 1983) suggests that this decline in urban activity was more widespread in the Redcliffe suburb, although possibly confined to the southern end. Further north at nos 1–2 Redcliff Street, late medieval buildings were demolished in the 17th century but immediately replaced (Hart, forthcoming).

Nonetheless, later 16th-century mapping (Smith 1568) shows the frontages of the properties at nos 55–60 St Thomas Street as built up, largely in the areas unavailable for excavation, under modern St Thomas Street. Although some of the tenement divisions were not archaeologically visible in the area of excavation in this period, it is apparent that the boundaries first identified in Period 1a were preserved at the street frontage, to be re-established at the rear of the plots in the later 17th century (Period 3 below).

Period 3: later 17th to mid 20th centuries

The structural remains dating from the later 17th to early 19th centuries (Period 3a) were those of a series of long, narrow buildings running back from St Thomas Street. Some building plans can be reconstructed by comparing the archaeological remains to documents of the properties at various dates, although due to 20th-century widening of St Thomas Street, the frontages of these buildings were beyond the limit of excavation. The remains of the Period 3 buildings were at cellar or basement level. The four plots were divided into six tenements. In the late 19th and 20th-centuries (Period 3b), much of the site was rebuilt for commercial purposes.

Period 3a: later 17th to early 19th centuries

Plot 1: no. 60 St Thomas Street
Parts of two rooms of Building 1 were revealed, but the main interest was the large stone cistern at the rear of the building. This had been modified in Period 3b so its original function

could not be ascertained. Its stone-flagged floor suggests it was built as a cess pit, but its relationship to the stone culvert that ran beneath it was not established, and it was big enough to have been a small cellar, although there was no means of access. It may relate to the use of the property as a public house, known by 1764 as The Artichoke (*The documentary evidence*, above). The Artichoke remained in existence at least until 1775. By 1800 the property was at least partly in multiple occupancy but neither the maps nor the archaeological record suggest this entailed alteration or extension to the property in this period.

Plot 2: nos 58–59 St Thomas Street
The Ordnance Survey (OS) map of 1882 (Fig. 21) shows that Plot 2 contained two mirrored houses with outbuildings to the rear, which appear to be the surviving Period 3a houses. The tiny walled front area, with the façade set very slightly back from the street, suggests an 18th to early 19th-century date for these, rather than earlier. The excavated remains of these on site were Building 2 to the south, and Building 5 to the north. More survived of Building 5 and the fragments match the map of 1882 in plan very well. The unexcavated well to the rear of the remains of Building 5 fell on the boundary of nos 58 and 59, and is shown with a pump in 1882. By 1800 the properties were in common ownership, but severally occupied.

Plot 3: nos 56–57 St Thomas Street
The remains of the house at no. 57 St Thomas Street (Building 6) were the best preserved of this period, largely because they were incorporated into the early 20th-century rebuild of the foundry which occupied these plots (and eventually all of the site) in later Period 3b. It can also be identified in a plan of the foundry of that period. Its plan was typical of the still evolving later 17th and early 18th-century urban terrace. Its central and presumably top-lit dogleg staircase was reached by a lateral corridor and was set between the front and rear rooms. The two post pads 779 and 780, excavated in the centre of this room, may represent stair supports. At the rear, separated from the body of the house by a courtyard, was a large detached room which survived well, including the stone-flagged floor and evidence of a fireplace. Excavation showed that this was a vaulted basement, large parts of whose brick-vault survived. It probably supported a room above which could have been a detached kitchen, or perhaps a workshop or warehouse, although access for goods would have been limited by the width of the lateral corridor in the frontage building.

These buildings occupied roughly over half of the tenement. East of the kitchen/workshop was a walled garden or courtyard, 10m x 5m. At its east end, centrally on the wall, was what appeared to be a drinking fountain or conduit linked to Well 6, in what was probably a well house (Building 10), only part of which fell in the excavated area. It is likely that the well was pumped, perhaps into a water tank at a high level. Overflow from this and the fountain was fed back into the culvert which ran under the garden and Building 6. It is not clear if this was later than Building 6 but it may well have been. Culvert 3 ran north from the east end of the vaulted basement, to drain into Culvert 4. The fact that the drain ran across the neighbouring property is of interest in that it implies rights of drainage to the Law Ditch and may explain the similar cross-boundary routes of the gullies and drains in Periods 1 and 2.

It seems probable that no. 57 St Thomas Street is that held by Samuel Wickham in 1725, described as a workhouse and yard. By 1730 it was held by Stephen Doggett, who had moved from no. 58. However, the history of nos 56 and 57 is confused as they were both owned by the Foster Charity from the late medieval period, and this may account for the record of only four properties (sometimes three) along St Thomas Street (south of the Law Ditch) until well into the 18th century. It seems that both were Samuel Wickham's workhouse and yard in 1725 and 1730, and the same description was given when Doggett became the occupant in 1735. The description, general as it is, fits no. 57 in Period 3a well, although as a workhouse yard the water feature excavated at the rear of the property is unlikely to have had an ornamental function.

An 1816 lease plan of no. 61 St Thomas Street, immediately south of the excavated area, includes a watercolour elevation (Fig. 20). This illustrates a mid to late 17th-century house of no great pretention, probably typical of what was being erected in Period 3a in this area. The house at no. 57 is a close match in plan to no. 61, but a little more advanced, reflecting its probable later date.

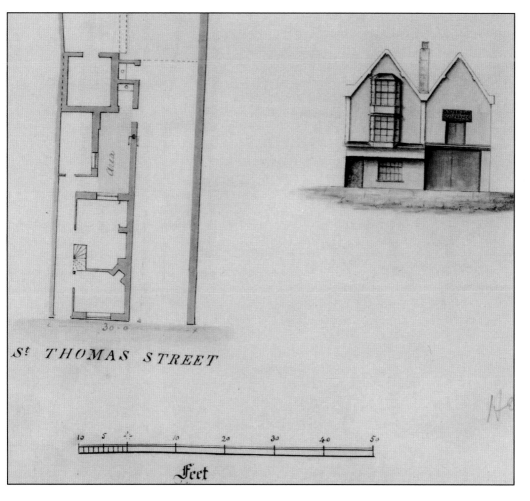

Fig. 20   Plan and elevation of no. 61 St Thomas Street, 1816–17 (BRO: P/StT/Ch/3/31 fol.4)

Plot 4: no. 55 St Thomas Street

The Law Ditch was culverted in this period (Culvert 4), thus removing any trace of earlier forms of this drain, which may have been left open until buildings in the flanking plots were extended in this period.

Pre-dating the construction of Building 7 were scraps of cobbling that may indicate a yard or workshop where the front room was later situated. Building 7 was originally a short building like Building 1, with a cess pit and two wells (Wells 2 and 4) in the back garden. This was extended by less than two metres when the rear wall was rebuilt, and then again when two heated rooms were added to the rear of the house along with a half-width room and a vaulted cess pit. This earliest phase of the building was probably early 18th century, as the underlying cobbled floors were dated to the late 17th century. In 1755 and 1802 this property was documented as the Ring of Bells public house (*The documentary evidence*, above), and business expansion may well account for its extension to the rear.

It is clear that, after some activity and building in the early part of this period, the development of this part of St Thomas Street took off in the 18th century and that the area was prosperous enough to support rebuilding, modifications and extensions. Tax returns from the later 17th century seem to show that St Thomas Street was only partly built up at this time, although Millerd's map of 1673 (Fig. 2) shows buildings all along the frontage. As late as 1695 only three of the potential five properties along St Thomas Street were listed, one being a house and stable (Ralph and Williams 1968, 115). The documentary evidence from here into the early 18th century indicates tenements, stables, warehouses and workshops as well as yards, but occupations are not given. Occupations are given in Sketchley's Directory from 1775 (grocer, carpenter, gent., victualler, etc.), but this does not necessarily reflect the activities in the properties themselves, except for the victuallers at nos 56 and 60, both public houses at this time. The remaining occupants places of work may have been off-site. The houses were built in typical late 17th and 18th-century Bristol fashion in sandstone rubble, and both the excavated and the documentary evidence shows that this was rendered. It was not possible to distinguish archaeologically between domestic or commercial/industrial property use (nor should we expect that the inhabitants did so).

Changes that led to the major upheavals in the early 20th century began when no. 57 was taken over by Gevers, an iron founder, in the 1810s. This foundry continued under various owners, growing with the acquisition of no. 56 by 1880. The latter property seems not to have been mentioned in rate and tax returns after 1830 and had most likely merged with no. 57 soon after that date. Until the 1930s the tenements south of no. 57 remained in domestic occupation.

Not much 18th-century pottery was recovered, which could reflect a lower residential density, but it more likely reflects a different loss pattern at this period, exacerbated by a lack of catchment, with more hard floors and fewer dug features.

Period 3b: 19th to mid 20th centuries AD

Rebuilding on the St Thomas Street frontage seems to have begun in the early 20th century. Archaeologically, the only structural traces from this period were remnants of the rebuild of no. 60 on Plot 1, a drain and well in no. 59 on Plot 2, and fragments of the rebuilding of the foundry that occupied nos 55 to 57 in Plots 3 and 4. Most of the concrete floors and other structures of this period were removed during preliminary site clearance.

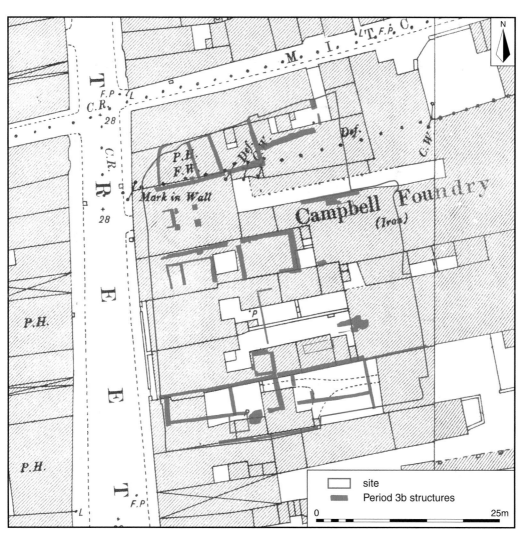

Fig. 21 Extract from 1882 1:500 Ordnance Survey map, with Period 3b (19th to mid 20th centuries) structures superimposed (scale 1:500)

At no. 60 the earlier house was rebuilt and divided into two long, narrow sections by a spine wall, but remained in one ownership. This does not appear to have happened before 1887 as its earlier form is on the Goad Fire Insurance Plan of that year (BRO; Fig. 6), although the construction of the ice house is identified, which was the brick-floored and walled room excavated at the rear of the property in Plot 1. Well 9 has been attributed to this period as it truncated cistern 573 of Period 3a and the later walls seemed to respect it, but it may have been a late Period 3a feature continuing in use into Period 3b, as it appears on the 1882 Ordnance Survey (OS) map as a pump (Fig. 20). The house had been rebuilt by 1938, as shown on plans relating to the road widening scheme of that year. By 1949

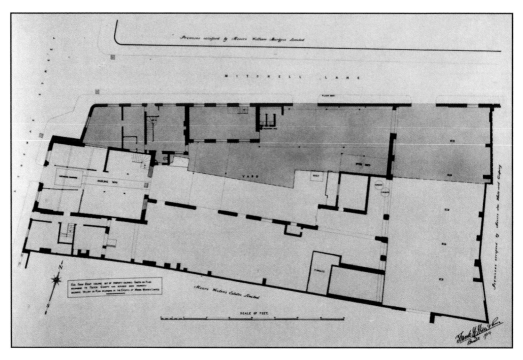

Fig. 22   Plan of nos 54–57 St Thomas Street, 1914 (BRO: 38041/BMC/12/PL3 fol.71)

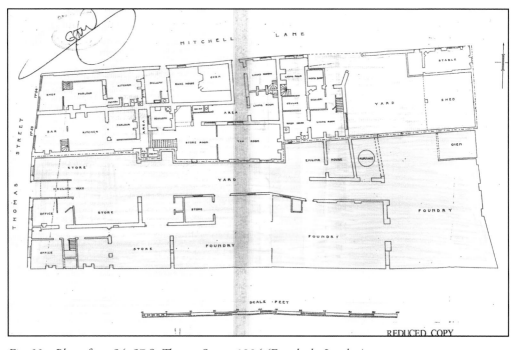

Fig. 23   Plan of nos 54–57 St Thomas Street, 1904 (Eversheds, London)

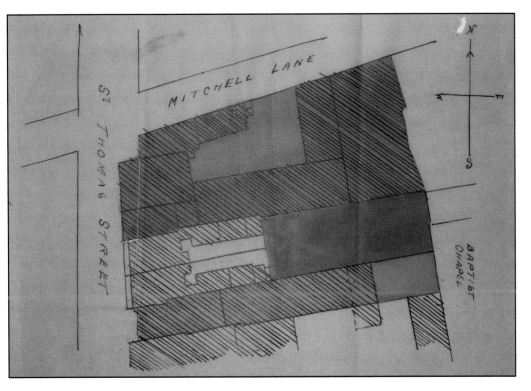

Fig. 24   Plan of nos 55–60 St Thomas Street, separate property holdings making up the estate of the Bristol Foundry Company, c. 1939 (BRO: 24529)

the site was a machine and erecting shop, part of the foundry (BRO: Goad *c*. 1949 Fire Insurance Plan).

The Period 3a houses at nos 58 and 59 St Thomas Street survived up to the road widening of 1939, as shown on a lease plan of 1939 (Fig. 23). In 1949 the properties were part of the foundry and were occupied by a machine shop and machine store (BRO: Goad *c*. 1949 Fire Insurance Plan).

At no. 55, the excavated remains can be equated with those shown in a survey plan of 1914 that seems to be of a recently built establishment (Fig. 21). In any case, these buildings do not appear on the Goad 1887 Fire Insurance Plan (BRO). On the Goad *c*. 1949 Fire Insurance Plan (BRO) these buildings were of the offices and a pattern shop behind, fronting Mitchell Lane. In no. 56, the remains were those of a weighbridge pit and the foundations for steel stanchions that flanked a 'hauling way' marked on the 1914 plan (Fig. 22). This led into a rear yard through the large room whose upper floor the stanchions supported. South of this the Period 3a house at no. 57 (Building 6), the original foundry from 1810, survived as offices incorporated in the rebuild, although its rear vaulted cellar was buried under the new floor. By the 1930s the foundry had taken over the entire block. Wholesale reorganisation and rebuilding of the area south of no. 55 followed the road widening of 1938, and by 1949 the area had been transformed. Between 1949 and the 1951 edition of the Ordnance Survey (OS) map the foundry had contracted to occupy only no. 55 St Thomas Street, with engineering works in nos 58–60. The 1959 OS map records a garage at no. 55. The buildings had been demolished before the 1974 revision of the OS map, and the site remained as an open space until the recent development.

Conclusions

The excavations at nos 55–60 St Thomas Street have shown that the earliest activities on the site seem to have been a little later than those to the north of the Redcliffe suburb, with only the slightest indications of pre-13th century utilisation. Substantive activity came in the mid to late 13th century, with the laying out of what proved to be long-lived property boundaries, typically long and thin urban tenements running back from St Thomas Street. The tenements were not destined to be intensively occupied through much of their history, however, and there is evidence to support the documentary references to gardens and small structures such as lodges and stables, from the general lack of substantial structural remains in Periods 1 and 2. On the other hand, lack of recognisable buildings does not preclude the use of the area for industrial activities as shown by the evidence for iron forging and, less certainly, for smelting and the casting of copper-alloy vessels, although these latter processes may derive from the immediate vicinity, rather than the site itself. Nonetheless, by the 15th century, if not before, and well into the 17th century, the excavated area was probably largely open, albeit with roadside buildings largely beyond the western limit of excavation, from which the domestic assemblages of animal bone and pottery may derive.

Development took off, at least in an archaeologically visible way, in the later 17th century, which reflects the boom in Bristol's trade in that period and through the 18th century (Manson 2000). Smith's map of 1568 suggests that the area was built up and Millerd's map of 1673 certainly shows the frontages all built up, but tax returns indicate a less intense occupation. By 1696 only three properties were listed here, and as far as the tax authorities were concerned the area was not fully developed until around 1725 (BaRAS 2002a). The first clear documented picture of occupation and development of all the properties does not come until Sketchley's Directory of 1775, but there can be little doubt that this density was reached much earlier in the century.

The framework provided by these developments seems to have served the area until the early 20th century, when properties were amalgamated and rebuilt for the foundry. This pattern appears to be typical of the 20th-century industrialisation of the Redcliffe and Temple suburbs in this period, largely removing the residential element that had been an integral part of the industrial use of the area previously.

ACKNOWLEDGEMENTS

The authors would like to thank Blenheim House Construction Ltd and CB Richard Ellis Investors Ltd (and in particular Mark Cowley) for enabling the funds to be available to complete the post-excavation work. The project was monitored by Bob Jones of Bristol City Council, whose comments during the excavation and on the post-excavation report were gratefully received. The fieldwork was directed by Mike Rowe and managed by Mary Alexander and Simon Cox. The post-excavation work was managed by Mary Alexander. Pete Moore prepared the illustrations. E.R. McSloy is grateful to Mike Ponsford, John Allan and John Shepherd for their advice. The project archives and finds will be deposited with Bristol City Museum and Art Gallery under accession number BRSMG 2006/6.

BIBLIOGRAPHY

Primary Sources

BRO (Bristol Record Office):
04041 fol.298
04335(5) fol.98
04335(7) fol.162
04335(9) fol.102
04044(1) fol.222
04479(2) fol.114
24529
24529(5)
38041/BMC/12/PL3 fol.71
Building Plan Book 47, fol.68
Building Plan book 174, fol.28
Goad 1887 Fire Insurance Plan
Goad *c.* 1949 Fire Insurance Plan
P/STMR/D/4/1
P/StT/Ch/3/31 fol.4
P/StT/D/1
P/StT/D/4
P/StT/D/15–16
P/StT/D/133–37
P/StT/D/139–40
P/StT/D/154

TNA (The National Archives):
PROB11/9 Dogett 9

Eversheds, London
Calendar of deeds for 55–60 St Thomas Street

Secondary Sources

Allen, J.R.L. and Rae, J.E. 1987 'Late Flandrian shoreline oscillations in the Severn Estuary: a geomorphological and stratigraphical reconnaissance', *Phil. Trans. Roy. Soc. London* **B315**, 185–230

Atkinson, D.R. 1965 'Clay tobacco pipes and pipemakers of Marlborough', *Wiltshire Archaeol. Natur. Hist. Mag.* **60**, 85–95

BaRAS (Bristol and Region Archaeological Services) 1999 'Archaeological Evaluation at 98–103 Redcliff Street, Redcliffe, Bristol', BaRAS unpublished report **608/1999**

BaRAS (Bristol and Region Archaeological Services) 2002a 'Archaeological Desktop Study of Mitchell Lane, Redcliffe, Bristol', BaRAS unpublished report **972/2002**

BaRAS (Bristol and Region Archaeological Services) 2002b 'Archaeological Evaluation of land at Mitchell Lane, Redcliffe, Bristol', BaRAS unpublished report **1043/2002**

Bayley, J., Dungworth, D. and Paynter, S. 2001 *Archaeometallurgy* Centre for Archaeology Guidelines **2001/01**, London, English Heritage

Behrensmeyer. A.K. 1978 'Taphonomic and ecologic information from bone weathering', *Palaeobiology* **4(2)**, 150–62

BGS (British Geological Survey) 1974 *1:50,000 Geological Survey of Great Britain (England and Wales), Solid and Drift, map sheet 264: Bristol* Keyworth, British Geological Survey

Blaylock, S.R. 2000 'Excavation of an Early Post-Medieval Bronze Foundry at Cowick Street, Exeter, 1999-2000', *Proc. Devon Archaeol. Soc.* **58**, 1–92

Boessneck, J. 1969 'Osteological differences between sheep (*Ovis aries* Linné) and Goat (*Capra hircus* Linné)', in D.R. Brothwell and E.S. Higgs (eds) 1969, 331–58

Brothwell, D.R. and Higgs E.S. (eds) 1969 *Science in Archaeology* London, Thames and Hudson

Butler, R. and Green, C. 2003 *English Bronze Cooking Vessels and their Founders 1350–1830* Honiton, Roderick and Valentine Butler

Burchill, R. 1987 'Excavations at Buchanan's Wharf, Redcliff Street, Bristol in 1985–6', *Bristol Avon Archaeol.* **6**, 17–23

Campbell, S., Hunt, C.O., Scourse, J.D., Keen, D.H. and Croot, D.G. 1999 'Southwest England', in D.Q. Bowen (ed.) 1999, *A revised correlation of Quaternary deposits in the British Isles* Geological Society Special Report **23**, London, Geological Society, 66–78

Challinor, D. 2009a 'The Wood Charcoal' in A. Norton and G. Cockin 2009, 'Excavations at The Classics Centre, 65–67 St Giles, Oxford', *Oxoniensia* **73**, 161–94, 193–4

Challinor, D. 2009b 'Charcoal', in R. Brown, *Excavations at Southampton French Quarter 1382* Specialist Download E5, Online Oxford Archaeology Library, http://library.thehumanjourney.net/55 (accessed 25th August 2010)

Challinor, D. (forthcoming) 'The Wood Charcoal', in R. Jackson, 'St James' Priory, Bristol: excavation of the cloisters 2004–2005', *Bristol and Avon Archaeol.*

Charleston, R.J. 1987 'The post-medieval glass (sixteenth to eighteenth century)', in S.S. Frere, P. Bennett, J. Rady and S. Stow 1987, *Canterbury excavations intra- and extra-mural sites 1945–55 and 1980–84: the archaeology Vol. 8* Maidstone, Kent Archaeological Society, 232–50

Clark, J. 1995 *Medieval Finds from Excavations in London 3: The medieval horse and its equipment c. 1150–1450* London, HMSO

Cronne, H.A. (ed.) 1946 *Bristol Charters 1378–1499*, Bristol Record Soc. **11**, Bristol, Bristol Record Society

Crummy, N. 1988 *The Post-Roman Small Finds from Excavations in Colchester 1971–85* Colchester Archaeol. Rep. **5**, Colchester, Colchester Archaeological Trust

Dobney, K. and Reilly, K. 1988 'A method for recording archaeological animal bones: the use of diagnostic zones', *Circaea* **5(2)**, 79–96

Donn, B. 1773 *Plan of the City of Bristol delineated from actual survey by Benjamin Donn* London, Benjamin Donn

Gale, R, 2006 'Charcoal from the 13th-14th century hearths', in R. Jackson 2006, 'Archaeological Excavations at the former Courage Brewery, Bath Street, Bristol, 2000-2001', *Bristol Avon Archaeol.* **21**, 1–58, 45–8

Good, G.L. 1987 'The excavation of two docks at Narrow Quay, Bristol, 1978–9', *Post-Medieval Archaeol.* **21**, 25–126

Good, G.L. 1989 'An excavation at the corner of St Thomas Street and Portwall Lane', *Bristol Avon Archaeol.* **8**, 20–9

Good, L. 1998 'Copper alloy', in R. Price with M.W. Ponsford 1998, 166–9

Goodall, I.H. 1980 *Ironwork in Medieval Britain: An Archaeological Study* Unpublished PhD thesis, University of Cardiff

Grant A. 1982 'The use of tooth wear as a guide to the age of domestic ungulates', in B. Wilson, C. Grigson, and S. Payne 1982, *Ageing and Sexing Animal bones from archaeological sites* BAR Brit. Ser. **109**, Oxford, British Archaeological Reports, 91–108

Griffiths, D. Philpott, R.A. and Egan, G. 2007 *Meols: The archaeology of the North-West Wirral Coast. Discoveries and objects in the 19th and 20th centuries with a catalogue of collections* University of Oxford School of Archaeology Monograph **68**, Oxford, University of Oxford School of Archaeology

Gutiérrez, A. 2007 'Pottery', in R. Jackson 2007, 'Excavations at the Old Council House, Corn Street, Bristol, 2005', *Bristol Avon Archaeol.* **22**, 47–78, 59–64

Hart, J. (forthcoming) *Excavations at nos 1-2 and no. 3 Redcliff Street, Bristol* Cotswold Archaeology Monograph, Cirencester, Cotswold Archaeology

Hebditch, M.G. '1968 Excavations on the Medieval Defences, Portwall Lane, Bristol', *Trans. Bristol Gloucestershire Archaeol. Soc.* **87**, 131–43

Higbee, L. (forthcoming) 'The Animal Bone', in J. Hart (forthcoming)

Higbee, L. 2004 'The faunal remains', in R. Jackson 2004, 45–7

Insole, P. and Jackson, R. 2000 'The excavation of a clay tobacco pipe kiln, Temple Quay, Bristol', *Bristol Avon Archaeol.* **17**, 129–38

Ireland, C. A. 1998 'The pottery', in D. Wilkinson and A. McWhirr 1998, 98–141

Jackson, R. 2004 'Archaeological excavations at nos 30–38 St. Thomas Street & no. 60 Redcliff Street, Bristol, 2000', *Bristol Avon Archaeol.* **19**, 1–63

Jackson, R. 2010 *The archaeology of the medieval suburb of Broadmead, Bristol. Excavations at Union Street, 2000* Bristol, Bristol and Region Archaeological Services

Jackson, R.G. and Price, R.H. 1974 *Bristol clay pipes: a study of makers and their marks* BCM Research Monograph **1**, Bristol, Bristol City Museum

Jones, A.P., Tucker, M.E. and Hart, J.K. 1999 'Guidelines and recommendations', in A.P. Jones, M.E. Tucker, and J.K. Hart (eds) 1999, *The description and analysis of Quaternary stratigraphic field sections* Quaternary Res. Assoc. Tech. Guide **7**, London, Quaternary Research Association, 27–76

Jones, J. 2010 'Plant macrofossil remains', in R. Jackson 2010, 77–95

Jones, J. (forthcoming) 'Plant macrofossil remains', in K. Brady, B.M. Ford and S. Teague (forthcoming), *Excavations at Finzel's Reach, Bristol, Avon* OA monograph, Oxford, Oxford Archaeology

Jones R.H. 1983 'Excavations at 68–72 Redcliff Street, Bristol, 1982', *Bristol Avon Archaeol.* **2**, 37–9

Jope, E.M. 1952 'Medieval Pottery', in H. O'Neil 1952, 61–76

Kellaway, G.A. and Welch, F.B.A. 1948 *British Regional Geology: Bristol and Gloucester District* London, HMSO

Leech, R.H. 2003 'The garden house: merchant culture and identity in the early modern city', in S. Lawrence (ed.) 2003, *Archaeologies of the British: explorations of identity in Great Britain and its colonies 1600-1945* One World Archaeol. Ser. Vol. **46**, London, Routledge, 76–86

Levitan, B. 1988 'Animal Bone', in B. Williams 1988, 160–3

Lewcun, M. 2004 'The clay tobacco pipes', in K. Rodwell and R. Bell 2004, 351–9

MacGregor, A. 1985 *Bone, Antler, Ivory and Horn: the technology of skeletal materials since the Roman period* London, Croom Helm

Manchee, T.J. 1831 *The Bristol Charities, Vols 1 and 2* Bristol, T.J. Manchee

Manson, M. 2000 *Bristol: Beyond the Bridge* Bristol, Past and Present Press

Matthews, W. 1870 *Bristol Directory* Bristol, J. Wright

McCarthy, M.R. 1974 'The medieval kilns on Nash Hill, Lacock, Wiltshire', *Wiltshire Archaeol. Natur. Hist. Soc.* **69**, 97–160

McSloy E.R. (forthcoming[a]) 'The Pottery', in J. Hart (forthcoming)

McSloy E.R. (forthcoming[b]) 'Medieval pottery', in V. Ridgeway and M. Watts (eds) (forthcoming)

McSloy E.R. (forthcoming[c]) 'Medieval ceramic roof tile', in V. Ridgeway and M. Watts (eds) (forthcoming)

Millerd, J. 1673 *An Exact Delineation of the Famous Citty of Bristol and Suburbs Thereof* Bristol

Millerd, J. *c.* 1715 *An Exact Delineation of the Famous Citty of Bristol and Suburbs Thereof* Bristol

MPRG (Medieval Pottery Research Group) 1998 'A Guide to the Classification of Medieval Ceramic Forms', *MPRG Occas. Pap.* **1**, Medieval Pottery Research Group

Munsell Color 2000 *Munsell soil color charts* New Windsor (NY), Munsell Color

Musty, J. 1973 'A preliminary account of a medieval pottery industry at Minety, North Wiltshire', *Wilts. Archaeol. Natur. Hist. Mag.* **68**, 79–88

Nicholson, R.B. and Hillam, J. 1987 'A dendrochronological analysis of oak timbers from the early medieval site at Dundas Wharf, Bristol', *Trans Bristol Gloucestershire Archaeol. Soc.* **105**, 133–45

Noël Hume, I. 1969 *A Guide to Artifacts of Colonial America* Philadelphia, University of Pennsylvania Press

O'Connor, T. 2000 *The archaeology of animal bones* Stroud, Sutton

O'Neil, H. 1952 'Whittington Court Roman Villa, Whittington, Gloucestershire: a report of the Excavations undertaken from 1948 to 1951', *Trans. Bristol Gloucestershire Archaeol. Soc.* **71**, 13–87

OS (Ordnance Survey) 1882 *1:500 series map*

OS (Ordnance Survey) 1951 *1:2500 series, map sheet 31/5872*

OS (Ordnance Survey) 1959 *1:1250 series map*

OS (Ordnance Survey) 1974 *1:1250 series map*

Oswald, A. 1975 *Clay pipes for the archaeologist* BAR Brit. Ser. **14**, Oxford, British Archaeological Reports

Pearce, J. and Vince, A. 1988 *A Dated Type-Series of London Medieval Pottery, Part 4: Surrey Whitewares* London Middlesex Archaeol. Soc. Spec. Pap. **10**, London, London and Middlesex Archaeological Society

Ponsford, M.W. 1988 'Pottery', in B. Williams 1988, 124–45

Ponsford, M.W. 1991 'Dendrological dates from Dundas Wharf, Bristol, and the dating of Ham Green and other medieval pottery', in E. Lewis (ed.) 1991, *Custom and Ceramics: essays presented to Kenneth Barton* Bristol, Wickham, 81–103

Ponsford, M.W. 1998 'Pottery', in R. Price with M.W. Ponsford, 136–56

Potter, E.C. 1992 'On being interested in the extreme (presidential address)', *J. Royal Soc. New South Wales* **125**, 79–91

Price, R., Jackson, R. and Jackson P. 1979 *Bristol clay pipe makers: a revised and enlarged edition* Bristol, published by the authors

Price, R., Jackson, R. and Jackson, P. 1984 'The Ring family of Bristol, clay tobacco pipe manufacturers', *Post-Medieval Archaeol.* **18**, 263–300

Price, R. with Ponsford M.W. 1998 *St Bartholomew's Hospital, Bristol: The Excavation of a Medieval Hospital 1976–8* CBA Research Report **110**, York, Council for British Archaeology

Rackham, O. 2006 *Woodlands* London, Collins

Ridgeway, V. and Watts, M. (eds) (forthcoming) *Cabot Circus, Bristol: the archaeology of the Broadmead expansion project, 2005–8* CAPCA monograph **1**, London, Cotswold Archaeology/Pre-Construct Archaeology

Rockware 2008 RockWorks v2006 http://www.rockware.com (accessed 20 May 2008)

Rocque, J. 1743 *A Plan of the City of Bristol. Survey'd and drawn by John Rocque. Engrav'd by John Pine 1742* Bristol, Hickey

Rodwell, K. and Bell, R. 2004 *Acton Court: the evolution of an early Tudor courtier's house* London, English Heritage

Rutter, J.A. and Davey, P.J. 1980 'Clay pipes from Chester', in P.J. Davey (ed.) 1980, *The archaeology of the clay tobacco pipe III* BAR Brit. Ser. **78**, Oxford, British Archaeological Reports, 41–272

Silver, I.A. 1969 'The ageing of domestic animals', in D.R. Brothwell and E.S. Higgs (eds) 1969, 283–302

Sketchley, J. 1775 *Sketchley's Bristol Directory* Bristol, James Sketchley

Smith, W. 1568 *Plan of Bristow*

Taylor, J. 1875 'The Church of Holy Cross, Temple, Bristol', *J. Brit. Archaeol. Soc.* **31**, 275–82

Tucker, M.E. 1982 *Sedimentary rocks in the field* Chichester, Wiley

Vince, A.G. 1977 'The medieval and post-medieval ceramic industry of the Malvernian region: the study of the ware and its distribution', in D.P.S. Peacock 1977, *Pottery and Early commerce* London, Academic Press, 257–305

Vince, A.G. 1984 *The Medieval ceramic industry of the Severn valley* Unpublished PhD thesis

Vince, A.G. (forthcoming) 'Medieval and later pottery', in J. Hart (forthcoming)

Vince, A. and England, S. 2004 'Medieval and later pottery', in K. Rodwell and R. Bell 2004, 294–331

Wadley, T.P. 1886 *The Great Orphan Book and Book of Wills* Bristol, Bristol and Gloucestershire Society

Warman, S. (forthcoming) 'Animal Bone', in J. Hart (forthcoming)

Watts, M. 2011 'Nos 26–28 St Thomas Street, Redcliffe, Bristol: excavations in 2002', in M. Watts (ed.) 2011, *Medieval and post-medieval development within Bristol's inner suburbs* Bristol and Gloucestershire Archaeol. Rep. 7, Cirencester, Cotswold Archaeology, 73–8

Whitehead, R. 1996 *Buckles 1250-1800* Chelmsford, Greenlight Publishing

Wilcox, T. 1980 'Clay tobacco pipes', in R. Wilcox 1980, 'Excavations at Farleigh Hungerford Castle, Somerset 1973-76', *Proc. Somerset Archaeol. and Natur. Hist. Soc.* **124**, 105–7

Wilkinson D. and McWhirr A. 1998 *Cirencester Anglo-Saxon church and medieval abbey* Cirencester Excavations **IV**, Cirencester, Cotswold Archaeological Trust

Wilkinson, K.N. 2008a *32–36* 'Victoria Street, Bristol: Borehole survey and monolith sampling. Assessment Report', ARCA unpublished report **0809-1** (Department of Archaeology, University of Winchester)

Wilkinson, K.N. 2008b '1–2 Redcliff Street, Bristol: Borehole survey. Assessment Report', ARCA unpublished report **0708-16** (Department of Archaeology, University of Winchester)

Wilkinson, K.N. and Head, K. 2008 'Broadmead Development, Bristol: Geoarchaeology and Bioarchaeology Analytical Report', ARCA unpublished report **0809-3** (Department of Archaeology, University of Winchester)

Williams, B. 1988 'The excavation of medieval and post-medieval tenements at 94–102 Temple Street, Bristol, 1975', *Trans. Bristol Gloucestershire Archaeol. Soc.* **106**, 107–68

Williams, B. and Ponsford, M. 1988 'Clay roof-tiles', in B. Williams 1988, 145–9

Winstone, R. 1987 *Bristol As It Was, 1937–1939* Bristol, Reece Winstone

26–28 ST THOMAS STREET, REDCLIFFE, BRISTOL: EXCAVATIONS IN 2002

by Martin Watts

Introduction

Between July and October 2002, Cotswold Archaeology carried out an archaeological excavation at nos 26–28 St Thomas Street, Redcliffe, Bristol (centred on NGR: ST 59187277; see Davenport *et al.* 2011 [this volume], fig. 1), at the request of CgMs Ltd and on behalf of Crown Dilmun (Redcliff Village) Ltd, in advance of proposed mixed-use redevelopment of the site. Preparatory work had comprised two desk-based assessments, for nos 26–28 St Thomas Street (BaRAS 2001a) and for a parcel of adjoining land in Three Queens' Lane (BaRAS 2001b), and a field evaluation (BaRAS 2002), all of which was undertaken in 2001. The evaluation trenches revealed features and deposits of medieval and post-medieval date, including garden soils, pits, ditches and masonry structures. Excavation followed in 2002 as a condition of planning permission. Post-excavation work continued into 2003 but came to a halt when the client ceased trading. A very brief summary of the site was published (Young 2003) and a post-excavation assessment report was ultimately completed (CA 2005), as were separate assessment reports on various environmental aspects of the project (Green *et al.* 2004; Vaughan-Williams and Branch 2004; Warman *et al.* 2004). This report presents a more detailed summary of the excavation, as it is understood at the assessment stage, to accompany the publication of the excavation undertaken on the opposite side of the road at nos 55–60 St Thomas St in 2006 (Davenport *et al.* 2011 [this volume]). The project archive is held at Bristol City Museum and Art Gallery under accession number BRSMG 2002/30.

The site is within the parish of St Mary Redcliffe, on the corner of St Thomas Street and Three Queens' Lane, at approximately 8m AOD. Covering an area of *c.* 700m², it comprised two former shop units on the St Thomas Street frontage, with a former garage building and car park to the rear. All buildings had been demolished prior to excavation. Redevelopment proposals included encroaching into St Thomas Street to create a narrower thoroughfare to the east. The underlying geology of the area is mapped as Triassic Redcliffe Sandstone and Keuper Marl (BGS 1974). This is overlain by alluvium forming the floodplain of the River Avon, which typically consists of a soft yellow clay, becoming dark blue-grey at depth.

Historical background

A general historical background to Redcliff Fee and St Thomas Street is provided elsewhere (see Davenport *et al.* 2011 [this volume], *Historical and archaeological background*). Like Mitchell Lane to the east, Three Queens' Lane was known as Hundenlane in the medieval period (Veale 1933, 214), and later Ivie Lane (on Millerd's plan of 1673; see Davenport *et al.* 2011 [this volume], fig. 3), but by 1742 it was '*The three Queen's Lane*', at least on some copies of Rocque's plan (e.g. Jackson 2004, fig. 6). Presumably it was named after the 'Three Queens Inn' depicted on the northern corner of the junction with St Thomas Street on Ashmead's plan of 1855 (ibid., fig. 20). On the southern corner, the current site formerly comprised seven tenements, nos 92–98 St Thomas Street, the plans of which suggest were originally medieval burgage plots. The original corner plot, no. 99, was lost to road widening in the late 19th century.

The earliest documented property on the west side of St Thomas Street south of Three Queens' Lane was nos 88–91 (now nos 30–38 St Thomas Street, immediately to the south of nos 26–28). This was first recorded in 1325, when it was described as 'a garden, house and land', and then again in 1346, when it was referred to as a 'grange' (Jackson 2004, 4). Documentary evidence for properties in St Thomas Street and Three Queens' Lane is sparse, and the earliest to clearly relate to the site is a lease of 1638 (though it is unclear precisely which tenement it refers to), which describes 'one stable, one backside or barton, a washing house, the use of half a well adjoining to the said washing house, also two grounds, then in one, in St Thomas Street' (BRO: 11533(2), quoted in BaRAS 2001a, 4). Millerd's plan of 1673 (Davenport *et al.* 2011 [this volume], fig. 2) shows nos 26–28 St Thomas Street as being occupied by buildings fronting St Thomas Street, with further buildings to the rear. By the 18th century the buildings fronting the street were known as nos 92–98, and an 18th-century lease describes no. 95 as comprising 'a messuage, tenement or dwellinghouse together with yard, workshops sheds and workhouse' (BRO: 11533(10), quoted in BaRAS 2001a, 4). Photographic evidence shows these buildings surviving into the 20th century as timber-framed, jettied and gabled properties of probable late 17th or early 18th-century origin (ibid., plate 3). From the early post-medieval period onwards the site was occupied by many different properties and trades, including Morgan, Walker and Company, one of the largest stoneware manufacturers of 18th-century Bristol, at no. 95, which later became the 'White Hart' public house. In the 1960s the roads were widened further and new shop units and offices constructed.

Method

Three areas were excavated, but nothing of significance was revealed in Area 3, a new service trench within the street just to the east of the former shop frontage. Area 1 extended to approximately 200m² within the property to the south of Three Queens' Lane; Area 2 covered an area of *c.* 500m² within the site of nos 26–28 St Thomas Street. All areas were stripped mechanically of modern surface and overburden. This was followed by selective hand excavation of exposed features and structures, and further machine excavation where appropriate. Truncation was substantial in places, with little to indicate the location of the former tenement boundaries other than the location of cellars and other features. However, where features survived intelligibility was generally good, with both negative features and upstanding remains surviving with well defined interfaces. Over 2000 sherds of pottery were recovered, which was related to the Bristol Pottery Type (BPT) fabric series (see Ponsford 1988).

Results

Period 1: medieval (11th to 13th centuries)
A layer of trampled alluvium, up to 0.15m thick, overlay natural alluvium at about 7m AOD. There were a number of features cut through the trampled alluvium (Fig. 1), mainly subcircular pits up to 5m in diameter and concentrated in the centre of Area 2, which could have been for quarrying alluvial clay. There were also a few shallow linear ditches at or near to the edge of excavation that may have been early land divisions and for drainage (though there was little

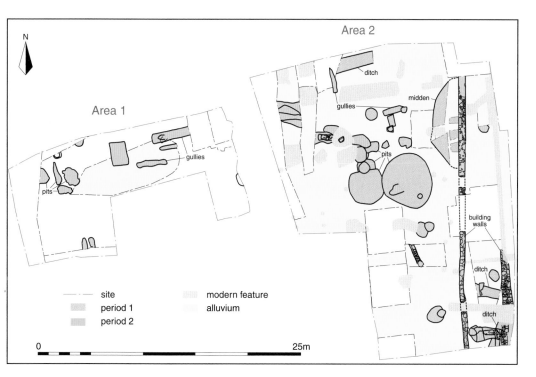

Fig. 1   Periods 1 and 2 (11th to early 16th centuries) (scale 1:350)

correlation with the plot divisions that lasted through to the 20th century) and the remains of a midden deposit to the north-east of the pit cluster. All of these early features appeared to have silted up rather than having been deliberately backfilled, with medieval finds from these and the trampled alluvium dating to the 11th to 13th centuries.

Period 2: late medieval (13th to early 16th centuries)

The earliest built structures dated to the late medieval period and comprised a pair of parallel stone walls on the eastern side of Area 2 (Fig. 1). These were almost certainly the remains of buildings that once fronted St Thomas Street, and survived to over 0.5m high, enough to indicate that construction had not been constrained by plot boundaries but had been undertaken in phases spanning several of the tenements evident from later maps. This implied either that this phase of construction pre-dated division of the area into tenements, or that the tenements were in common ownership when first developed.

To the rear of these buildings, in the western part of the site, were substantial soil layers that together were approximately 1m thick. There were a few pits and gullies of probable late medieval date within the soil layers, but no other structures could be assigned to this period with any certainty. It was unclear if the soil layers were the result of deliberate importation of cultivation soil or the slow build-up of domestic and perhaps industrial waste. The relationship between the soils and the early structures fronting St Thomas Street was lost to truncation.

Period 3: post-medieval (16th to 18th centuries)

This period was characterised by the remains of stone walls, surfaces and other structural

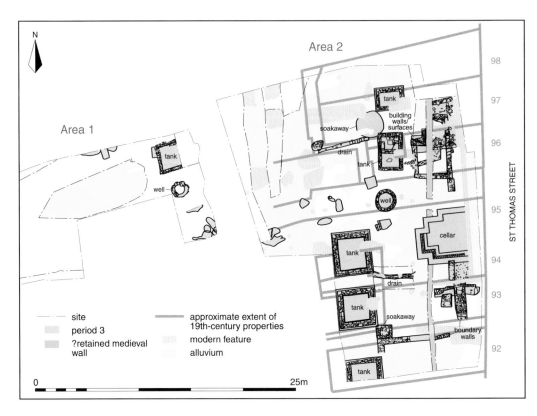

Fig. 2   Period 3 (16th to 18th centuries) (scale 1:350)

elements of buildings on the St Thomas Street frontage in Area 2. In addition, to the rear or west of these, was an array of subterranean tanks, soakaways, drains and wells. Some of the building walls cut through or were built over the parallel stone walls of the Period 2 buildings (Fig. 2), but it was not possible to determine if these were additions/alterations to the earlier buildings, or new structures following their demolition. They included the remains of a large cellar, with a floor level at 6.8m AOD and walls surviving up to 1m high, which featured a drainage channel running around its periphery. To the west, the tanks, which were up to 2.5m² internally, were also constructed in stone, with flagstone floors at 6.9m AOD and rendered stone walls surviving up to 0.9m high. These appeared to have served as cisterns or water storage tanks.

Truncation had removed almost all evidence of contemporary tenement boundaries but the distribution of features gave a clear indication that development in the post-medieval period had proceeded on a plot-by-plot basis (Fig. 2). Thus it would appear that, from south to north, the southernmost two square tanks were located within nos 92–93 St Thomas Street; the large cellar, adjacent tank and well were part of nos 94–95, which by the mid 19th century formed a single plot; the double tank and adjacent building remains were those of no. 96; and the remaining rectangular tank was in the back part of no. 97, with no structural remains surviving from no. 98.

The finds

Medieval pottery amounted to 1286 sherds, approximately half of which was recovered residually from post-medieval contexts. The bulk of the stratified material came from the Period 1 alluvium deposits, pits and other features sealed by the Period 2 cultivation soils. It comprised mainly locally made wares with a small quantity of regional and continental imports. With the exception of a few sherds of Ham Green A type jugs, none of the medieval pottery needs to have been any earlier than the 13th century, and most medieval contexts probably dated to between 1250 and 1350. The overwhelming bulk of the glazed ware was of Bristol Redcliffe type (BPT 118), almost all consisting of jugs of known form, including some moulded anthropomorphic designs. However, waster pits of the type identified at the neighbouring site of nos 30–38 St Thomas Street (Burchill 2004, 26–8) were not present. The most abundant of the coarseware fabrics comprised Ham Green products (BPT 32), handmade and with vessel forms and decoration closely comparable to examples known from the production site (Barton 1963, fig. 112). These were mostly simple jars (cooking pots) with everted rims. There was also a highly unusual probable lamp of Minety ware (BPT 84). Continental imports were relatively rare and regional imports were poorly represented, presumably due to the dominance of local products.

A total of 1052 sherds of post-medieval pottery was recovered. It spanned the 15th/16th to 18th centuries, with the bulk from the 16th and 17th centuries. Included were Malvernian redware, 'Tudor Green' and Cistercian wares, types which were in production before 1500 but which continued well beyond. As with the medieval assemblage, continental imports were not abundant. The bulk of the utilitarian coarsewares appeared to be regional imports and made up of internally glazed earthenwares. Malvernian redwares were well represented, as were Somerset red earthenwares and North Devon gravel-tempered wares. Forms included pipkins, 'basket-handled' and other jars, and pancheon-type flanged bowls. Tablewares were less abundant and consisted of cups and small jugs in Tudor Green and Cistercian wares, and slipware or *sgraffito*-decorated plates. The absence of 'household' forms (e.g. chamber pots and stoneware tankards), which were abundant from the early to mid 18th century, suggested that the bulk of the post-medieval assemblage dated to before *c.* 1700–1720.

Other notable medieval finds included glazed ridge tile, of likely 14th-century date; Pennant sandstone and Delabole slate roof tiles; a copper-alloy shield-shaped harness mount and seal matrix, and a variety of lace-ends and dress-pins. Post-medieval finds included further metal objects, clay pipes (mostly of mid 17th to early 18th-century date), 18th-century bottle glass and some lozenges of 16th to 17th-century window glass.

Biological evidence

A small assemblage of well preserved animal bone was recovered, the majority from medieval (Period 2) contexts. It was dominated by domestic stock species (cattle, sheep/goat and pig) but also included horse, dog, cat, chicken and goose as well as wild species such as roe deer and rabbit. A few fish vertebrae were recovered, as was a single bone from a dolphin.

Charred plant remains recovered from Period 1 deposits included some cultivated cereals, including emmer/spelt wheat, bread wheat and barley, with the rest of the assemblage assoc-iated with human diet (fig, blackberry, plum, sloe and grape) or the deposition of animal or human waste (fat hen and nettle). Period 2 deposits contained evidence for the continued utilisation of cultivated cereals, notably emmer/spelt wheat and barley, with bread wheat possibly increasing in importance, but only limited evidence for human diet (e.g. plum). The composition of the assemblage was mainly of charred grain, suggesting the area was used to dump material associated with domestic occupation rather than for horticultural purposes.

Bibliography

BaRAS (Bristol and Region Archaeological Services) 2001a 'Archaeological Desktop Study of 26/28 St Thomas Street, Redcliffe, Bristol', BaRAS unpublished report no. **928B/2001**

BaRAS (Bristol and Region Archaeological Services) 2001b 'Archaeological Desktop Study of a site in Three Queens Lane, Redcliffe, Bristol', BaRAS unpublished report no. **928A/2001**

BaRAS (Bristol and Region Archaeological Services) 2002 'Archaeological Evaluation at 26/28 St Thomas Street, Redcliffe, Bristol', BaRAS unpublished report no. **958/2002**

Barton, K.J. 1963 'A medieval pottery kiln at Ham Green, Bristol', *Trans Bristol Gloucestershire Archaeol. Soc.* **82**, 95–126

BGS (British Geological Survey) 1974 *1:50,000 Geological Survey of Great Britain (England and Wales), Solid and Drift, map sheet 264: Bristol* Keyworth, British Geological Survey

Burchill, R. 2004, 'The Pottery', in R. Jackson 2004, 24–33

CA (Cotswold Archaeology) 2005 '26–28 St Thomas Street, Redcliffe, Bristol: Post-Excavation Assessment', CA unpublished report no. **05144**

Davenport, P., Leech, R. and Rowe, M. 2011 '55–60 St Thomas Street, Redcliffe, Bristol: excavations in 2006', in M. Watts (ed.) 2011, *Medieval and post-medieval development within Bristol's inner suburbs* Bristol and Gloucestershire Archaeol. Rep. **7**, Cirencester, Cotswold Archaeology, 1–72

Green, C.P., Kemp, R., Canti, M., Hunter, R., Swindle, G. and Branch N.P. 2004 '26–28 St Thomas Street and Three Queens Lane, Bristol: Report on the Geoarchaeological Investigations', Archaeoscape unpublished report

Jackson, R. 2004 'Archaeological excavations at nos. 30–38 St. Thomas Street & no. 60 Redcliff Street, Bristol, 2000', *Bristol Avon Archaeol.* **19**, 1–63

Millerd, J. 1673 *An Exact Delineation of the Famous Citty of Bristol and Suburbs Thereof* Bristol

Ponsford, M. 1988 'The pottery', in B. Williams, 'The excavation of medieval and post-medieval tenements at 94–102 Temple Street, Bristol, 1975', *Trans. Bristol Gloucestershire Archaeol. Soc.* **106**, 107–68, 124–46

Vaughan-Williams, A. and Branch, N.P. 2004 '26–28 St Thomas Street and Three Queens Lane, Bristol: Report on the Archaeobotanical Investigations', Archaeoscape unpublished report

Veale, E.W.W. 1931 *The Great Red Book of Bristol* Bristol Rec. Soc. **2**, Bristol, Bristol Record Society

Warman, S., Branch N.P. and Athersuch, J. 2004 '26–28 St Thomas Street and Three Queens Lane, Bristol: Report on the Archaeozoological Investigations', Archaeoscape unpublished report

Young, R. 2003 'BRISTOL: 26–28 St Thomas St, ST 59187277', in J. Wills (ed.) 2003, 'Archaeological Review No. 27, 2002', *Trans Bristol Gloucestershire Archaeol. Soc.* 121, 270

HARBOURSIDE, BRISTOL:
INVESTIGATIONS FROM 2003–2008

by Mary Alexander and Chiz Harward

with contributions by
Edward Besly, Dana Challinor, Sarah Cobain, Lorrain Higbee, Reg Jackson,
Roger Leech, E.R. McSloy, Hannah Russ, B. Silva, Jennie Stopford,
Penelope Walton Rogers, Sylvia Warman and Keith Wilkinson

INTRODUCTION

Archaeological investigations were carried out between January 2003 and February 2008 by Cotswold Archaeology on land to the south of Anchor Road, Bristol (Fig. 1). The work was undertaken on behalf of Nicholson Estates (now Crest Nicholson Regeneration Ltd) prior to the redevelopment of the Harbourside area.

Given the historic importance of the location of the site, close to the former Abbey of St Augustine (now Bristol Cathedral), conditions attached to planning consent required archaeological work to be undertaken in advance of and during construction. Initial works comprised the monitoring and recording of geotechnical and archaeological bore-holes (Wilkinson and Tinsley 2005), and a desk-based review of all the archaeological, geotechnical and cartographic data pertinent to the development area (CA 2003). Archaeological evaluation followed later in 2003, followed by excavation of specific areas in 2003 and 2004. An intermittent watching brief was also undertaken during specific phases of development from 2004 until 2008.

Location, geology and topology

The development area covers a total of 7.3ha of low-lying land on the Avon floodplain next to the Floating Harbour. The site lies at approximately 9m AOD and is bounded to the north by Anchor Road, to the east by @Bristol, to the south by the Floating Harbour and to the west by Gas Ferry Road (centred on NGR: ST 58157245; Fig. 1). Prior to re-development, the site comprised two areas of car parking and derelict oil gas works. The underlying geology of the area is mapped as Redcliffe Sandstone of the Triassic Keuper series, covered by estuarine alluvium (BGS 1974).

Archaeological and general historical background

The site lies to the south-west of the historic centre of Bristol in the parish of St Augustine-the-Less and within the historic area of Canon's Marsh (Fig. 1). The site is approximately 150m to the south-west of the former Abbey of St Augustine, founded by Robert FitzHarding in *c.* 1140, the church of which is now Bristol Cathedral. The northern part of the site lay within the former precinct of the abbey, with the southern part being within Canon's Marsh, which was endowed to the abbey in the 1150s (Bryant 1995).

By the end of the 12th century the abbey had probably begun to manage its holdings on a systematic basis, with water management being a major requirement for the improvement

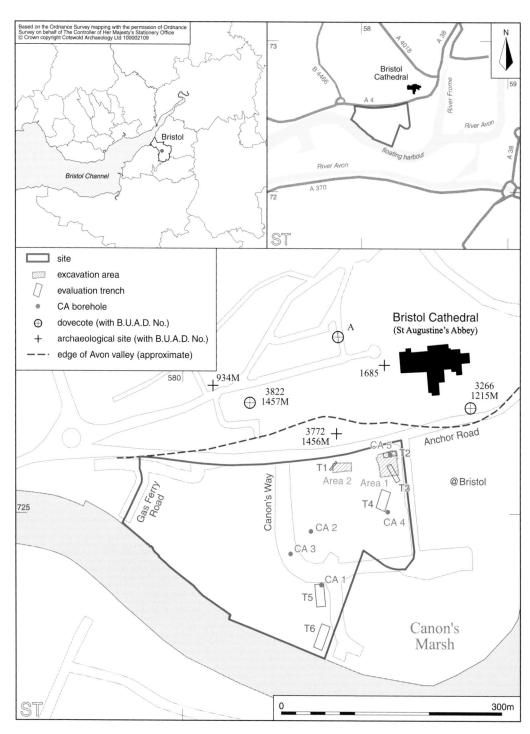

Fig. 1   Site location plan, with excavation areas and evaluation trenches (scale 1:5000)

of the Canon's Marsh area (Cox *et al.* 2006, 64–5). Documentary evidence suggests that a water supply to the abbey was established by the mid 13th century (ibid., 66) and that hay crops were being gathered from the marsh by the 15th century (Beachcroft and Sabin 1938, 28, 112–13, 148). Fishponds shown on Rocque's map of Bristol (1743) also may have been created in the medieval period (Fig. 2).

The monastery was granted licences to make rope in 1491 and 1512, and the ropewalk shown on numerous later maps may have been established at this time (Beachcroft and Sabin 1938, 278–9). The Abbey of St Augustine was suppressed in 1539, and in 1542 many of its holdings, including the area of the site, were transferred to the Dean and Chapter of the newly created Bristol Cathedral, although the landscape remained largely unchanged. Ropemaking continued after the Dissolution, with ropewalks shown on De Wilstar's survey of 1738 (BRO: DC/E/3/4 fols.24–5), Rocque's map of 1743 (Fig. 2), Plumley and Ashmead's map of 1828 (Fig. 9) and the Ordnance Survey (OS) map of 1885. In the 19th century, Canon's Marsh was increasingly developed for manufacturing and industry.

The review of the archaeological, geotechnical and cartographic data (CA 2003) concluded that there was potential for deposits of medieval, post-medieval and modern date

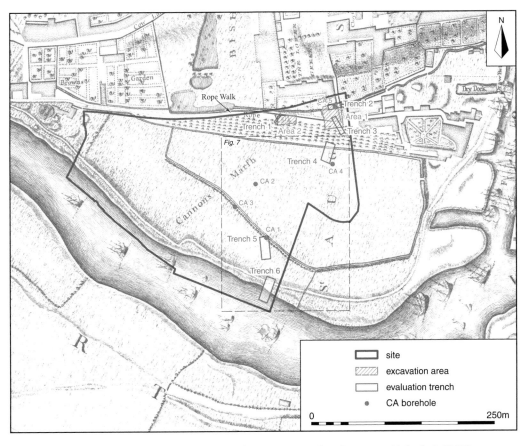

Fig. 2   Excavation areas and evaluation trenches superimposed on Rocque 1743 (scale 1:5000)

to survive within the development area, although it also showed that much of the area was likely to be heavily truncated by the 19th-century industrial development of the site.

Methodology

Six evaluation trenches (Trenches 1–6), were excavated to investigate the areas of high archaeological potential identified in the review (CA 2003). Trenches 4–6 were located on banks and ditches shown on Rocque's map of Bristol of 1743 (Fig. 2). This was followed by two open-area excavations totalling 1090m², investigating features of archaeological interest identified in Trenches 1–3 in the north-eastern part of the development area (Areas 1 and 2). Within the open-area excavations, modern surface material and overburden was excavated mechanically, and archaeological features thus exposed were hand-excavated to the bottom of stratified archaeological deposits. Where widespread homogeneous deposits were identified, these were mechanically removed under archaeological supervision. Environmental samples were obtained from appropriate deposits. Five boreholes were drilled into the underlying stratigraphy in Canon's Marsh. The cores were examined in conjunction with the borehole stratigraphy obtained from a geotechnical survey of the Harbourside development area (by Geotechnical Engineering Ltd). The results of the borehole study and the evaluation trenches have been synthesised with the subsequent excavation; the detailed contextual information, finds and geoarchaeological reports are summarised below; detailed reports can be consulted within the archive.

RESULTS

Geoarchaeological sequence, by Keith Wilkinson

Study of the borehole data suggests that the geological substrate of the Triassic Mercia Mudstone Group is overlain on the southern part of the site by gravels of the Late Pleistocene Avon Formation. Silts, clays, organic muds and peats of the Holocene Wentlooge formation occur above the gravels, and the sequence is capped by made ground deposited during the medieval and post-medieval periods.

Sedimentological and palynological analysis of organic sediments within the Wentlooge formation from a borehole in the centre of Canon's Marsh (CA 2; Fig. 1) provided a detailed palaeoenvironmental history. This suggests that the lowest elements of the Wentlooge formation accumulated in an intertidal salt marsh during the Middle Holocene (c. 7000–5000 BC). The radiocarbon date obtained from this part of the sequence dated to 6230–6060 cal. BC (7287±42 BP, Wk 16708). Following this, sediment deposition exceeded rises in river/sea level and as a result the area emerged from the river for a short time, during which sedge communities colonised the site. Organic deposits from these deposits were radiocarbon-dated to 5680–5530 cal. BC (6694±39 BP, Wk 16707). Later still, the area once more became inundated as a result of rising sea levels, and mud flats developed. A radiocarbon date from these sediments of 7750–7570 cal. BC (8619±47 BP, Wk 16706) was obviously too old, and may have derived from reworked older carbon-rich material within the organic laminae used for the AMS measurement. This cast doubt on the integrity of the lower two dates, which do not tally with the accepted vegetation history of South-West England, suggesting contamination of the stratigraphy had occurred.

The wider vegetation throughout this succession comprised woodland of lime and oak on the high ground that surrounded the site. Evidence for human impact was slight during accumulation of the organic deposits, but sedimentological evidence indicated one possible episode of ash deposition onto the mud flats. As discussed above, chronological control on these events is uncertain.

Archaeological sequence

The archaeological remains survived as structures, layers and below-ground features, but had suffered from truncation by ground levelling and the construction of substantial industrial buildings. This had an impact on the understanding and interpretation of the more complex sequences of archaeological remains, most notably in Area 1, where Great Western Railway transit sheds were constructed in the 19th century. The sequence was divided into five periods:

Period 1: medieval (12th to mid 15th centuries)
Period 2: late medieval to post-medieval (mid 15th to 17th centuries)
Period 3: 18th century
Period 4: 19th century
Period 5: 20th century

Period 1: medieval (12th to mid 15th centuries)

Archaeological remains from Period 1 were poorly dated with only 24 sherds of medieval pottery recovered. The scant ceramic evidence appeared to date from the later 13th century onwards, consisting primarily of Bristol Redcliffe wares (BPT 118); however, this pottery was nearly all recovered from garden features or the later Building 1 and there was no direct dating evidence for the earliest structures. The dating for the period is therefore largely relative and mostly based on limited stratigraphic relationships. The ceramics suggest a date of *c.* 1270–1300 for the earliest remains; however, given the paucity of datable material and the undated nature of the earliest deposits, Period 1 is perhaps best defined as starting with the foundation of St Augustine's Abbey in *c.* 1140.

The top of natural alluvium was recorded across the site at between 7.65m and 6.9m AOD. The archaeological sequence had been heavily disturbed by later truncation but the earliest archaeological activity appeared to relate to the laying out of the Abbey precinct.

A substantial 0.5m-wide masonry wall excavated in both Area 1 (9257, Fig. 3) and Area 2 (1078/8042/8113, Fig. 6) represents the earliest structural activity, although no dating evidence was recovered. The position of the wall correlates with one shown on Rocque's map of 1743, which would appear to mark the southern boundary of the precinct of St Augustine's Abbey (Fig. 2). The wall was later rebuilt (wall 9150, Fig. 3). In Area 1, this returned to the north (walls 9278 and 9281) to enclose an open area, interpreted as a garden. A fragment of roof tile from wall 9150 may date to the 15th or 16th century, although this is not certain.

The garden area was accessed through a gap in wall 9278. Within the garden was a homogeneous soil and a stone-kerbed pavement (9249) along the eastern garden wall; a fragment of ceramic louvre recovered from the pavement probably dates to *c.* 1300 to 1450. Other features included a stone-filled foundation (9210), possibly indicating the wall of a lean-to structure against the precinct wall, and a drain (9239). A large section of

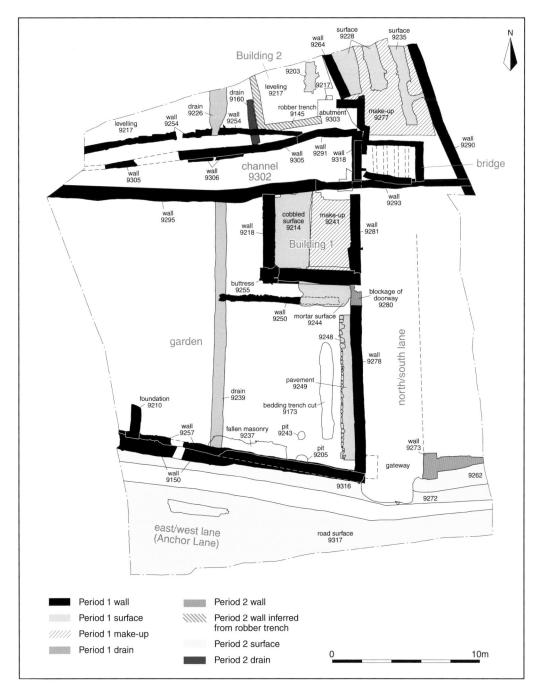

Fig. 3   Area 1, Period 1 (12th to mid 15th centuries) and Period 2 (mid 15th to 17th centuries) (scale 1:250)

fallen masonry (9237) lay to the north of precinct wall 9150. Within the garden a masonry wall (9250) may have marked a subdivision of the garden and contained pottery dating to the late 12th to 13th centuries. Pottery recovered from the lean-to structure and garden soil dates to the mid 13th to 14th century.

To the north of the garden was an east/west-aligned drainage channel (9302), revetted by masonry walls 9293 and 9301 (not shown); there was no evidence for an earlier timber revetment and it is likely that the channel was masonry-built from the outset. The channel was originally approximately 3m wide, narrowing to the west. The north wall of the channel was repaired with a new masonry wall (9254), and later the north and south channel walls were both rebuilt in sandstone as walls 9291, 9295 and 9305. The north wall (9305) was rebuilt on a new alignment, narrowing the channel to a width of 1.1m to the west in Area 1. The area between this new wall (9305) and the previous repair (9254) was infilled with dumps of silt and stone.

A masonry bridge was built over the channel (Figs 3 and 4). The bridge was 4.7m wide with a span of approximately 2.6m and was originally formed of a single span with four sandstone ribs and Bathstone facing, keyed into the channel walls. At the north end of the bridge, the addition of abutment 9303 strengthened the west wall of the bridge, which on its south side was probably keyed into wall 9281. The eastern side of the bridge had been truncated. It may have been constructed at the same time as the precinct and garden boundary walls, although the complex construction sequence, subsequent repairs and rebuilds, and severe truncation obscured the finer detail of the sequence.

The bridge served to carry a north/south lane across the channel. To the north of the

Fig. 4   Channel 9302 with bridge to rear, Area 1, Period 1, looking east (scales 2m)

bridge, the lane took a northwest/southeast alignment, bounded by walls 9264 and 9290. Wall 9264, on the west side of the lane, butted bridge abutment 9303. The surface of the lane was cobbled, and had been repaired several times (9228 and 9235). No such surfaces survived to the south of the bridge from this period, but a lane connecting the bridge to Anchor Lane is inferred by the later evidence (see below, Period 2).

To the north of the channel, the area to the west of wall 9264 was levelled up (9217); a surface of stones (9203) surviving over part of the levelling (this surface may have been contemporary with Period 2 Building 2, but the robbing of the walls had destroyed the stratigraphic relationship). The levelling contained ceramics dating to the 14th to 15th centuries. To the west of these deposits was a stone drain (9226), discharging into the channel.

A building (Building 1), measuring 5.1 m² internally, was constructed to the south of the channel, post-dating channel revetment wall 9295 and reusing wall 9281 for its east wall. The building may have had slight external buttresses at its south-western corner (9255), although much of the south and west wall had been robbed out at a later date. Internally, make-up layer 9241 formed the base for cobbled floor 9214. Late forms of Bristol Redcliffe ware pottery (BPT 118l) from make-up layer 9241 suggest a mid 14th to 15th-century date for construction.

An arched culvert (9306) was built over the channel west of Building 1, springing off from revetment walls 9305 and 9295. The culvert almost certainly continued eastwards, to the north of Building 1, as later maps show buildings spanning the channel in this location (Fig. 9), although no archaeological evidence for this had survived. To the south of Building 1, a mortar surface (9244) sealed the demolition of garden wall 9250 and may have been a garden path leading to an entrance to the lane. Later in Period 1, this entrance was blocked by masonry insert 9280.

To the south of precinct wall 9150 there was little evidence for activity, although there appears to have been some ground raising in Area 2. This may have been for a lane along the south side of the wall, depicted on later maps as Anchor Lane, but there was no direct evidence for this in this period.

There was no archaeological evidence in Trenches 4, 5 and 6 for any activity in this period within Canon's Marsh, and the area probably remained as open and largely unimproved marshland in this period.

Period 2: late medieval to post-medieval (mid 15th to 17th centuries)

There is a slight increase in the amount of pottery recovered from this period compared to Period 1, and dating of contexts is aided by clay tobacco pipes, although there is some intrusive material. The pottery includes Iberian micaceous-type wares (BPT 282), with a date range of 1250–1600, and Black-glazed Cistercian types (BPT 275) dating to between *c*. 1500 and 1650, but these were found in combination with later pottery types such as East Somerset glazed earthenware (BPT 96) and tin-glazed earthenware (probably Bristol manufacture) (BPT 99), which extended the sequence into the late 17th century. However, Period 2 contexts are generally poorly dated and overall the period relies on stratigraphic relationships for relative dating.

In Areas 1 and 2 the major structural features survived with little or no change. Within the garden in Area 1 (Fig. 3) soil built up, sealing earlier features, and was cut later by pits 9243 and 9205, and bedding trench 9173. Pottery from these features gives a date range of *c*. 1550–1650, but a clay pipe fragment from pit 9205 suggests a later (17th-century) date for these features. To the north of the channel, robber trench 9145 marked two sides of a building (Building 2), measuring 5.2m east/west by at least 3.6m north/south. A stone drain (9160), which issued into the channel, was built against the west wall of this building.

At the junction of the north/south lane and Anchor Lane, a pillar (9273) of well dressed Bath stone and sandstone blocks was constructed in 17th-century style, with buttresses to the north and south, and with an iron pintle for a hinged gate. This was probably the eastern side of a gateway into the former precinct, but the corresponding western pillar at the corner of wall 9150/9278 had not survived. The pillar lay at the west end of a length of wall that continued the line of the precinct wall beyond the eastern limit of excavation.

The first clear evidence for Anchor Lane dates to this period. A series of metalled surfaces (9262, 9272, 9316 and 9317) indicated that it was resurfaced on several occasions. Dating evidence from these surfaces included clay pipe from the late 17th/early 18th-century from surface 9262. The level of the north–south lane was also raised, although the actual road surface had been truncated.

In Trench 6 (within Canon's Marsh), a bank approximately 1.2m high composed of two thick deposits of clay (6052 and 6039) was constructed from a level of *c.* 7m AOD on the natural alluvium next to the Avon (Figs 7 and 8). The upper bank deposit (6039) contained two copper-alloy farthing tokens dating to 1652. The bank survived to a width of 3.5m (it was probably originally over 4m wide, but had been truncated on its landward side; see below). The bank was constructed in two episodes with a shallow gully separating the two 'lifts' of the bank. The top of the bank was covered by a thin layer of cinders, clinker, ash and charcoal (6038), which formed a protective surface and walkway on the bank. Dating evidence from this layer included a fragment of clay pipe manufactured between 1699 and 1728. The bank was later raised to *c.* 8m AOD with the addition of another dump of clay (6037). A residual 13th-century decorated floor tile was found in this deposit.

The landward side of the riverside bank was cut away to form a channel or pond (6050). Pollen from the lower deposits of this feature suggest there was an environment of open vegetation cover, probably dominated by grassland; pond species (including pondweed, yellow water lily and reed mace) from upper fills 9041 and 9051 confirm that this feature once contained water. It partly silted up, but also included glassworking waste and a pipe fragment from the upper fill dating between 1677 and 1716. It was infilled to 7.7m AOD and cinder track 6036 was built over it (Fig. 8).

Period 3: 18th century

Period 3 deposits generally contained sufficient quantities of pottery and clay tobacco pipe to allow contexts to be dated with some certainty, although stratigraphy remained a key element in the relative dating of the sequence. Many ceramic types recovered from Period 3 contexts were first introduced in the late 17th century (for instance tin-glazed earthenware BPT 99; yellow slipware BPT 100, North Devon gravel-tempered ware BPT 112, and Somerset earthenware types BPT 96 and BPT 285), so some deposits may have been slightly earlier than 1700.

Within Area 1, Building 1 was demolished, its south and west walls (9131 and 9246) removed and layers of demolition material (9140 and 9141) were spread over the cobbled floor (Fig. 5). Immediately to the south a buttress (9206) was built against the garden wall entrance (9280) blocked in Period 2. A new building (Building 3) was constructed in the south-eastern corner of the garden; its south wall was keyed into the surviving

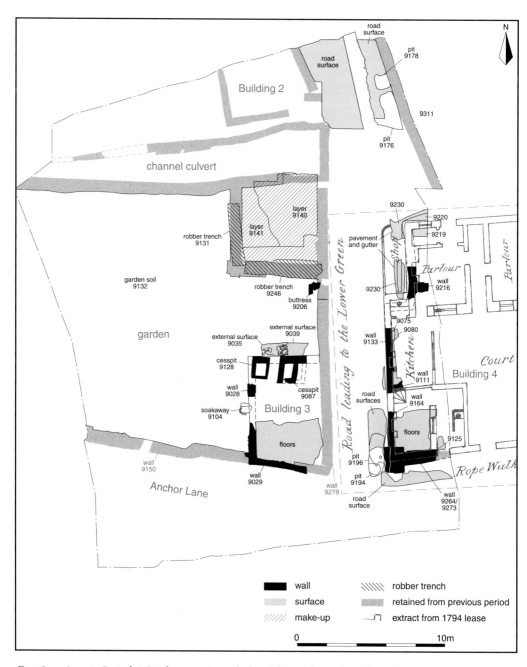

Fig. 5   Area 1, Period 3 (18th century), with detail from a lease plan of 1794 (BRO: dc/e/40/38/1) (scale 1:250)

precinct wall (9150) and the building also reused the existing wall (9278) for its eastern side. The northern part of this building was truncated, but it can be assumed to have been on the northern edge of brick and stone cesspits 9087 and 9128, to the south of external surfaces 9035 and 9039. Building 3 was 4.3m east/west and 7.2m north/south. The surviving internal surfaces were a frequently repaired sequence of clay and mortar floors with ingrained ash, charcoal and dirt layers. Soil layers built up further in the garden area (9132) and a soakaway (9104) was later dug to the west of Building 3.

The level of the north/south lane was raised and resurfaced both to the north and south of the bridge crossing, and numerous pits were dug in the road, possibly to repair potholes (e.g. 9178, 9194 and 9196), although some were also used to dispose of domestic refuse (e.g. 9176). Building 4 was constructed to the east of the lane, incorporating boundary wall 9273 into its southern wall 9264. A fragment of a late 15th or early 16th-century decorated tile in the foundations of this building may derive from earlier building on the east side of the lane. There was archaeological evidence for at least two rooms, divided by wall 9111, with a series of trampled floor deposits in each room. The surviving evidence matches a lease plan of 1794 (BRO: DC/E/40/38/1) and from this it can be deduced that the stub of a wall (9125) running north from wall 9264/9273 divided the southern room into two (Fig. 5). The building extended to the north (9216) and a pavement (9220) and gutter (9230) ran to the west of wall 9216 and round the north side of the building. A fragment of a bone syringe (Fig. 14, no. 1) was recovered from gutter 9230.

Anchor Lane was repaired and remetalled with glassworking waste and clinker. Within Area 2, the former precinct wall was rebuilt during this period (8044) and Anchor Lane was enclosed on the south by a new stone wall (8007, Fig. 6) creating a 3.5m-wide lane.

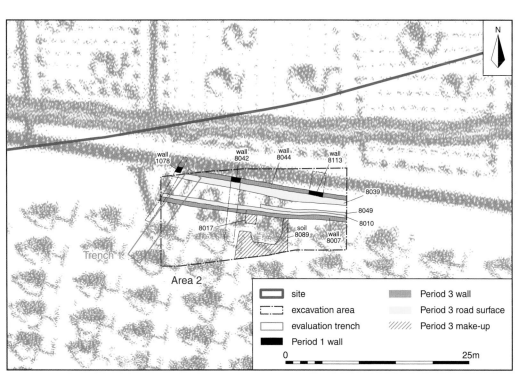

Fig. 6   Area 2, Period 1 (12th to mid 15th centuries) and Period 3 (18th century), superimposed on Rocque 1743 (scale 1:500)

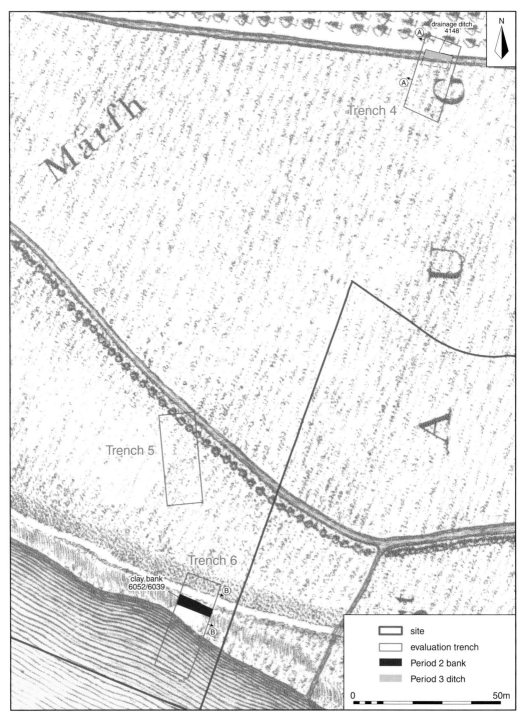

Fig. 7   Trenches 4–6, Period 2 (mid 15th to 17th centuries) and Period 3 (18th century), superimposed on Rocque 1743 (scale 1:1250)

There was no evidence for a south wall to the lane in Area 1. In Area 2 the lane was resurfaced several times using glassworking waste, mortar and ash (8010, 8039 and 8049). Soil layers 8017 and 8089 were dumped in the area immediately south of Anchor Lane, which is shown on Rocque's map as being planted with trees.

In Trench 4, the surface of Canon's Marsh was located at *c.* 7.7m AOD. Drainage ditch 4148 was cut through the marsh on an east/west alignment. It was 1.15m deep and survived to a width of 1.55m; if reconstructed with a symmetrical profile, the ditch would have measured over 3m wide (Figs 7 and 8). This was almost certainly the remains of a linear ditch shown on Rocque's plan of 1743 edging the south side of a ropewalk (Fig. 2).

Period 4: 19th century
Whilst the buildings in Area 1 were only slightly altered in this period, Canon's Marsh was subject to significant development.

Trench 4; section AA

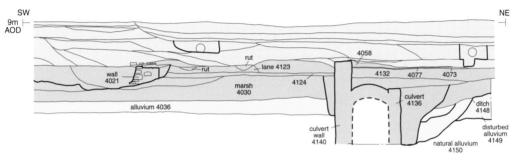

Trench 6; section BB

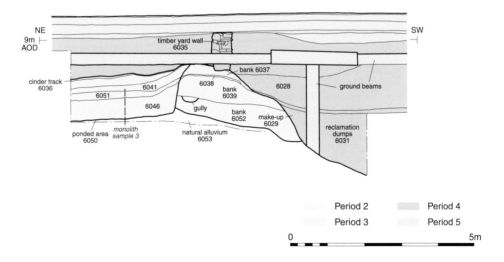

Fig. 8   Sections AA (Trench 4) and BB (Trench 6) (scale 1:100)

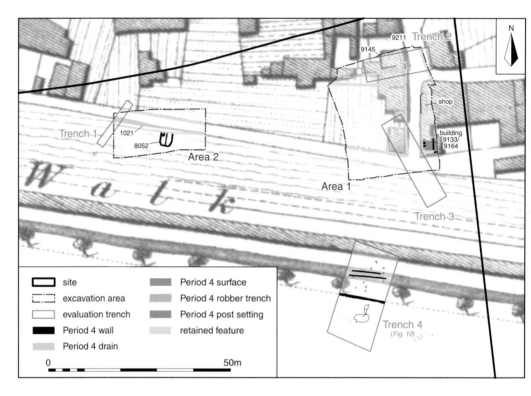

Fig. 9   Areas 1–2 and Trenches 1–4, Period 4 (19th century), superimposed on Plumley and Ashmead 1828 (scale 1:1000)

To the north of Anchor Lane in Area 1, the site appears to have largely retained its earlier character, although numerous minor structural alterations were made to the various buildings, and Building 2 to the north of the channel was demolished. Sewers were dug along the north/south lane and a major culverted sewer (1021) inserted beneath Anchor Lane (Fig. 9).

In Trench 4, marsh deposits of disturbed alluvial silts (4030), up to 0.68m thick and containing 19th-century pottery, were cut by a brick-and-stone barrel-vaulted culvert (4136, Figs 8 and 10) with an integral inspection chamber, which replaced the drainage ditch (4148) of Period 3. The south wall (4140) of the culvert survived above the contemporary ground level to a height of 0.35m along the line of the earlier ditch. To the north of the wall, clay surface 4132 was laid down and featured several parallel ruts (e.g. 4161, 4163). Two spherical cast-iron objects found within these ruts may have been weights used for tensioning rope. Postholes and stakeholes cut through the clay surface may indicate that the ropewalk was divided into lanes or walkways separated from the ropemaking area. The clay surface was repaired with clinker and stone patches, before being sealed by a new surface of ash, clinker coal and cinders (Fig. 8; 4073/4077). Six fragments of coir cordage were found in surface 4077, and a further fragment of cordage was found in demolition deposit 4058, which overlay this surface (*The cordage*, below). These features are broadly contemporary with Plumley and Ashmead's Map of 1828 (Fig. 10). The drain depicted on

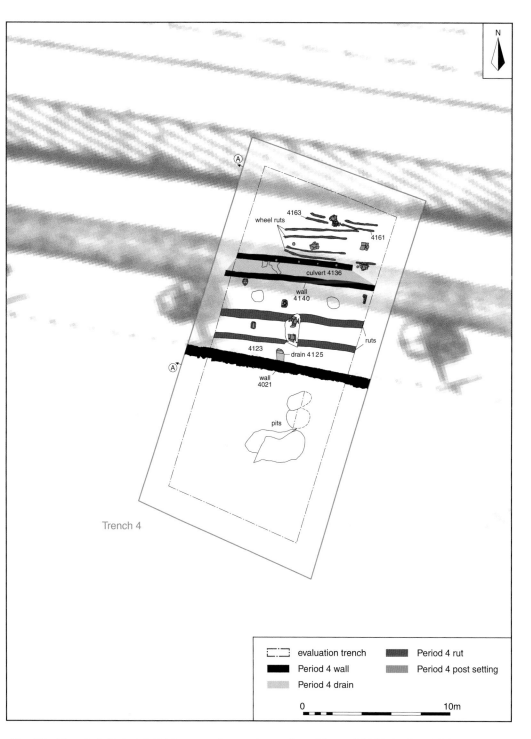

Fig. 10   Trench 4, Period 4 (19th century), superimposed on Ashmead 1828 (scale 1:250)

this map would appear to match culvert 4136, but there is no trace of the ropewalk building depicted to the north of this, which may have lain just beyond the north edge of Trench 4.

To the south of wall 4140, a cobbled lane surface (4123) was established on bedding layer 4124 laid over marsh surface 4030 (Figs 8 and 10). The surface was badly worn and marked by two parallel ruts. Wall 4021 was cut into the south of the lane and separated it from Canon's Marsh to the south. A drain (4125) took rain water from the lane through the wall and onto the marsh, which featured several pits in this area. Lane 4123 was cut by a series of post-settings, some fairly substantial, which may have been part of a later building of the 'Wire and Hemp' rope manufactory shown on the OS map of 1885.

In Trench 2 a small polygonal building (8052) had been constructed against the Anchor Lane south wall (Fig. 9) and can be identified on the 1885 OS Map opposite a fountain, within ornamental gardens.

Within Trench 5, evidence from this period was heavily truncated by later activity. Little survived other than a series of dumps to raise ground level, and a stone drain (not illustrated). The river bank in Trench 6 was rendered redundant as industrial waste and riverine silts (6028 and 6031; Fig. 8) were dumped to reclaim land from the River Avon. The earlier deposits (6031) were possibly associated with the construction of the Floating Harbour in 1809; the later deposits (6028) perhaps served to raise and level the ground for the construction of the timber yards shown on the 1885 OS Map (wall 6035, Fig. 8). Most of the archaeological remains relating to this late 19th-century industrial period had been horizontally truncated by later activity.

Period 5: 20th century

The beginning of the 20th century saw significant transformation of the site, when the buildings north of Anchor Lane were demolished for road realignment and the construction if the new Dean's Marsh Road, as shown on the 1907 OS Map (not illustrated). The features dating to this period that truncated earlier activity were not recorded in detail but can be related to various industries and industrial features recorded on the 20th-century OS maps. To the south in Trenches 4, 5 and 6, the remains of wall foundations for 19th-century saw mills and a box factory (shown on the 1903 OS map) were recorded. Anchor Lane was realigned to the north (as Anchor Road), and a large transit shed was built for the Great Western Railway in the north-western corner of the site (as shown on the 1918 OS map), which truncated archaeological remains in Area 1 and Trench 4. Following demolition of the transit sheds and industrial buildings, the site was levelled and used as a car park in the later 20th century.

THE FINDS

The Pottery, by E.R. McSloy

A total of 1519 sherds of pottery weighing 31.4kg was recovered; the majority of the assemblage was hand-recovered during excavation, while a further 438 sherds were retrieved following processing of bulk soil samples. The assemblage was quantified by sherd count and weight, and pottery fabrics were recorded by context. Recording of pottery types has been adapted from the Bristol Pottery Type (BPT) series (Ponsford 1988, 1998). Vessel form was recorded where possible (typically from rim sherds) and rim sherds were used to provide rim EVES (Estimated Vessel Equivalents). Modern material (Periods 4 and 5) was recorded to a basic level, consisting of sherd count and weight by context, and a list of pottery types from the modern material is contained in the archive.

Medieval pottery

Small quantities of medieval pottery amounting to 68 sherds (1118g) were recovered, of which only 24 sherds were stratified within Period 1 deposits. The assemblage is insufficient to draw conclusions relating to the status or function of the area investigated or to compare with monastic or secular assemblages from the city and elsewhere. The group is therefore described in relation to its significance as dating evidence.

All of the medieval pottery identified conforms to types previously recorded and described from the city. Overall, ware types known to have been made in or near Bristol dominate, and Bristol jug types (BPT 118; 118l) are particularly prominent. This, together with the scarcity of unglazed coarsewares of the kind common in the 12th to 13th centuries, suggests that most material relates to the period after *c.* 1300 and in some instances probably after *c.* 1350. Non-local material is present as Minety type (BPT 84), a type known throughout the medieval period but common in its wheelthrown form in the 14th and 15th centuries. Continental imports are present as a single south-west French glazed ware jug sherd (BPT 156).

Post-medieval pottery

The vast majority of the recorded assemblage, 1388 sherds weighing 29.3kg, dates to the post-medieval period, *c.* 1500–1750. The overall assemblage composition is tabulated in the archive. The range of types present is typical for the city over the period represented.

Material belonging to the earlier post-medieval period to *c.* 1650 is relatively scarce. Types which would be expected to be most common from this period (e.g. BPT 81; 82; 197) amount to only 93 sherds or 6.8% of the post-medieval group. A proportion of the Somerset glazed earthenwares, particularly Nether Stowey types (BPT 280; 280sg) might also belong to this period but there are none of the characteristically 'early' vessel forms (Good 1987), and most material probably dates to after *c.* 1650. As with the medieval assemblage, the pottery of 16th/earlier 17th-century date is too small for meaningful analysis or comparison with other sites, but has helped to date the archaeological sequence.

The remaining and larger portion of the assemblage dates to the period after *c.* 1650, with most seemingly from the early to mid 18th century. The dating for pottery of this period is well established and may be precise, founded in some instances on documented dates for the local potteries, including for tin-glazed earthenwares manufactured in Bristol from the second half of the 17th century (Jackson *et al.* 1991, 89–90). Dating for the utilitarian types, where vessel forms are less liable to development or are less exhaustively studied, can be broad. The 'end' dates for the common coarsewares, including the Somerset glazed earthenwares (BPT 96; 285), North Devon gravel-tempered (BPT 112) and yellow slipware (BPT 99) are imprecise, but circulation probably lessened in the second half of the 18th century.

Characteristically for the period, much of the pottery, particularly the coarsewares, was supplied from sources to the south and south-west. Most abundant is North Devon gravel-tempered ware (BPT 112), produced in kilns near to Barnstaple and Bideford. Represented forms in this type are a mix of open vessels (bowls/pancheons) and jar-proportioned vessels including 'lid-seated' crocks. The gravel-free variant BPT 108 from the same source is present only rarely as plates/bowls with the characteristic yellow slip and fine *sgraffito* decoration revealing brown underslip.

Certain glazed earthenware types can be difficult to distinguish either from the fabric or form, whether from south Somerset (centred on Donyatt) or southeast Somerset from the area of Wanstrow. Good (1987) and subsequently Ponsford (pers. comm.) have been of the opinion that the bulk of material supplied to Bristol was from the latter source, which was considerably closer. Recorded forms are mainly bowls/pancheons, pipkins and jugs. The bowls and jugs infrequently feature slip-trailed decoration. *Sgraffito*-decorated dishes, commonly with concentric cut designs, are almost certainly from south Somerset and of the later 17th to mid 18th centuries (Allan 1984, 150–2).

Pottery made in Bristol and its environs are the light-bodied types BPT 99, BPT 100 and BPT 211, which make up 43% of the total according to sherd count. Tin-glaze earthenware (BPT 99) comprises the most common type. Most or all are Bristol products and the presence of biscuit-fired sherds (BPT 99b), possibly in use as seconds, is recorded. Forms consist of tablewares, mainly flatwares, and chamber pots. Occasional plate sherds with leaded undersides (Fig. 11, no. 4) are probably later 17th century in date. The majority,

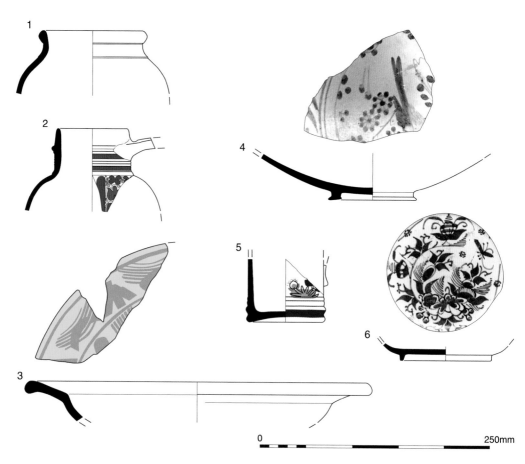

Fig. 11   Post-medieval pottery, nos 1–6 (scale 1:4)

including simplified plates and bowls (Fig. 11, no. 6; Fig. 12, no. 7) with all-over tinned glaze and, more unusually, a polychrome-painted tankard from Period 3 garden soil 9199 (Fig. 11, no. 5), belong to the 18th century. The small number of painted vessels which can be dated by their decoration are 18th century, and one plate with Chinese-derived blue painted 'rhomboid leaf' foliate decoration (Fig. 11, no. 6) probably dates to *c.* 1730–50. The mark to the rear of this vessel, probably a '3' with an oblique slash, is not paralleled from surviving Bristol vessels, though the overall style and 'exuberant misuse of a Chinese design' suggests such an origin (Rod Dowling, pers. comm.).

Yellow slipware BPT 100 and mottled brown glazed-ware types BPT 211 imitate Staffordshire production, but it is likely that most material was manufactured in Bristol from the final quarter of the 17th century. Thrown cup forms (Fig. 12, no. 8) are amongst the earlier yellow slipwares. A colander with three-slipped decoration might be a Staffordshire product (Fig. 12, no. 10). Mottled brown glazed wares (BPT 211), including the hard-fired 'tiger wares', are represented by tankards and a cup, mainly of 18th-century type (Fig. 12, no. 9).

White salt-glazed stonewares are dated as early as 1720, and together with tin-glazed products were rendered obsolete by Midlands-produced refined whitewares by *c.* 1770/80. The largest-scale production was in Staffordshire although other centres of production are known, possibly including Bristol. Bristol-made stonewares, characterised by a grey fabric and teardrop-shaped voids visible to the break (BPT 277), were in production as early as the 1690s (Price 2003), and continued throughout the 18th century and beyond. Vessel forms for the stonewares are mainly tankards and cups, with one plate.

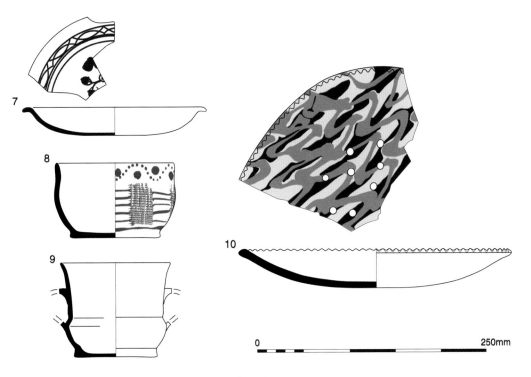

Fig. 12   Post-medieval pottery, nos 7–10 (scale 1:4)

Continental imports follow a pattern typical for Bristol assemblages from the later 17th and 18th centuries. The small quantities of Iberian wares (BPT 81, BPT 281 and BPT 282) and north Italian wares (BPT 82) probably date before to *c.* 1650/1700. Only the Westerwald stoneware (BPT 95), round-bodied drinking jugs (Fig. 11, no. 2) and tankards occur in reasonable quantities, these probably dating from 1690–1750.

Summary

The majority of the recovered material dates to the later post-medieval period, *c.* 1650–1770, and with most dating to after *c.* 1690/1700. The assemblage is broadly reflective of pottery use in the city in this period and compares quite closely with the comparably dated group from Welsh Back (Burchill and Jackson 2010). The emphasis is on utilitarian wares, serving a variety of kitchen or storage-related functions. The drinking and tablewares were for the most part supplied from local sources, with tin-glazed wares most common among the 'flatwares'. Porcelain, including high-quality Chinese or English imports for display or 'prestige' tableware, is virtually absent, and may reflect the relatively lowly status of the populations using the pottery discarded at this site. The small assemblage of imports overall is evidence of the self-sufficiency of Bristol in terms of its requirements in this period, both for utilitarian wares and for tablewares. Pottery with specific or 'industrial' use was present rarely in the form of unglazed earthenware sugar-cone mould or syrup-collecting vessel fragments (BPT 310). The quantities of such material (three fragments) are insufficient to suggest sugar refining was ongoing close to the site.

Catalogue of illustrated sherds

No. 1   BPT 286. Frechen stoneware jar(?) Period 4 residual from floor surface 3092.
No. 2   BPT 95. Westerwald stoneware globular-bodied mug/drinking jug. Period 3 make-up layer 3061.
No. 3   BPT 268sg. South Somerset redware dish with *sgraffito* decoration (broad blade through yellow slip and with patchy copper colouring in glaze). Period 3 garden soil 9199.
No. 4   BPT 99. Tin-glazed earthenware (probably Bristol) charger/large dish with foot ring, lead glaze to undersurface, blue/yellow painted bird design, probably later 17th century. Period 3 garden soil 9199.
No. 5   BPT 99. Tin-glazed earthenware (probably Bristol) tankard with polychrome painted decoration, 18th century. Period 3 garden soil 919.
No. 6   BPT 99. Tin-glazed earthenware (probably Bristol) bowl(?) with blue-painted design featuring 'rhomboidal' leaves, marked with numeral to underside, 18th century (probably 1730–50). Period 3 layer 3092.
No. 7   BPT 99. Tin-glazed earthenware (probably Bristol) bowl (punchbowl?) with blue-painted design, 18th century. Period 3 layer 3092.
No. 8   BPT 100. Yellow slipware cup with combed slip decoration, probably *c.* 1690–1720. Period 3 make-up layer 9081
No. 9   BPT 211. Mottled brown glazed earthenware cup. Period 3 make-up layer 9081.
No. 10   BPT 100. Yellow slipware variant (with three slips) press-moulded strainer bowl, 'Pie-crust' decoration to rim. Period 4 make-up layer 3090.

The clay tobacco pipes, by Reg Jackson

The excavation produced 471 clay-pipe fragments from 84 contexts, plus three bags of unstratified material. Of these, 132 were pipe bowls or bowl fragments; 47 bowl fragments were too small to be dated.

Where possible the pipes were dated by the use of the general bowl typology developed by Oswald (1975), which has been refined by further research into pipe production in Bristol (Jackson and Price 1974). The position, type and style of a pipemaker's mark are often indicative of a likely date and place of manufacture, and it is often possible to assign the initials or full name on the mark to a particular pipemaker whose working dates have been determined by documentary research. Most of the pipes found at Harbourside were made in Bristol and the pipemakers working in the city have been extensively researched (Price *et al.* 1979). Quantification, description and dating of all the clay tobacco pipes by context is available in tabulated form in the archive.

Mid to late 17th century

The earliest pipes date from the mid to late 17th century and the majority were made by either Philip Edwards I or II. They are all stamped on the heel with the initials 'PE'. A spurred bowl with the initials 'IL' in a circle in relief on the side of the bowl was probably made by John Lewis II, while one with the initials 'RN' stamped on the heel was made by Richard Nunney.

A bowl with the three-line mark 'EC/IN.CH/ARD' stamped on the heel from the fill of pit 9205 in Area 1 was made by Edward Collins of Chard in Somerset, who was working from about 1663 to 1673 (M. Lewcun, pers. comm.; Fig.13, no.1). Similarly marked pipes have been found in Taunton (Pearson 1984, 146, figs 9 and 10) but, as far as the writer is aware, this is the first to be recorded in Bristol.

Two pipes are similar in bowl form and style of mark to those made in Broseley, Shropshire, during the late 17th and early 18th centuries. One, from lane surface 9109 in Area 1, has the initials 'WK' in relief in a rectangular panel on a broad, tailed heel (Fig. 13, no. 2). However, neither Atkinson (1975) nor Higgins (1987) has identified a pipemaker with the initials 'WK' working in Shropshire. The other, from 8073 in Area 2 has a three-line mark in relief within a rectangular panel on a large heel; the first line of the mark probably reads 'THOM' while the rest is illegible (Fig. 13, no. 3).

There were a number of pipes made by Bristol makers whose working dates span the late 17th and early 18th centuries. These include a spurred bowl made by James Abbott with the three-line mark 'I/ABBO/TT' in a circle in relief on the side of the bowl; a spurred bowl made by Devereux Jones with the two-line mark 'D/IONES' in a circle in relief on the side of the bowl; a heeled bowl made by Thomas Owen I with the initials 'TO' stamped in the back of the bowl; and spurred bowls made by William Taylor with the two-line mark 'W/TAYLOR' in a circle in relief on the side of the bowl.

18th century

Most of the pipes date to the 18th century and are all spurred bowls with the pipemaker's initials either in relief on the side of the bowl (George Ebbery; Thomas Harvey I; John Macey I; John Squibb), the pipemaker's full or partial name in relief on the side of the bowl (Henry Edwards; Thomas Harvey; Edward Reed) or the pipemaker's initials stamped into the back of the bowl (John Bryant; George Ebbery; Thomas Harvey I; Henry Hoar; Maurice Phillips; Edward Reed; John Squibb).

19th century

Fragments of seven pipe bowls from a Period 4 levelling layer (5051) are decorated in relief with the Prince of Wales feathers across the rear of the bowl, beneath which is the motto 'ICH DIEN' ('I serve'), together with elaborate sprays of leaves and flowers on the front

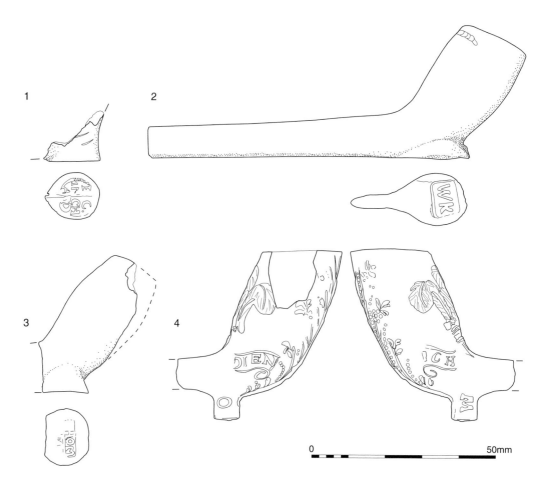

Fig. 13   Clay tobacco pipes (scale 1:1)

of the bowl and the initials 'W' and 'O' on each side of the flattened spur (Fig. 13, no. 4). Pipes decorated in this way were made at a number of production centres across England from the mid 18th to mid 19th centuries (Atkinson and Oswald 1980). The bowl typology of those from Harbourside suggests a date in the early 19th century and it is possible they were made by the Bristol pipemaker William Okeley.

Other 19th-century pipes include a bowl fragment decorated in relief with the prow, foremast and sails of a square-rigged ship and another which has four talons holding the bowl, with the skin of the talons, which extends down the stem, being textured with small circles in relief.

Coins and tokens, by Edward Besly

Two examples of Bristol-type tokens issued between 1651 and 1670 were found in the clay bank (layer 6039) in Trench 6. The City of Bristol was a pioneer in England in the issuing of small change in copper-alloys, having first issued such tokens in the reign of Elizabeth I, from 1577. Following Parliamentary suppression in 1644 of the 'royal' farthings of James I and Charles I, the city was again a prolific issuer of farthing tokens. Although primarily intended for local circulation, these large issues passed widely, notably in south Wales, and their design influenced a number of other municipal tokens (Thompson 1988). When an official regal coinage in copper was introduced in 1672, local tokens were banned and disappeared from circulation within a few years (Boon 1973). It is likely, therefore, that these tokens were deposited at some time between 1652 and the middle of the 1670s.

No. 1   City of Bristol, copper-alloy farthing token, dated 1652. Corroded but not much worn. From layer 6039, Period 3.

No. 2   City of Bristol, copper-alloy farthing token, similar. The date is obscured but probably reads 1652. Corroded, some wear? From layer 6039, Period 3.

No. 3   Halfpenny of Victoria. Dated 1865. Very worn. From backfill 3143 within drain 3142, Period 5.

Worked bone and metal objects, by E.R. McSloy

A total of 232 items of metal and worked bone was recovered from the excavations. Items of intrinsic interest are described below; the remainder are summarised in the archive.

Worked Bone (Fig. 14)

No. 1   Tubular object with threaded rebate. This is the final 'needle' element from a four-piece medical syringe of later post-medieval type. Missing are a collar, joining the barrel-like container for the medicament, and the syringe plunger. More complete examples are known from the prison hospital at Portchester Castle, dating to *c.* 1800. Use for the delivering of enemas has been suggested (Garratt 1994, 117). L. 88mm. From fill 9229 of gutter 9230, Area 1, Period 4.

No. 2   Apple corer or cheese scoop. Similar objects are known from 18th-century contexts (MacGregor 1985), though this example is unusual in having a well made, lathe-finished handle. L. 156mm; D. (max. at handle) 21mm. From layer 4030, Trench 4, Period 4.

No. 3   Fragment of object of unknown function, adapted from cow-sized rib (Sylvia Warman, pers. comm.). Polished from use and concave-convex in section, with repeated deep grooves/cuts to its internal (dished) surface. L. 90mm; W. 13mm. From wall 9250, Area 1, Period 1.

Iron

(n.i.)   Cast iron spherical weight(?) with suspension loop. Given the documented use of the site for rope manufacture, the most likely function is as a weight supplying tension. D. 105mm; weight 4.6kg. From fill 4162 of rut 4161, Trench 4, Period 4.

(n.i.)   Cast iron spherical weight or cannon ball. As with above, this probably functioned as a weight, used in rope manufacture. The absence of a suspension loop may indicate a former use as 'roundshot', possibly dating to before *c.* 1850. D, 108mm; weight 4.6kg. From fill 4164 of rut 4163, Trench 4, Period 4.

Glass and glass waste, by E.R. McSloy

A total of 647 fragments of vessel glass (23.6kg) and a small quantity of window glass (16 fragments, 108g) was recovered. The majority of the glass was hand-recovered, with additional quantities (4.1kg) retrieved following sorting of bulk soil samples. The assemblage comprises mostly wine or spirit bottles, with some thin-walled pharmaceutical phials, but virtually no drinking vessels or other tableware. In addition to the glass, material relating to glass manufacture (including crucible fragments) amounted to 11kg. Further quantities were recovered from soil samples (651g), this material frequently comprising a mix of waste and vessel glass.

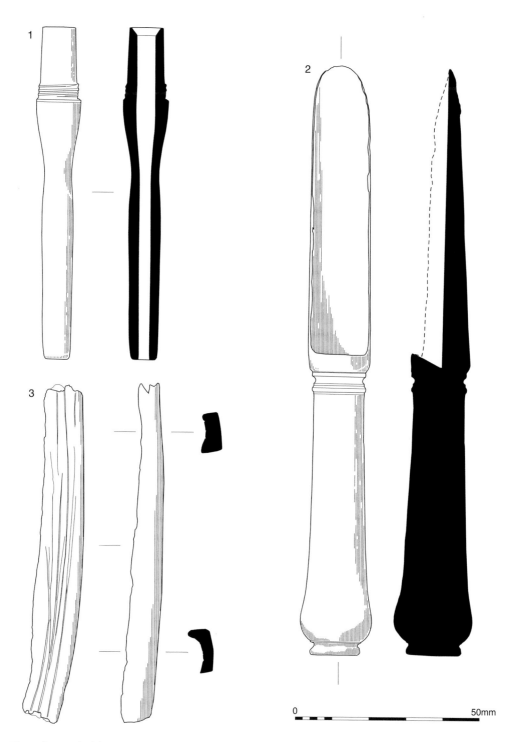

Fig. 14   Worked bone artefacts (scale 1:1)

Vessel glass

The bulk of the vessel glass consists of dark green fragments of thick-walled wine or spirits bottles, typical of the mid 17th to the later 19th centuries (Dungworth 2005a), for which closer dating is not possible. Amongst the rim fragments, 'strung' bottle rims are common, suggesting that most material dates before *c.* 1800. A small number of more closely datable elements are present, including a group from garden soil 9199 (Area 1, Period 3), which consists of sizeable fragments from short-necked 'free-blown' bottles with string rims and low, bulbous bodies, which probably date before *c.* 1720 (Hume 1969, 63–4). A large group from fill 9063 of cesspit 9128 (Area 1, Period 4), which consists of fully mould-made cylindrical bottles dates after the early 19th century, and faceted brown-coloured bottles from this deposit suggest later 19th-century dating. The same deposit produced the only example of glass tableware, part of a drinking glass stem, almost certainly of leaded crystal.

A small number of glass pharmaceutical phials were recovered, principally from Area 1 from Periods 3 and 4. These are of tall cylindrical form with well made flattened rims; all probably date to the 18th century.

Window glass

A few fragments of green-coloured diamond lights from post-medieval leaded windows were found in Periods 3 and 4 contexts in Area 1. The remainder consists of later 18th or 19th-century window glass from Periods 4 and 5, and seven fragments of clear glass from the construction trench for polygonal building 8052 (Area 2, Period 4), with painted floral decoration of late 19th-century date.

Glass waste

The glassworking waste derives primarily from Period 3 make-up and levelling layers. Industrial waste was commonly incorporated into deposits in the city intended to raise the ground levels, and as this material could have come from a number of sources its origin cannot be known (David Dungworth, pers. comm.). One possible source is the Limekiln Lane glasshouse, shown on Rocque's map of 1743 approximately 300m to the west of the site. Analysis on a very limited scale has previously been undertaken on waste material from the Limekiln Lane site (Dungworth 2005b), one focus of which was the manufacture of specialist laboratory apparatus.

The recovered material is typical of glassworking waste of the type encountered at glasshouse excavations in Bristol and elsewhere, and is likely to have been associated with bottle manufacture between the later 17th and 19th centuries. Included are quantities of dark green-coloured blocky lumps, made up of 'high lime low alkali' (HLLA) glass and some material discoloured to an opaque cream or blue, probably representing 'overcooked' HLLA glass. In addition there are various spills, runs/pulls and strings, all probably relating to glass manufacture, including test pieces used to assess consistency and viscosity (Dungworth 2005b, 20).

A number of small fragments of ceramic crucible, used in glass manufacture, were recovered. These are derived large, thick-walled (20mm) vessels or 'pots' made from hard grey-firing refractory clay and with distinctive vitrified surfaces.

Medieval floor tiles, by Jennie Stopford

The medieval floor tile assemblage consisted of seven tiles or fragments dating variously between the 13th and 15th centuries. Four are decorated, two are plain-glazed and one was a quarry fragment. The floor tiles were residual or had been reused in their contexts. Given the proximity of the abbey, it is probable that this was where some were first used. The assemblage has been divided into four types, described below.

Type 1

A single decorated tile fragment from floor surface 9227 (Period 3) measures 92mm x 68mm and is 20mm thick, and is possibly a quarter of the complete tile. The design is geometrical, in deep counter-relief, possibly with a small central *fleur de lys* motif with an olive-green glaze (Fig 15, no. 1). Parts of two scooped keys are visible on the lower surface, cut out using a blade. The rounded edges of the design suggest the tile was produced in a mould rather than using a stamp, where the impressed edges are usually straight, but this is not conclusive. The distinctive granular, laminated body fabric has a high content of course (*c.* 1mm) quartz sand and some grog. The tile is dated to the 13th century on typological grounds.

Type 2

One decorated half tile (unstratified) and a small corner fragment from bank deposit 6037 (Period 3) are probably of the same type, based on fabric and keying. The larger fragment measures 134mm across the upper surface and is 24mm thick. It has a design of an animal in a circle with an attached *fleur de lys* at each corner, inlaid with white clay (Fig. 15, no. 2). Traces of glaze on the tile edge suggest that the design would have been yellow against a brown-olive background. The white inlay has worn away in the centre of the tile. Parts

Fig. 15   Medieval floor tile, types 1–3 (scale 1:2)

of three scooped keys are visible on the lower surface. The fabric is poorly mixed, with the upper half of the quarry laminated with some very large (up to 10mm) pieces of grog. The lower part is better mixed, with a fine quartz, white clay and grog. The tile is dated to the 13th century on typological grounds.

Type 3

Two largely complete and unworn decorated tiles represent this type, one in good condition with a heraldic design (unstratified; Fig. 15, no. 3), the other reused in wall 9133 (Period 3; not illustrated). They are not the same size, measuring 113mm x 27mm and 137mm x 29mm, but are similar in other respects. The heraldic design formed part of a multi-tile arrangement and includes the shield of Westminster Abbey (Eames 1980, II, design 2897). The design on the second tile is unclear but has an inscribed border, possibly with a central circle containing entwined initials. The inlaid decoration is of white clay and the glaze had fired brown over the body fabric and yellow over the white clay. The fabric is fine and generally homogeneous, but with some grog and voids and occasional pebble. The lower surface is unkeyed, with a sandy base. The tiles are dated to the later 15th/early 16th century on comparative and typological grounds.

Type 4 (not illustrated)

Two plain-glazed fragments of the same tile (probably less than a quarter complete) from levelling deposit 4057 (Period 5) and a further fragment of the same tile or similar from fill 4146 (Period 3). The depth is incomplete at 36mm. The upper surface is completely unworn with a thick, crackled glaze, which has formed a white opaque glass layer, with a translucent streaked dark brown/black layer above. The quarry has been completely reduced in firing and partly vitrified; the unworn upper surface and vitrified fabric and lower surface may indicate that this tile was discarded as a waster. The fabric is hard, fine and homogeneous with grog and glaze inclusions and occasional organics resulting in voids on break lines. The tile is typologically of medieval date.

Comparative material

The limited research carried out for this report has not found material directly comparable to the counter-relief tile of Type 1. The simple geometrical design on the tile and the ubiquitous *fleur de lys* motif do not help to date the tile typologically.

The tile of Type 2 conforms to the characteristics of Eames' Wessex group with its inlaid design, dimensions and keying (Eames 1980, I, 186–200). The encircled animal is likely to be either a lion passant or griffin but many variants of these designs are known (see for example Eames 1980, II, designs 1781–8 and 1867–9). Other examples of Wessex tiles from Bristol include some of those from Mary-le-Port (Watts and Rahtz 1985, 145–6), and the Carmelite Friary (British Museum collection, cat. nos 11645–55).

Tiles of both the designs of Type 3 have previously been found in Bristol. The heraldic design is one part of a 16-tile arrangement known from Great Malvern Priory in Worcestershire, and at Gloucester Cathedral, and with derivative versions at other sites such as Acton Court, Avon, and in the Canynges' House pavement in Bristol (Eames 1980, I, 236–54; British Museum design 2897). The second tile of Type 3, with the black-letter inscription, may be the same as an example illustrated by the Clifton Antiquarian Club journal (vol. V, 1900-1903, Plate XXXI, no. 28). This design was also found at Great Malvern and Gloucester Cathedral. The circular inscription was read as *'Fiat misericordia tua domine super nos'* and the initials in the centre were thought to be IN, commemorating John Newland, who was abbot of St Augustine's, Bristol, 1481–1515. A tile of John Newland was recovered from College Green in 1968 (Fowler 1970, 55). The Malvern school of tiles is dated from the mid 15th to earlier 16th centuries.

Medieval ceramic roof tile, by E.R. McSloy

A total of 34 fragments weighing 2573g was identified from 20 deposits, primarily from Area 1. A single fragment of flat roof is recorded, the remainder comprises glazed ridge tile. This small group compares with medieval material previously recorded from the city and has been matched against published type descriptions (Williams and Ponsford 1988).

Only 12 fragments weighing 939g were from stratified medieval deposits, with most deriving from post-medieval deposits, either redeposited or representing survivals of medieval structures. The roof tile was recorded by type with codings, adapted from Williams and Ponsford's scheme, and with such attributes as crest form or other decoration described. Ten tile fragments preserve triangular knife-cut crests, some with stabbed 'decoration'. A full description is available in the archive.

The majority of the medieval tiles accords with published fabric Types 1–5, which share characteristics with Bristol Redcliffe pottery type BPT 118, known to be produced in Bristol *c.* 1250–1450. The Bristol-made ridge tiles are thought to be mainly 14th century in date, with Malvern-type tiles probably dominant from the 15th and 16th centuries. Glazed ridge tiles suggest a level of building above that of a peasant dwelling, although they are commonly found in excavations in Bristol (e.g. Burchill 2004, 33; McSloy forthcoming) and are not indicative of highly sophisticated structures.

The cordage, by Penelope Walton Rogers

Seven lengths of cordage were recovered from Period 4 levels, one from demolition deposit 4058 and six from surface 4077. They are 4–7mm thick, 70–240mm long, and all seven are two-plied, the primary strands being twisted in the Z-direction and then laid together in the S-direction (Z2S). Some of the pieces are frayed and worn, while others appear relatively fresh and have at least one cut end. Three representative samples were submitted to Dr A.R. Hall, who identified them as coir (coconut fibre). A full report of this identification is available in the archive.

Similar coir cordage has been recorded from a number of sites along the lower Thames. These include the 18th and 19th-century dockyard at Greenwich, where there was the greatest number (Walton Rogers 2004), the 18th-century backfill of a side channel at 165 Rotherhithe Street, Southwark (Walton Rogers 2002), and from a 19th-century river lighter excavated at Erith in Kent (Dawkes *et al.* 2009, 83–5). All of these examples are either two-plied, Z2S, 3–6mm in diameter, or thicker ropes made by combining the Z2S cords in multiples. This Z2S element seems to be how the material was traded from the main area of production, which was Ceylon (Sri Lanka) and the southern tip of India (Bally 1956, 18, 24). The Dutch, who took possession of Ceylon in 1740, exported the cordage to Europe until the British took over both the island and the trade in 1802 (ibid., 15). Although the Harbourside cords will almost certainly have originated in Ceylon, it is likely that they were used in the manufacture or repair of thicker rope in the ropewalk.

THE BIOLOGICAL EVIDENCE

Animal bone, by Sylvia Warman and Lorrain Higbee

This report comprises a summary of the animal bone, both hand-collected and from processed samples, recovered from secure contexts dated to Periods 1, 2 and 3. Animal bone from deposits dated to Periods 4 and 5 totalled 814 fragments from 842 bones, of which 194 were identified to species. These comprised horse, cattle, sheep, sheep/goat, pig, dog, cat and chicken; further information on this material is available in the site archive.

Period 1: medieval (12th to mid 15th centuries)
A total of 25 fragments of animal bone was recovered from the fills of ditches, drains and channel 9032 in Areas 1 and 2 from this period, with an additional 1015 fragments recovered from processed samples. Cattle, sheep/goat and pig bones were identified, and the size of some of the fragmented material suggested that goose, chicken and small mammals were also represented. It is not clear whether this material represented butchery or household waste.

Period 2: late medieval and early post-medieval (mid 15th to 17th centuries)
Animal bone totalling 16 fragments was recovered from rubbish pit 9205 and bedding trench 9173 in Area 1; an additional 527 fragments were recovered from processed samples. Cattle and sheep bone were identified, and fragments of mouse-sized and goose-sized animals were also recovered. Evidence for butchery was seen on a single sheep/goat bone fragment, and some bones had been gnawed by dogs. Some of the bone fragments from sample <10> from fill 9242 of pit 9243 had been burnt, and the colour change to white/grey is indicative of higher temperatures than those normally reached in domestic cooking fires. The feature is interpreted as a rubbish pit, but it would seem the material discarded in it may not be entirely domestic in origin.

Period 3: 18th century
The assemblage was considerably larger than that seen for the earlier periods and drawn from a greater number of deposits. It comprised 374 hand-collected fragments and 1408 fragments from processed samples. The range of species present was wider than for Periods 1 and 2, comprising cattle, sheep, sheep/goat, pig, red deer, dog, cat, rabbit, chicken and duck.

Animal bone recovered from surfaces, both internal and external, had suffered weathering and breakage, and some had been burnt. Make-up deposit 9037 beneath stone surface 9035 comprised cattle horn cores. These are robust items but also porous, a property for which they may have been selected if drainage was an issue in this part of the site. The use of animal bone to repair surfaces was noted at Newport Street Worcester (Warman, forthcoming[a]).

Quantities of animal bones were also recovered from deposits interpreted as garden soils and from cut features. Deposit 9107, from pit 9108 beneath Building 3 in Area 1 (not illustrated), produced a fragment of red deer antler, the only evidence for deer species at the site.

Summary
The species seen at Harbourside are commonly present in much larger assemblages such as those from Cabot Circus (Warman forthcoming [b]), and are likely to represent the deposition of animal bone from domestic waste. The presence of butchery marks suggests

that beef and mutton/lamb were consumed, although pork, chicken and duck were utilised in smaller quantities. Given the monastic element to the site, greater quantities of game species would have been expected in the assemblage, although other assemblages in Bristol have also lacked game, or include only very small quantities, for example at Cabot Circus.

Fish bone, by Hannah Russ

A total of 311 fragments was recovered, largely from flotation samples. In general the fish remains were well preserved. Ribs and spines, which represented over half of the assemblage, showed some fragmentation, which is common for these elements in any archaeological assemblage. Vertebrae were well preserved with many retaining their neural and haemal spines. Cranial elements were virtually absent from the assemblage.

The fish bone from Period 1 was identified as cod family, herring, salmon/trout and flatfish. Herring was identified from a single sample in Period 2. Thornback ray, European eel, herring, flatfish and cod family were identified from Period 3. Flatfish, cod family and ling were identified from Period 4. Burning of some specimens was recorded in deposit 9030, Period 4, from a stove base, and a few other contexts. Cut-marks were observed on the vertebrae of ling.

A range of edible marine species was seen, some of which also inhabit estuarine and freshwater environments during their lifecycle (e.g. eel and salmon). The size of the ling vertebrae from Period 4 indicates an adult that lives in waters up to 400m deep (Dipper and Powell 1984, 184), which supports evidence for deep-sea fishing in the 19th century. The other species present suggest fishing in shallower coastal waters. An absence of cranial elements suggests the presence of processed fish but is more likely a result of taphonomic processes. Little can be said about such a small assemblage, although an increase in the range of species in Period 3 may suggest diversification in fishing strategies in the late post-medieval period.

The charcoal and plant macrofossil remains, by Dana Challinor and Sarah Cobain

Nineteen samples were processed, comprising flots from 1mm and 0.5mm fractions, and material sorted from the residues. Two bags of hand-collected charcoal from Area 1 were also examined. The flots and charcoal from the residues were scanned under a binocular microscope at up to x45 magnification. Charcoal caught on a 2mm sieve was identified and quantified; and some fragments were examined in transverse section for the identification of ring porous taxa (e.g. oak and ash). The flots were also scanned for the presence of any other plant remains.

The charcoal was generally small in size, although the preservation was quite good. A range of taxa was recovered including coniferous species, elm, walnut, beech, oak, alder/hazel, *Maloideae* (hawthorn, apple, pear, service) and ash. With the possible exception of the coniferous and the walnut charcoal, the wood is likely to have come from native tree species. The walnut was introduced to Britain by the Romans, but the identification here is tentative. The coniferous charcoal found in Periods 3 and 4 exhibited resin canals in transverse section, which are characteristic of pine or other species such as spruce or larch which were introduced to Britain in the 15th and 17th centuries respectively (Cutler and Gale 2000), although the pine is also likely to have been imported in this period. The presence of possible introduced or exotic species is of interest but not unexpected for the post-medieval period at a major trading port like Bristol.

There was only one sample which produced carbonised plant macrofossil remains. A single carbonised wheat grain was identified from fill 9225 of drain 9226 (Period 1). The majority of the waterlogged plant macrofossil material derived from channel 9302 and the fill of drain 9226 (Period 1), and pit 9243 (Period 2). There were also occasional fragments in ditch 8006 (Period 3), cultivation layer 8002 and garden soil 8059 (Period 4). Although none of these was charred they are all from plants with robust woody seeds which resist decay and are therefore likely to be contemporary with the deposits. Single fragments of hazelnut and cherry pip represent food remains. The remaining plant macrofossil assemblage was made up of elder, sedge and water pepper, all of which are species that tolerate damp conditions, and raspberry, bramble, fat hen, dock, cinquefoil, sow thistle, common chickweed, grass, fumitory, fool's parsley, mustard/cabbage and stinking chamomile, which are opportunistic species that establish in disturbed areas (Rose 2006). As with the charcoal, the material within these drains and deposits could have come from several sources and there is a lack of any plant macrofossils with any economic significance.

Pollen, by B. Silva
Four sub-samples were extracted from monolith sample <3> in Trench 6 for pollen analysis. These comprised a layer of marsh alluvium 6053 at 6.39–6.40m AOD, and three fills from channel or pond 6050: fill 6046 at 6.75–6.76m AOD; fill 6051 at 7.20–7.21m AOD; and fill 6041 at 7.30–7.31m AOD. The pollen was extracted from a standard volume of samples sediment (1ml). Full details of the methodology are available in the archive. The sub-samples processed for the pollen analysis were also assessed for diatoms, but no diatom frustules were preserved in the sedimentary succession.

The results indicate that alluvium 6053 contained a low concentration of pollen grains and spores dominated by pine, ribwort plantain and male fern. Fill 6046 also contained low concentrations of pollen, with pine, male fern, grass family and campion family. Fill 6051 contained pine, male fern, sphagnum moss, pondweed and yellow water lily in low concentrations. Fill 6041 contained willow, ribwort plantain, male fern and reedmace/bulrush in low concentrations. Although the pollen is poorly preserved and in low concentrations, the results indicate an open vegetation cover, probably dominated by grassland. The presence of pondweed, yellow water lily and reedmace pollen is particularly interesting since these taxa indicate the presence of open water.

DISCUSSION
(Including documentary and historical information by Roger Leech)

Geoarchaeological sequence

The Middle Holocene (*c.* 7000–5000 BC) strata examined in the borehole deposits gave little indication of prehistoric human impact on the area, which was characterised by salt-marsh environments subjected to periodic inundation and sedimentation. One episode of ash deposition may have been an indication of human activity, but radiocarbon dating proved unreliable, and the episode cannot be dated with any security. There was little evidence for occupation or exploitation of the floodplain prior to the establishment of the abbey of St Augustine in *c.* 1140, situated on higher ground to the north of the site. Before this, the majority of the site was likely to have been poorly drained land that may have been used for seasonal grazing.

St Augustine's Abbey and its precincts

The majority of Area 1 and the northern part of Area 2 lay to the north of a substantial east–west wall. Its identification as the abbey's outer precinct wall is an extrapolation from later cartographic evidence, which shows this alignment as a major boundary between buildings and gardens backing on to Lower College Green and the marsh (Fig. 2). By the 1150s the abbey was in possession of the lands between the abbey and the river (Bryant 1995), and this part of the floodplain became known as Canon's Marsh.

The timescale involved in the initial laying out of the precinct of St Augustine's Abbey after its foundation is unknown, but it is likely to have been soon after the foundation, alongside the establishment of boundaries and a water management infrastructure. The Great Gatehouse on the north side of the precinct dates from the 1170s (Rogan (ed.) 2000, 19) and it is likely that the whole precinct was enclosed by a masonry wall at an early date.

The lack of good ceramic dating from Period 1, combined with the high levels of truncation in both Areas 1 and 2, means that it has not been possible to provide a clear date for the construction of the earliest features excavated in these areas. Later activity enclosed by the precinct wall dates to *c.* 1270–1300. It is likely that wall 9257 was constructed shortly after the foundation of St Augustine's Abbey, to formally enclose the outer monastic precinct, and separate this area from the abbey's lands on the marsh. It is probable that the east/west lane (later Anchor Lane) running along the outside of this wall originated at this time, although it may have been little more than a cart track.

Subdivision of the monastic precinct into distinct areas was demonstrated by the rebuild of precinct wall 9150 and the construction of garden wall 9278. Although these elements were also undated, it is likely that they formed part of the wider development of the abbey and its precinct in the 13th or 14th century, when numerous new buildings were constructed across the precinct, including at least three dovecotes (Boore 1979; Hansell and Hansell 1988, 79; Cox *et al.* 2006), and an aisled barn which formed the western side of the outer court immediately to the north of Area 1 (see Cox *et al.* 2006, fig. 1). Later maps (e.g. Rocque 1743; Fig. 2) indicate that Area 1 lay within the block of land forming gardens at the rear of buildings flanking the south side of the outer court. The construction date of the channel excavated in Area 1 also cannot be established archaeologically; however, water supply was key to all monastic houses and it is likely that some form of water management system was instigated early on in the abbey's development. It has been suggested that the monastic water supply was in place by the mid 13th century (Cox *et al.* 2006, 64–6).

The precinct wall excavated in Areas 1 and 2 marked the limit of the abbey outer precinct. The north/south lane excavated in Area 1 would have provided access from the outer court of the precinct to Canon's Marsh as well as into the precinct from the south and west. No evidence for the lane survives from the early period, but it is assumed that access would have been regulated by a gate; the iron pintle set into the 17th-century pillar (9273) shows that access could still controlled in the post-Dissolution period. Unlike the Great Gatehouse which controlled access into the inner monastic precinct from the north, this access point between the outer court and Canon's Marsh was relatively minor, and probably did not require a formal gatehouse. The entrance is marked as the Lower

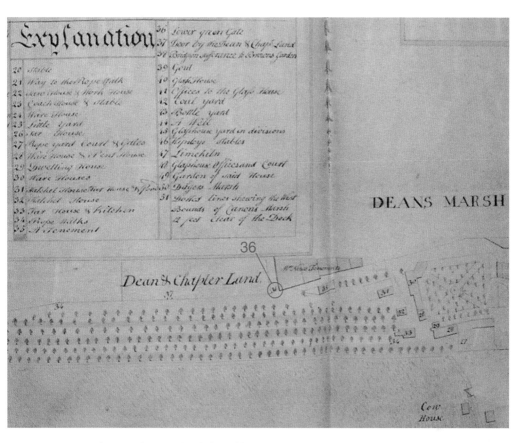

Fig. 16   A map of 1791, showing lands leased by Thomas Clement (BRO: DC/E/40/8/1)

Green Gate (no. 36) on the plan of John Clement's estate in 1791 (Fig. 16), which is based on Cooke's copy of a plan of 1738 by John Jacob de Wilstar.

Within the precinct, the area west of the north/south lane appears to have been used initially as a garden, with a stone pavement alongside the garden wall. The exact function of Building 1 abutting the bridge was unclear; its cobbled floor and location within a probable garden near to the gateway may indicate that the ground floor was used as a stable, although access to the lane was by a narrow doorway, which was subsequently blocked. Some fragments of 14th-century glazed ridge tile from later deposits in this area may give some idea of the character of this building. To the east of the lane no structural evidence earlier than *c.* 1700 was excavated. Much of this area may also have been gardens, and the three fragments of decorated floor tile, two of 13th-century date, the other late 15th or early 16th-century date, are more likely to have come from the monastic and abbey buildings to the north than medieval structures in this location.

Whilst the site was clearly peripheral to the inner precinct of the abbey, the excavated evidence casts some light on the development of the outer precinct. Although the early sequence of construction cannot be dated, it is apparent that the original layout of precinct wall and drainage channel formed a framework for later structural developments.

The former precinct in the post-medieval period

The general plan of the buildings and roadways excavated in Areas 1 and 2 survived into the immediate post-Dissolution period, although the buildings may have been put to different uses. The lands were now held by the Dean and Chapter of the newly established Bristol Cathedral. Both Rocque's map of 1743 and Plumley and Ashmead's map of 1828 show the lane leading to Lower Green, within the former abbey precinct, as built up on both sides (Figs 2 and 9). The details of the buildings on either side of the precinct lane could not be correlated with Rocque's schematic outline, although this early map fitted well with the excavated location of the precinct wall in Area 2, and bank and ditches in Trenches 4 and 6. However, the location of the 18th-century buildings to either side of the north/south lane matches well with those on Plumley and Ashmead's map of 1828. This and later cartographic evidence from a plan of 1895 (Fig. 17) show a narrow alley running westwards from the lane where surface 9035/9039 was recorded, although access to this alley through the lane wall was not apparent in the archaeological record. No evidence survived for the building mapped to the north of this alley, other than possibly the small fragment of wall 9206 of Period 3. To the north of the channel culvert, the maps depict a building approximately equal in size and dimensions to the robbed walls of Building 2 dated to Period 2 (1450–1700) (Figs 3 and 9). The absence of evidence for a successor to Building 2, where a building is clearly depicted on the 18th and 19th-century maps, may be explained by later truncation, which was severe, although it is also possible that the datable artefacts found in association with the robbed structure were residual.

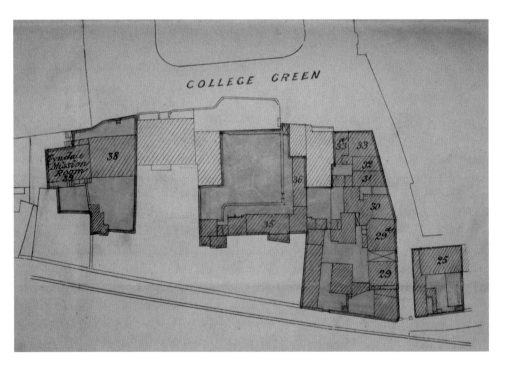

Fig. 17   A plan of 1895, showing the Revd Thomas Barlow's prebendal house (nos 29–30) (BRO: DC/E/40/39/1)

The area occupied by buildings and gardens to the west of the lane can be identified as having belonged to successive holders of the second prebendal stall, i.e. a seat held by a canon with a fixed income drawn from the abbey estates; following the Dissolution, the title was maintained as an honorary post in some dioceses (Cutts 1895, 476). By 1895, the second prebendal stall was held by the Revd Thomas Barlow (Fig. 17, nos 29 and 30).

Evidence from leases sheds light on some aspects of life within the Area 1 buildings in the 18th and 19th centuries. A lease of 1794 shows that no. 1 Ropewalk (Anchor Lane) clearly matches and complements the excavated evidence of Building 4 (Fig. 5; BRO: DC/E/40/38/1). The lease shows a house of two rooms (both parlours) with a courtyard and kitchen range (partially excavated) extending south to Anchor Lane. Fronting the road leading to the Lower Green was a shop which appears open-fronted, referred to in leases of the property as 'a shop adjoining to a vault or house of easement', the room and seat for the latter clearly visible on the plan (although it did not survive in the archaeological record). Part of a bone medical syringe and fragments of glass pharmaceutical phials, both of 18th-century date, found in the gutter running through the shop area may cast light on the commercial use of this building, although phial fragments were also found in several contexts associated with Building 3 to the west of the lane, and in the lane surface to the north of the bridge.

A watercolour of 1826 by Thomas Rowbotham (Fig. 18), painted from immediately in

Fig. 18 'The way from Canon's Marsh to the Butts, looking east', watercolour of 1826 by T.L. Rowbotham, looking east along Anchor Lane (M2540) © Bristol's Museums, Galleries and Archives

front of no. 1 Ropewalk and looking east, shows the sign of 'The Ship', no. 2 Ropewalk in 1775, and ships (probably in dry dock) beyond. The painting is of interest in that it shows the construction of the precinct wall to be blocks of dressed ashlar, quite unlike most boundary walls of this date in Bristol (which were generally of coursed or uncoursed rubble). The quality of construction lends weight to the assumption that this was the medieval boundary to the abbey's outer precinct.

Canon's Marsh

The land later known as Canon's Marsh was given to the abbey in the 1150s and functioned as an abbey grange (Brett 2005, 31). Part of the marsh was conveyed to the town to allow the diversion of the Frome via St Augustine's Reach in *c.* 1240, the low price of 9 marks suggesting the land was of limited economic value to the abbey at this time (Walker (ed.) 1998, 375–6). The marsh is first mentioned in the accounts of St Augustine's Abbey for 1491–2, when a rent of 23s 4d per annum was paid for 'that pasture called le Warthe next to le Canonmershe' (Beachcroft and Sabin 1938, 148). The abbey would have drawn an income from the sale of the first crop of hay from the marsh, 'a large home pasture between the monastery and the Avon' (ibid., 28). A survey of 1595 refers to Canon's Marsh as 'two marshes commonly called Canones Marshes adjoyinge to the cathedral churche aforesaid, of the yearly rent of 53s 4d' (BRO: DC/E/1/1(c)).

Draining the marsh would have allowed its exploitation as an agricultural resource; 18th-century maps such as Rocque's (Fig. 2) show a large area of the marsh enclosed by a ditch or channel, with a further channel to the north crossing the former abbey precinct. This northern channel was associated with fishponds in Bishop's Park to the west of the abbey, which may well be of medieval origin (Cox *et al.* 2006, 65). This was the channel excavated in Area 1, which also appeared to date from relatively early in the medieval period; the ditch on the marsh was excavated in Trench 4 (ditch 4148) and probably also originated in the medieval period.

The Sea Banks were built in the 17th century to protect the increasingly valuable marsh land from flooding. This name was retained for a lane running around the southern edge of the marsh, as shown on Plumley and Ashmead's map of 1828 (Brett 2005, 40). The recovery of two copper-alloy farthing tokens dating to 1652 from the clay bank indicates a construction in the 3rd quarter of the 17th century for the sea bank.

The presence of a building labelled as 'Cow House' on the map of lands leased by Thomas Clement in 1791 (Fig. 16) suggests that the marsh was still used for pasture at the end of the 18th century. Pollen recovered from the pond excavated in Trench 6 suggests the area immediately behind the sea banks was subject to localised or more widespread flooding in the later part of the 17th century.

19th-century ropemaking and industry on Canon's Marsh

The flat and open nature of Canon's Marsh, and its location to the west of St Augustine's Reach, made it ideally suited for making rope, an industry requiring long stretches of level land. The earliest reference to ropemaking on the abbey lands is between 1491 and 1512, when the abbey received sums derived from the 'Rent of house and licence to make rope on green within the Sanctuary' (Beachcroft and Sabin 1938, 278–9). It is probable that the specified location was of the rented property only, and the actual ropemaking took place to the south of the abbey precinct. Early ropemaking may have taken place on the lane to the south of the precinct wall, coinciding with metalling of the lane surface in the 15th or 16th century. The lane is shown on Rocque's map of 1743 where it is labelled 'Ropewalk' (Fig. 2). It was still known as Ropewalk on the 1794 lease; however, by 1795 it was known as Anchor Lane and it may be that both names were interchangeable to some extent (BRO: DC/E/40/38/1).

The map of lands leased by Thomas Clement in 1791 shows the Ropewalk as a clearly demarcated area separate from Anchor Lane to the north, and from the Great Ground and Lower Ground of Canon's Marsh to the south (Fig. 16). The Ropewalk is illustrated as a series of long avenues between six lines of trees, which may have been planted to shade the workers. Buildings at the eastern end of the ropewalk are associated with the Ropewalk; these include a tar house and kitchen, warehouses, and 'Rope Yard Court and Gates'. On the north side of the Ropewalk (later Anchor Lane), John Evans, ropemaker, is recorded as leasing no. 1 Ropewalk (Building 4) in 1766 and 1773 (Little 1971, 30).

The ditch excavated in Trench 4 on the south side of the Ropewalk was replaced by culvert 4136 in the 19th century, whose southern wall would have been visible above ground (Figs 8, 9 and 10). On Plumley and Ashmead's map of 1828 most of the lines of trees appear to have been cleared and a long narrow building is shown to the north of the ditch or channel. The lanes of an external ropewalk to the north of the ropewalk building are indicated by a series of parallel lines on Plumley and Ashmead's map. Ropewalks were originally entirely open-air; the development of enclosed ropewalk buildings for spinning and laying ropes was pioneered by naval ropeyards in the early 17th century (Coad 1987, 211–12). The building of a fully enclosed ropewalk was a considerable expense and could only be justified by continuous operation, and it is possible that the side(s) of the ropewalk was/were left open (ibid., 211–12, fig. 8). Although there appears to be a gap between the culvert and the building depicted on Plumley and Ashmead's map, the evidence from Trench 4 suggests this area was also utilised for ropemaking. Parallel ruts cutting the clay surface in this area suggest the passage of the forming machine travelling along the aisles of the ropewalk, and two cast-iron spherical objects found within the ruts may have been weights used to tension the rope on the forming machine. Fragments of cordage excavated from the later surfaces appear to have been made in Sri Lanka from coir, suggesting that by the 19th century, the initial processing of the raw materials was being undertaken abroad. Dating of the evidence in Trench 4 is imprecise, and the wheel ruts and surfaces may belong to the larger building marked as the 'Wire and Hemp Rope Manufactory' on the 1885 OS map. This map also depicts a polygonal building amongst ornamental gardens, which were partially excavated in Area 2.

The construction of the Floating Harbour in c. 1809 led to an increase in the development of Canon's Marsh and the area to the east of the Ropewalk (Brett 2005, 390; BRO: DC/E/3/4), and Plumley and Ashmead's map of 1828 shows two dry docks and a timber yard as well as shipyards. Yards were also being built along the southern edge of Canon's Marsh, adjacent to the Sea Banks, which had been extended up to the Floating Harbour using dumps of industrial waste and river-dredged silt to create wharves for shipping. Leases for no. 1 Ropewalk, and the adjacent tenement 'The Ship', record occupations closely linked to shipbuilding and seafaring: victuallers, ropemakers and riggers are recorded in the mid to late 18th century (BRO: DC/E/40/38/1; DC/E/1/1 fol.457; DC/E/40/16; CC49632).

Development was not restricted to maritime industries: the developing wharves and flat open land of Canon's Marsh meant raw materials could be easily unloaded. By 1903, Canon's Marsh was almost entirely occupied by a wide variety of industrial and manufacturing buildings, with the gas works occupying the western part of the marsh and a box manufactory, several marble works, saw mills, timber yards and wharves on the east (OS 1907). The foundations of buildings associated with these industries were identified in Trenches 4–6 where they truncated earlier deposits.

The major change in the early 20th century was the arrival of the Great Western Railway and a number of railway transit sheds, the construction of which required the demolition of many buildings, including the ropewalks and the buildings excavated in Area 1, and the alteration of the street layout.

ACKNOWLEDGEMENTS

The archaeological investigations and this publication were funded by Crest Nicholson Regeneration Ltd. The fieldwork was managed by Simon Cox. The evaluation was led by Richard Young and the excavation by Dave Cudlip. Post-excavation was managed by Annette Hancocks and Mary Alexander. Pete Moore, Lorna Gray and Jon Bennett prepared the illustrations. Thanks are due to Bob Jones of Bristol City Council who monitored the site and commented on an early draft of this report. We are grateful to the specialists who contributed to this report and Martin Watts for his comments on an earlier draft of this article. The authors would like to thank Jonathon Butler (Pre-Construct Archaeology), John Chambers (Chatham Historic Dockyard Trust) and Peter Insole (Bristol City Council Historic Environment Record) for their assistance during research for this report.

Cotswold Archaeology is grateful to Michael Ponsford and Rod Dowling for advice on the pottery, M. Lewcun for advice on the clay tobacco pipes, and David Dungworth for advice on the glass waste. Keith Wilkinson (University of Winchester) would like to thank Nick Branch and Gemma Swindle (ArchaeoScape, now Quest), Simon Cox, Jon Webster and Richard Young (Cotswold Archaeology), Geotechnical Engineering Ltd., Bob Jones (Bristol City Council), Ove Arup Ltd and Vanessa Straker (English Heritage). The finds and archive will be deposited with Bristol City Museum and Art Gallery under accession number BRSMG 2006/73.

BIBLIOGRAPHY

Primary Sources

BRO (Bristol Record Office):
> CC49632
> DC/E/3/4 fols.24–5
> DC/E/40 Estate records relating to the study areas, Records of the Dean and Chapter of the Cathedral, part of the Diocese of Bristol collection
> DC/E/40/38/1
> DC/E/1/1(c)
> DC/E/1/1 fol.457
> DC/E/40/16

Secondary Sources

Allan, J.P. 1984 *Medieval and Post-medieval finds from Exeter 1971–1980* Exeter Archaeol. Rep. **3**, Exeter, Exeter City Council and University of Exeter

Atkinson, D.R. 1975 *Tobacco pipes of Broseley, Shropshire* Saffron Walden, Hart-Talbot

Atkinson, D.R. and Oswald, A. 1980 'The dating and typology of clay pipes bearing the Royal Arms', in P.J. Davey (ed.) 1980, *The archaeology of the clay tobacco pipe III* BAR Brit. Ser. **78**, Oxford, British Archaeological Reports, 363–91

Bally, W. 1956 'Coir', *Ciba Review* **116** (August-September 1956), 2–32

Beachcroft, G. and Sabin, A. (eds) 1938 *Two compotus rolls of Saint Augustine's Abbey, Bristol (for 1491–2 and 1511–12)* Bristol Rec. Soc. **9**, Bristol, Bristol Record Society

BGS (British Geological Survey) 1974 *1:50,000 Geological Survey of Great Britain (England and Wales), Solid and Drift, map sheet 264: Bristol* Keyworth, British Geological Survey

Boon, G.C. 1973 *Welsh Tokens of the Seventeenth Century* Cardiff, National Museum of Wales

Boore, E.J. 1979 'Bristol Cathedral School Classroom Extension – Watching brief', *Bristol Archaeol. Res. Group Bull.* **6(8)**, 198–200

Brett, J.R. 2005 'Bristol Urban Archaeological Assessment, 2nd draft', Bristol City Council, unpublished report

British Museum Collections (accessed 13 Janaury 2012) http://www.britishmuseum.org/research/search_the_collection_database.aspx

Bryant, J. 1995 'Archaeological Desktop Study of Bristol Harbourside Development', BaRAS unpublished report **BA/D133/134**

Burchill, R. 2004 'Ceramic roof tile' in R. Jackson 2004, 'Archaeological excavations at Nos 30–38 St Thomas Street and No. 60 Redcliff Street, Bristol, 2000', *Bristol Avon Archaeol.* **19**, 33–4

Burchill, R. and Jackson, R. 2010 'Pottery', in R. Jackson 2010 'Archaeological work at 22–25 Queen Square and 42–44 Welsh Back, Bristol, 2002–2006', *Bristol Avon Archaeol.* **23**, 23–33

CA (Cotswold Archaeology) 2003 'Land at Harbourside, Bristol: Archaeological Data Review', CA unpublished report **03004**

CA (Cotswold Archaeology) 2009 'Land to the south of Anchor Road, Harbourside Development Area, Canon's Marsh, Bristol: Post-Excavation Assessment and Project Design', CA unpublished report **08115**

Coad, J.G. 1987 'Manufacture of cordage in the royal dockyards, 1760–1815', *Guerres et Paix 1660–1815*, 211–29

Cox, S., Barber, A. and Collard, M. 2006 'The archaeology and history of the former Bryan Brothers' Garage Site, Deanery Road, Bristol: the evolution of an urban landscape', *Trans. Bristol Gloucestershire Archaeol. Soc.* **124**, 55–71

Cutler, D.F. and Gale, R. 2000 *Plants in Archaeology - Identification Manual of Artefacts of plant origin from Europe and the Mediterranean* Kew, Westbury Scientific Publishing

Cutts, E.L. 1895 *A Dictionary of the Church of England, 3rd edn* London, Society for the Promotion of Christian Knowledge

Dawkes, G. Goodburn, D. and Walton Rogers, P. 2009 'Lightening the load: five 19th-century river lighters at Erith on the River Thames, UK', *Int. J. Naut. Archaeol. Underwater Explor.* **38/1**, 71–89

Dipper, F. and Powell, A. 1984 *Field guide to the water life of Britain* London, The Reader's Digest Association Limited

Dungworth, D. 2005a *Assessing Evidence for Post-Medieval Glassworking* English Heritage unpublished paper

Dungworth, D. 2005b *Investigation of 18th-Century Glass and Glassworking Waste from Limekiln Lane, Bristol* English Heritage Res. Dept Rep. Ser. **7/2005**, London, English Heritage

Eames, E.S. 1980 *Catalogue of medieval lead-glazed tiles earthenware tiles in the Department of Medieval and Later Antiquities* London, British Museum

Fowler, P. J. 1970 *Medieval Archaeology Review Part 4* Bristol, University of Bristol

Garratt, B. 1994 'The small finds', in B. Cunliffe and B. Garratt 1994, *Excavations at Portchester Castle Vol. V: post-medieval 1609–1817* London, Society of Antiquaries of London, 98–129

Good, G.L. 1987 'The excavation of two docks at Narrow Quay, Bristol, 1978–9', *Post-Medieval Archaeol.* **21**, 25–126

Hansell, P. and Hansell, J. 1988 *Doves and Dovecotes* Bath, Millstream Books

Higgins, D. 1987 *The interpretation and regional study of clay tobacco pipes: a case study of the Broseley District* University of Liverpool PhD thesis

Hume, I.N. 1969 *A Guide to Artefacts of Colonial America* Philadelphia, University of Pennsylvania Press

Jackson, R.G. and Price, R.H. 1974 *Bristol clay pipes: a study of makers and their marks* BCM Research Monograph **1**, Bristol, Bristol City Museum

Jackson, R. Jackson, W. and Beckey, I. 1991 'Tin-glazed earthenware kiln waste from the Limekiln Lane Potteries, Bristol', *Post-medieval Archaeol.* **25**, 89–114

Keen, L. 1969 'A series of seventeenth and eighteenth century lead glazed relief tiles from North Devon', *J. Brit. Archaeol. Assoc. 3rd ser.* **32**, 144–70

Little, B. (ed.) 1971 *Sketchley's Bristol Directory 1775* Bath, Kingsmead Reprints

MacGregor, A. 1985 *Bone, Antler, Ivory and Horn* London, Croom Helm

McSloy, E.R. (forthcoming) 'Medieval ceramic roof tile', in V. Ridgeway and M. Watts (eds) (forthcoming)

OS (Ordnance Survey) 1885 *1:500 map series, Gloucestershire, sheet LXXV.4.4*

OS (Ordnance Survey) 1907 *1:2500 map, (revised 1903–5) Bristol District sheets 250–1*

OS (Ordnance Survey) 1918 *1:2500 map*

Oswald, A. 1975 *Clay pipes for the archaeologist* BAR Brit. Ser. **14**, Oxford, British Archaeological Reports

Pearson, T. 1984 'Clay tobacco-pipes', In P. Leach 1984, *The archaeology of Taunton* Western Archaeol. Trust Excavation Monograph **8**, 145–51

Plumley J. and Ashmead G.C. 1828 *Plan of the City of Bristol and its Suburbs* Bristol, G.C. Ashmead

Ponsford, M.W. 1988 'Pottery', in B. Williams 1988, 'The excavation of medieval and post-medieval tenements at 94–102 Temple Street, Bristol, 1975', *Trans. Bristol Gloucestershire Archaeol. Soc.* **106**, 124–45

Ponsford, M.W. 1998 'Pottery', in R. Price, with M.W. Ponsford 1998 *St Bartholomew's Hospital, Bristol: The Excavation of a Medieval Hospital 1976–8* CBA Res. Rep. **110** York, Council for British Archaeology, 136–56

Price, R. 2003 'Late 17th-century stoneware waste from the Tower Harratz Pottery, Bristol', *Post-Medieval Archaeol.* **37.2**, 217–20

Price, R., Jackson, R. and Jackson P. 1979 *Bristol clay pipe makers: a revised and enlarged edition* Bristol, published by the authors

RBG Kew (no date) Coir: information sheet http://www.rbgkew.org.uk/ksheets/coir.html (consulted 15th November 2004)

Ridgeway, V. and Watts, M. (eds) (forthcoming) *Cabot Circus, Bristol: the archaeology of the Broadmead expansion project, 2005–8* CAPCA monograph **1**, London, Cotswold Archaeology/Pre-Construct Archaeology

Rocque, J. 1743 *A Plan of the City of Bristol. Survey'd and drawn by John Rocque. Engrav'd by John Pine 1742* Bristol, Hickey

Rogan, J. (ed.) 2000 *Bristol Cathedral History and Architecture* Stroud, Tempus

Rose, F. 2006 *The Wild Flower Key* London, Penguin Books

Thompson, R.H. 1988 'Bristol farthings, 1651-70', in R.H. Thompson 1988, *The Norweb Collection, Cleveland, Ohio, USA: Part 2, Dorset, Durham, Essex and Gloucestershire* London, Spink and Son, ix–xxxiii

Walker, D. (ed.) 1998 *The Cartulary of St Augustine's Abbey, Bristol* Gloucestershire Rec. Ser. Vol. **10**, Bristol, J.W. Arrowsmith for the Bristol and Gloucestershire Archaeological Society

Walton Rogers, P. 2002 'Cordage and caulking materials from 165 Rotherhithe Street, Southwark, London', unpublished Museum of London Archaeology Service Textile Research Associates Report **ROZ00**

Walton Rogers, P. 2004 'Cordage and caulking', in D. Divers *et al*, 2004, 'Excavations at Deptford on the site of the East India Company dockyards and the Trinity House almshouses, London', *Post-Medieval Archaeol.* **38.1**, 17–132, 79–84

Warman, S. (forthcoming[a]) 'Animal bone', in P. Davenport (forthcoming) *Excavations at Newport St. Worcester, 2005: Roman roadside activity and medieval to post-medieval urban development on the Severn floodplain* Cotswold Archaeology Monograph, Cirencester, Cotswold Archaeology

Warman, S. (forthcoming[b]) 'Animal bone', in V. Ridgeway and M. Watts (eds) (forthcoming)

Watts, L. and Rahtz, P. 1985 *Mary-le-Port, Bristol, Excavations 1962–3* CBMAG Monograph **7**, Bristol, City of Bristol Museum and Art Gallery

Wilkinson, K. and Tinsley, H. 2005 'Harbourside Development Area, Bristol: The geoarchaeology of borehole stratigraphy', Archaeostrat. unpublished report **05/06-3**

Williams, B. and Ponsford, M. 1988 'Clay roof-tiles', in B. Williams 1988, 'The excavation of medieval and post-medieval tenements at 94–102 Temple Street, Bristol, 1975', *Trans. Bristol Gloucestershire Archaeol. Soc.* **106**, 145–9

CABOT HOUSE, DEANERY ROAD, BRISTOL: INVESTIGATIONS IN 2008

by Ray Holt and Roger Leech

with contributions by
Mary Alexander, E.R. McSloy and Keith Wilkinson

INTRODUCTION

Between June and August 2008 Cotswold Archaeology undertook a programme of archaeological investigation, comprising excavation, a borehole survey and a watching brief, at the site of Cabot House, Deanery Road, Bristol (centred on NGR: ST 581726; Fig. 1). Work was carried out at the request of Westmark Developments ahead of the redevelopment of the site for offices within the area formerly occupied by Cabot House and its car park, bounded by College Street to the east, Brandon Street to the north, St George's Road to the west and Deanery Road to the south. College Street and Brandon Street were relocated in the 1950s when Cabot House was constructed but previously had been partly within the development area (Fig. 2). The underlying geology is of the Redcliffe Sandstone Formation, part of the Mercia Mudstone Group (BGS 1996). The site occupies part of a dry valley, infilled before the late 18th century; the ground surface now lies between 9.5m and 13.8m AOD, sloping upwards towards the northwest.

Archaeological and historical background

Borehole surveys previously undertaken at the nearby sites of the former Bryan Brothers' Garage (Deanery Road) and Harbourside (Fig. 1) revealed organic strata containing pollen evidence for human manipulation of the early Holocene woodland (Wilkinson *et al.* 2002; Cox *et al.* 2006; Wilkinson and Tinsley 2005; Alexander and Harward 2011 [this volume]). Other than these borehole investigations, there was no other evidence known locally for activity pre-dating the medieval period.

In the medieval period the site belonged to the abbey of St Augustine and lay approximately 200m to the west of the abbey precinct. At the Dissolution in *c.* 1540 the abbey church was retained to become Bristol Cathedral. The abbey lands were divided, most passing to the Dean and Chapter of the cathedral but some passing to the Bishop, including the 'Bishop's Park' (Leech 2006, 67), a steep valley to the west of the cathedral over which the site lay. Excavations to the south at the former Bryan Brothers' Garage, which was also within the former Bishop's Park, revealed the remains of a probable medieval dovecote beneath *c.* 2m of 18th-century deposits (Cox *et al.* 2006).

The area was developed for housing in the later 18th century, and the excavations revealed the remains of surfaces and houses from College Street, Brandon Street and St George's Road (formerly Limekiln Lane) of this 18th-century development. An Act of Parliament obtained in 1770 enabled the Bishop of Bristol to grant a 'Lease or Leases of a Close of Ground, commonly called The Bishop's Park, in the Parish of Saint Augustine otherwise called Saint Augustine the Less, within the City of Bristol, or the Suburbs thereof' (HLL:

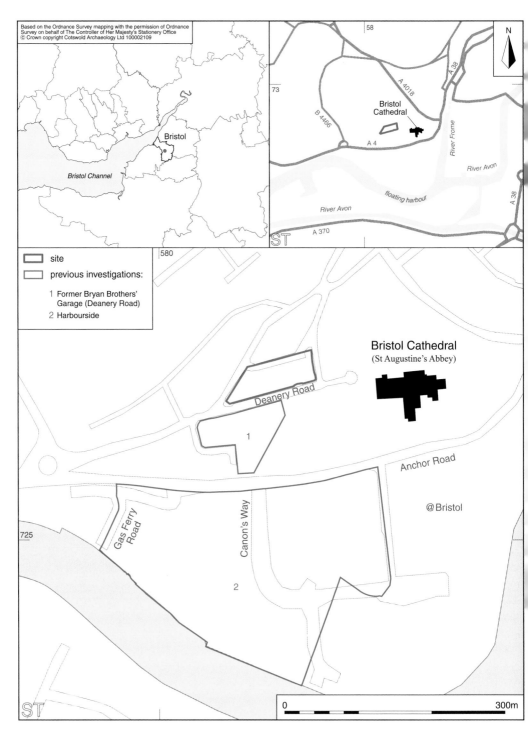

Fig. 1   Site location plan (scale 1:5000)

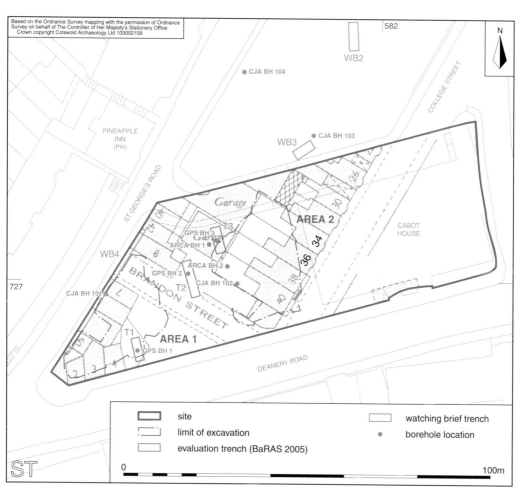

Fig. 2   Excavation areas and evaluation trenches superimposed on OS 1951 (scale 1:1000)

Private Act, 10 George III, c.5). In 1772 the land was leased for 99 years at £63 p.a. to Samuel Worrall, a gentleman property developer living in Clifton and Town Clerk to the Corporation of Bristol from 1787 until 1819 (BRO: 12149; EP/E/5/1). The lease stated that 'Samuel Worrall had formed a plan for covering the said ground with buildings' (BRO: 34631(6)a). Unfortunately this plan does not appear to survive in any of the relevant archives.

Several surviving building leases show that individual plots were leased to building craftsmen, such as Benjamin Tucker, a house carpenter, who in 1788 mortgaged his plot to Mr Joseph Blatchley, a banker, who was probably intending either to live in the house or to speculate on its onward sale (BRO: 34631(6)a). Edward Rosser, a mason, took out a lease on a plot extending from College Street back to Lamb Street. His source of finance for a subsequent mortgage was another mason, William Lamb, who possibly gave his name to this street on the estate (BRO: 05492(1-26)). Thomas Stocking, a tiler, and Thomas Sims, a carpenter, took leases on the plots which became nos 34–36 and 38–40 College Street, within the excavated area (below). The street nos 34, 36, 38 and 40 first appeared in the street directory for 1888; prior to this the houses were numbered consecutively from 55 to 58 in descending order from north-east to south-west, and no. 54 College Street occupied the corner plot with Brandon Street. These earlier street numbers correspond to those on Plumley and Ashmead's map of 1828 (Fig. 7).

The construction of the Deanery Road viaduct in 1869 across the valley between Hotwells and College Green involved the demolition of some 18th-century housing on College Street (including the property next to no. 40 College Street, no. 54 on Plumley and Ashmead's map of 1828) and in adjacent streets. Archaeological evaluation of the site in 2005 identified the remains of structures relating to 18th to 20th-century buildings, as well as deep underlying deposits (BaRAS 2005), the latter confirmed by three boreholes (Fig. 2: GPS BH1–3) which recorded 4.5–6.8m of 'made ground' infilling the natural valley below the site (Wilkinson 2006).

The 20th-century use of the area included garages and car parking, with extensive and progressive demolition of buildings across the site. This also saw the reordering of the street pattern in the area, with alterations to the position of Brandon Street and College Street. The office block of Cabot House, constructed in 1957, occupied the south-east corner of the site, and the rest of the site area was used for car parking (Fig. 2).

Methodology

The surface deposits of tarmac and rubble were stripped to identify the areas of greatest preservation. Two areas measuring 270m² and 288m² (Areas 1 and 2) were selected for further investigation in accordance with written methodologies approved by the Bristol City Council Archaeologist (Fig. 2). The structural remains in both areas were hand-cleaned and recorded following the removal of demolition infill deposits by machine. Two dwellings typical of the 18th-century development were then selected for more detailed examination in Area 2, where limited excavation took place within the former nos 38 and 40 College Street. Two small hand-dug trenches were also excavated, to the rear of no. 40 College Street and beyond its garden wall at the back of the properties fronting St George's Road, and a machine-dug trench was excavated into the upper levels of the valley infill to the rear of no. 36 College Street (Fig. 4).

Following excavation, an archaeological watching brief was undertaken during the removal of the Cabot House foundations, during various piling operations and during the installation of services in the car park area to the north of the new building.

Two boreholes were drilled during the excavation of Area 2 to augment information from those undertaken during the evaluation and from previous geotechnical boreholes (Wilkinson 2006). The initial borehole (ARCA BH1) was unable to penetrate the sequence below the 2m of deposits overlying archaeological horizons. A second borehole (ARCA BH2) successfully penetrated these deposits and cores were recovered from the underlying stratigraphy. Cores were investigated under laboratory conditions; sub-samples were analysed for palynological and diatom analysis and for sedimentological testing. A single radiocarbon date was also obtained to resolve chronological problems raised by the dates obtained from the evaluation stage. Full details of the methodologies employed and a full report of the results are available in the archive.

RESULTS

Based on analysis of the structural and stratigraphic relationships and dating evidence, the results of the evaluation, excavations, boreholes and watching brief have been phased into three broad periods of activity:

Period 1: pre-18th century development (pre- *c.* 1770)
Period 2: late 18th to mid 20th centuries (*c.* 1770–*c.* 1967)
Period 3: mid 20th century and later (*c.* 1930+)

There is an overlap between Periods 2 and 3 in the 20th century, as there was no single event across the site which allowed chronological differentiation within the complex structural remains. The division between the two periods is essentially functional: Period 2 represents the construction and use of the buildings found on the site, with a sub-Period 2a for with the construction of Deanery Road and adjacent properties in 1869, whereas Period 3 represents the disuse, demolition and redevelopment of the site in the 20th century.

Period 1: pre-18th century development (pre- *c.* 1770), by Keith Wilkinson

The deeper stratigraphy of the site was recorded principally by borehole investigation. Basal Triassic deposits of the Redcliffe Sandstone Formation (part of the Mercia Mudstone Group) were recorded at or below 7m AOD across most parts of the site, but with a valley running through the centre of the site recorded at below 4.35m AOD. This palaeovalley was infilled and overlapped on its southern flank by deposits of the Wentlooge formations found in ARCA BH2 between 5.65m and 4.35m AOD (4.1–5.4m below ground surface). Two local pollen assemblage zones were noted from individual analyses of ten palynological sub-samples from these sediments. Analysis of pollen grains from the lower zone indicates the presence of damp woodland growing within fen carr and/or on the margins of flowing water, but also the presence of dry woodland species. Pollen from the upper zone suggests an increase in pollen taxa representative of ground flora and aquatic vegetation, as wetter conditions prevailed. Some species suggest a saline influence. Unfortunately diatom preservation was too poor to determine whether these fine-grained deposits of the Wentlooge formation were deposited in intertidal or freshwater conditions. A radiocarbon date from organic-rich sediments demonstrates that strata of the Wentlooge formation began to be deposited around 2870–2500 cal. BC (Wk 25622, 4100±31 BP), consistent with the Middle/Late Neolithic period. This date range is slightly later than the radiocarbon dates obtained for equivalent deposits from the former Bryan Brothers' Garage (Wilkinson *et al.* 2002; Cox *et al.* 2006) and Harbourside (Wilkinson and Tinsley 2005; Alexander and Harward 2011 [this volume]). Previous radiocarbon dates obtained for these deposits from GPS BH3 during the evaluation stage indicated a late medieval/ early post-medieval origin. The dates obtained from ARCA BH2 demonstrate that the earlier radiocarbon dates were erroneous. Sedimentological analysis suggests no effects of human activity on these deposits, although some species from the upper pollen zone that are indicative of disturbed ground possibly reflect some impact from human activity.

Above these deposits ARCA BH1 and BH2 recorded 'made ground' consisting of silts, sands and ash containing frequent mortar, brick and ceramic structural remains, as well as pottery and bone fragments. Measurements from ARCA BH2 and earlier geoarchaeological and geotechnical investigations show that up to 6m of 'made ground' existed below the current ground levels, representing a significant effort to level a substantial area in which the 18th-century housing development took place.

The earliest deposits encountered during the excavations were revealed within two sondages excavated in the rear yards of nos 36 and 40 College Street in Area 2 (Fig. 4). A series of dumped deposits lay immediately beneath garden soils and represent the upper levels of deliberate infilling of the natural valley prior to the construction of the Period 2 properties. Similar deposits of late 18th-century date were recorded in Trenches 1 and 3 in the evaluation (Fig. 2; BaRAS 2005).

Period 2: late 18th to mid 20th centuries (*c. 1770–c. 1967*)

Period 2, Area 1 (Fig. 3)
Within Area 1, remains of upstanding walls, drains and surfaces of properties at nos 46, 48 and 50 St George's Road, and nos 3, 5 and 7 Brandon Street were recorded, as well as the edge of the original alignment of Brandon Street. Some later alterations to the properties were noted. Those that can be related to the construction of the Deanery Road viaduct are discussed in Period 2a below.

The surface of Brandon Street was revealed aligned northwest/southeast along the northern edge of Area 1, as well as part of the pavement, kerb and cobbled guttering. Bounded by Brandon Street to the north and St George's Road to the west, no. 7 Brandon Street consisted of two rectangular stone-built cellar rooms with a dividing brick wall between. Accessed via doorway 476 from room 483 of this property was a narrow L-shaped alleyway running behind room 482 (no. 46 St George's Road) which could also be entered from no. 48 St George's Road to the south and may have led to a communal area 459 behind nos 3 and 5 Brandon Street.

No. 46 St George's Road consisted of a single cellar room in plan (482), with a wall separating it from the alleyway behind to which there was no access at this level. No. 48 St George's Road consisted of two cellar rooms with a dividing wall (467) between. The northern room (446) had a mortar, brick and stone floor. Doorway 505 led into the alleyway behind no. 46 St George's Road, and two further doorways (503 and 504) were located in the rear property wall. All three doorways had later been blocked. The blocking of doorway 504 occurred before wall 462 was constructed in Period 2a (see below). The southern room (481) had a small stone-built structure (465) in its southeast corner and a stone-built drain in the northeast corner. No. 50 St George's Road consisted of a single room (418). Remnants of two small internal walls on its north side were probably the side walls of a fireplace.

Part of room 417 was identified immediately to the south of no. 50 St George's Road. This is depicted as the location of the Ship Public House, at the intersection of St George's Road and Deanery Road, on the 1951 OS 1:2500 map, and room 417 was probably part of that building. As in room 418, two small sections of wall were interpreted as the side walls of a fireplace.

At the north end of the area, the cellar (491) of no. 5 Brandon Street was accessed by a doorway and steps from the street, which was subsequently blocked (475). The room had a flagstone floor and a spiral stone stair in the southeastern corner leading to the ground floor of the property. Alongside this, in the southeastern wall (437) were two corbels (486 and 487), which may be interpreted as the supports for a chimney breast on the floor above.

To the rear of room 491 was a single room (493), with a central drain (455) and fire-

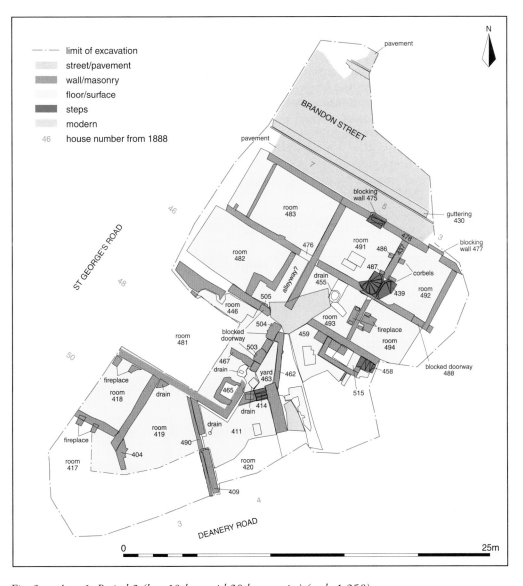

Fig. 3   Area 1, Period 2 (late 18th to mid 20th centuries) (scale 1:250)

place. Although the demolition backfill within these rooms was not removed during the archaeological works it would appear that there was no doorway between the two rooms. Room 493 was tentatively interpreted on site as having a higher floor level than room 491 and so could potentially be accessed from the room above 491. This would suggest rooms 491 and 493 were part of the same residential property, if we assume the rooms above them were connected.

With a similar plan to rooms 491 and 493, rooms 492 and 494 represent the cellar and adjacent room of no. 3 Brandon Street. They shared party walls and a dividing wall, and had similarly positioned spiral stairs and corbels. The door leading onto Brandon Street from room 492 was also blocked (477). The hearth in room 494 was slightly larger than that in 493. In contrast to the adjoining property, a doorway (488, later blocked) linked the two rooms and confirmed they originally formed part of the same property.

To the rear of rooms 493 and 494 was a small probable washroom, 515, with steps 458 leading down to an adjacent property. This washroom projected into a polygonal area of flagstone flooring 459, which probably represents a yard. Before wall 462 was built (see below) this area may also have been accessed from no. 48 St George's Road.

Period 2a, Area 1 (Fig. 3)
Walls and surfaces revealed on the south side of Area 1 can be related to the alteration of the back end of existing properties fronting St George's Road and the construction of properties on Deanery Road in 1869. Parts of nos 3 and 4 Deanery Road were identified.

No. 3 Deanery Road consisted of a single-room cellar, 419, formed by walls 404 and 409 which abutted the rear of nos 48 and 50 St George's Road. Within the eastern wall (409), a doorway opened into the adjacent structure, 420; this had been subsequently blocked in by an additional wall (490), built over the flagstone floor surface of the cellar. A stone-built drain was identified in the north corner of the room.

No. 4 Deanery Road consisted of an irregularly-shaped cellar, (room 420) with walls abutting no. 48 St George's Road to the north. As with no. 3 Deanery Road, this indicated a reconstruction and realignment of properties subsequent to the construction of Deanery Road. A ceramic drain cut through the surviving flagstone cellar floor. The addition of wall 462 at the back of no. 4 Deanery Road built against the blocked the rear door (504) of no. 48 St George's Road created a small triangular yard area 463 with a new flagstone floor. This wall cut off any access there may have been from no. 48 St George's to the yard space behind nos 3 and 5 Brandon Street. Access to yard 463 from the room 446 may have been through doorway 503, although this too was subsequently blocked. A doorway from room 481 of no. 48 St George's Road appears to have been a later alteration and may have been added at this time. A flight of brick steps (414) led up from the rear of no. 4 Deanery Road into the small yard. It would appear that no. 4 Deanery Road shared this yard with the household at no. 48 St George's Road.

Period 2, Area 2 (Fig. 4)
Demolition deposits were fully removed within nos 38 and 40 College Street in Area 2 to reveal upstanding walls and surfaces and the complete plan of these properties. To the south a small area of Brandon Street was recorded, and to the north of nos 38 and 40 the incomplete plans of nos 34 and 36 College Street were also identified.

A section of the northern pavement and kerb of Brandon Street was revealed similar to the southern pavement revealed in Area 1. A small area of concrete surface 550 between this and no. 40 College Street is thought to represent the remnants of a later garage or similar non-domestic structure. Historic plans and documents show that this area was originally occupied by a house identical in plan to no. 40 College Street, which was demolished in 1865 for the construction of Deanery Road (Fig. 8).

No. 40 College Street
The complete cellar plan of no. 40 College Street was revealed, with two main basement rooms, each extending to the full width of the property, with a narrower single room

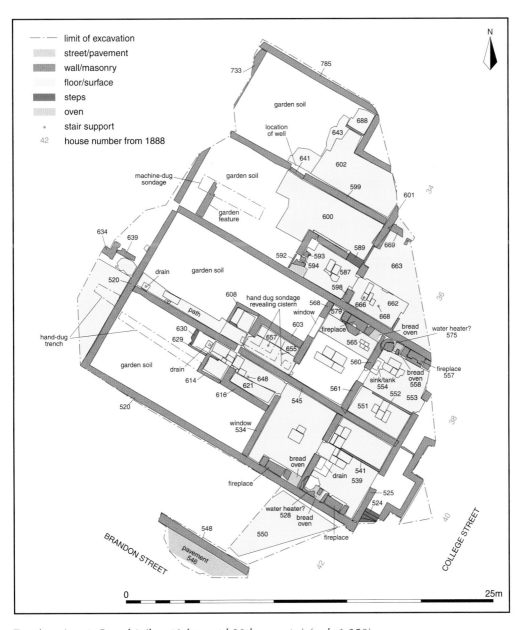

Fig. 4   Area 2, Period 2 (late 18th to mid 20th centuries) (scale 1:250)

extending into the back yard. As with all the recorded properties, the initial wall build consisted of rough red sandstone blocks, rendered with plaster internally and unrendered on all external surfaces. These walls formed the original structure. The southern boundary wall was a continuous extension of southern house wall 520 and therefore contemporary, as was its return at the end of the garden, which formed the rear boundary wall to this and the adjacent property.

The cellar was entered from College Street via stone steps 524, down into a narrow alleyway in front of the buildings, with a small alcove across the alley opposite the front door. The alcove would be accessible from the street for the delivery of coal.

The internal floor surfaces in all rooms predominantly consisted of thin flagstones, probably original. A small area beneath the stairs had a concrete surface, 621, contemporary with the adjacent flagstones leading to the back door. Near the edge of the concrete surface the flagstones had a shallow square cut, 648, consistent with the use of wooden support posts for the stairs which led up to the next floor. Fragments of the wooden staircase structure were still adhering to the exterior wall. In the front room, built against the south wall, was a large central fireplace with some surviving ironwork of the range, supplemented by a bread oven, and a brick-built curving recess, 528, that may have held a water-heating copper. This was subsequently plaster-lined and showed coal staining, suggesting the space was reutilised for fuel storage. The middle room contained a smaller central fireplace with a bread oven, also built against the south wall. Two windows were identified, still containing remnants of wooden window frames. One looked out the front of the property into the small alleyway, the other (534) from the middle room into the garden at the rear. Garden soil banked up against the rear window sill was heavily stained with coal dust.

Some secondary features were apparent. In the front room the flagstone floor to the north of the small internal brick dividing wall (541) was covered with linoleum. A later brick extension, 614, had been added to the rear of the property and contained a toilet. Beyond this a short length of wall and a stone kerb divided off a small part of the back yard where a drain was located. This area probably served as a washroom. A hand-dug trench excavated across the rear yard revealed garden soils extending to the rear boundary wall. Modern domestic pottery and coal was recorded within the garden soil.

No. 38 College Street

No. 38 College Street shared a party wall with and was a mirror image of no. 40, including later alterations and additions, and was contemporary in construction. However there were a few minor changes and additions that differentiated the two properties.

Beneath the narrow rear room of no. 38 a brick-vaulted water cistern was revealed within a hand-dug sondage. This was a primary feature of the house and had been included within the foundations. The walls of the cistern were constructed of red sandstone blocks of a similar type to the main structural walls above; the interior was concrete-rendered and still held a large volume of water. A cast iron drainpipe brought in rain water from the roof into the cistern and this was subsequently pumped towards the front of the house through a large-diameter lead pipe, perhaps to the brick tank or sink 554 found in the front room. The vaulted roof of the cistern was covered by a series of levelling deposits and finally flagstone flooring. An entry hatch into the cistern appears to have been concreted over at a later point and re-covered by the original flagstone floor. No. 40 College Street may have had a similar cistern but this was not investigated.

The fireplaces and associated features in the front and middle rooms followed the same arrangement as in no. 40 College Street but were better preserved and showed minor differences. Built against the party wall with no. 36 College Street, the main fireplace (557) in the front room was narrower, and the bread oven (558) and curved recess (575) assumed to be for a water heater were of slightly different design (Fig. 5). A sample of brick from oven 558, dating to the 19th or 20th century, is from later alteration. The bread oven in the

Fig. 5   Front room of no. 38 College Street: recess for water heater 575, bread oven 558 and fireplace 557. Area 2, Period 2, looking northeast (scales 1m and 2m)

middle room had been blocked in with brick and a later quarry tile floor, 565, was laid in front with a small area of the original flagstone floor (579) remaining between the fireplace and wall 568. Brick extension 608, containing the toilet at the rear of the property, was of slightly different design to that in no. 40, although the bricks did appear to be of the same type suggesting broadly contemporary construction. Remnants of a wooden staircase were revealed on the interior face of wall 603 leading to the ground floor with two rectangular notches, 655 and 657, for stair supports cut into the flagstone floor. A flagstone garden path with integral drain led to the rear property wall. Kerbing along the edge of the path retained the garden soil.

To the west of the rear garden wall of no. 38 College Street, short lengths of stone and brick walling were identified (walls 634 and 639). These did not relate to any structures on the 19th-century mapping and may date to the later use of this area of the site as a garage (as depicted on OS 1951).

No. 36 College Street
The front room and most of the middle room of No. 36 College Street had been truncated during the construction of Cabot House. Only the western part of the middle room, the narrower rear room and back garden illustrated on the 1951 OS map were visible.

The property shared a dividing wall on its south side with No. 38 College Street and is considered broadly contemporary. The remaining walls were built against this, also in red sandstone blocks. The internal floor surfaces predominantly consisted of thin flagstones, contemporary with the initial build. This property differed from nos 38 and 40 in some internal details, the most notable of which was the absence of a fireplace in the middle room (although the north wall of this room was largely absent). In an area next to the south wall in this room, two rectangular notches (666 and 668) cut into flagstone floor 662 may indicate an internal staircase, as they were similar to those found with other evidence for stairs in the back extensions of nos 38 and 40.

Later alterations included the brick blocking (592) of a door into the rear garden area from the narrow back room, and a fireplace and bread oven 594 built against the blocking. A brick sample of 19th or 20th-century date from this bread oven suggests a date for these alterations. A further doorway with steps 589 led out through the north wall of the rear room onto a flagstone courtyard surface (600) with integral drains (not shown). However it was not possible to ascertain whether this doorway was contemporary with the initial construction, or a later addition compensating for the blocked doorway, although the latter seems more likely. A brick extension containing a toilet had at one time been added to the rear of the property, covering the blocked doorway, but few remnants of the structure remained. Access to the toilet would have been via the paved back yard. Rough brick walling within the back garden suggested a degree of terracing or a garden feature.

Underlying the dividing garden wall between nos 34 and 36 College Street and covered by flagstones, a brick-lined well was noted but not excavated. This potentially supplied water to both properties but was subsequently capped and wall 641 built over it.

No. 34 College Street
This was a mirror image of no. 36 and of one build, sharing party wall 669. Only the narrower rear room and back garden of no. 34 College Street was visible, the rest of the property had been removed during the construction of Cabot House. A brick extension with a toilet (688) had been added to the rear of the property; access would have been via the paved back yard. The initial flagstone yard surface (643) had a later concrete surface (602) added; the rear end of the property was a garden.

Period 2, watching brief areas 2, 3 and 4
Remnants of the street frontage walls pertaining to nos 42, 44, 46 and 48 St George's Road were recorded during a watching brief for piling works along the north-east limit of the site (Fig. 2: WB 4). In the interest of safety the trenches could not be accessed to allow detailed recording and the walls were not planned.

Period 3: mid 20th century and later (*c.* 1930+)

The demolition of properties fronting Brandon Street, including nos 3 and 5, can be related to slum clearance in the 1930s (*The Documentary Evidence*, below). Demolition waste was dumped within the cellars and basements of the properties in Areas 1 and 2 in order to level the area. Properties fronting College Street were purchased in 1957 for the construction of Cabot House; the remaining buildings on Deanery Road and St George's Road were also demolished in the late 1950s (*The Documentary Evidence*, below). The most recent use of the site as car parking adjacent to Cabot House was shown by rubble and hardcore levelling deposits and tarmac surfaces sealing all the earlier deposits.

A number of brick-built walls were revealed during a watching brief on geotechnical pits (Fig. 2, WB 2 and 3). Along with quantities of building rubble backfill, these deposits and features were of 20th-century date and probably relate to the use of the site for garages. Modern pottery was recorded within the rubble deposits but not retained.

FINDS SUMMARY
by E.R. McSloy

A small assemblage of 63 sherds of pottery and porcelain (2726g) was derived from cellar backfills in Area 1. This material was scanned by context, quantified by sherd count and weight, and the medieval and post-medieval pottery fabrics matched against the Bristol Pottery type (BPT) series (Ponsford 1988; 1998). The bulk of material dates to the earlier 20th century and probably relates to the last use or demolition of the buildings.

A single sherd (44g) of residual medieval pottery was recovered from cellar backfill 454. This is a wide strap handle fragment from a jug in Bristol glazed ware type BPT 118, dating to between the later 13th and 15th centuries. Post-medieval pottery was also recovered from cellar backfill 454. The fabrics represented, North Devon gravel-tempered ware (BPT 112), Bristol or Staffordshire yellow slipware (BPT 100) and tin-glazed earthenware (BPT 99), are commonly seen from among Bristol groups between the later 17th and later 18th centuries. Identifiable forms comprise a press-moulded plate in type BPT 100 and a bowl in type BPT 112. The majority of the ceramic assemblage is modern, consisting of flatwares and cups in refined whitewares, and stoneware bottles.

Ten complete glass bottles and a glass marble were recovered from cellar deposits. All bottles are fully mould-made in clear or green-coloured glass and all are modern, considered to date to the 1930s or later.

Eleven metal items were recovered. Most were not identifiable but derive from modern deposits and probably date accordingly. Identified items include a copper-alloy coin (a halfpenny) of post-medieval or modern type, and thimbles of pressed sheet metal (brass) from deposits 443 and 616, dated to after the mid 17th century and probably to the 18th or 19th centuries.

Complete bricks taken as samples from within individual properties or associated with structural alterations were quantified and measured. With the exception of frogged bricks associated with no. 38 College Street (from oven 558) and no. 36 College Street (from oven 594), which probably date to the later 19th or early 20th centuries, the size and other characteristics of the bricks suggest broadly consistent dating, within the 18th or early/middle 19th-century range.

THE DOCUMENTARY EVIDENCE
by Roger Leech

Development of Area 1

No. 7 Brandon Street and nos 46–52 St George's Road
This plot (no. 19) was leased by Samuel Worrall on 30 May 1772 to John Crouch of Hanham, quarryman, for 96 years commencing 24 June 1772 at a rent of £11 8s 6d p.a. It was 100ft wide against Limekiln Lane, bounded on the north-east by Brandon Street and on the south-west by part of the Bishop's Park not yet granted for building (BRO: EP/E/4/3 fol.21); the location is identified from the measurements and abuttal to Brandon Street; building leases from Samuel Worrall to Roach, Marriott, Hobbs and Willis (BRO: 05503) are now mislaid but listed in the schedule (BRO: 06495(1)). By 1839 the properties on plot no. 19 (occupants in parentheses) were in Limekiln Lane: a public house (R. Kethro), a

house and another public house (A. Miller) and a smith's forge (Wm Haydon). In Brandon Street: two houses with shops (John Isles and Thomas Searle) and a public house (James Fedden) (BRO: EP/E/4/3 fols.230). The excavations provided evidence for a row of three houses of identical depth fronting Limekiln Lane (later renamed St George's Road), one of which was at the corner with Brandon Street, and also for two houses of identical plan in Brandon Street, each two rooms in depth and set at right angles to the street. These were probably the two shops of John Isles and Thomas Searle.

Nos 3–5 Deanery Road

These were plots of land sold freehold for building by William Tanner in 1874, following the construction of Deanery Road (Fig. 6). Both plots, nos 13 and 14, were sold to George Cooke, a carpenter and builder of Canon's Marsh close by; the allocation of plot numbers may indicate that Tanner had sold these at auction (BRO: 20940-1).

The house built as no. 3, together with a cottage at the rear, all then in the occupation of Joseph Pelling and William Matthews, was then sold in 1880 by Cooke to a Mary Phillips of Brixton, Surrey, most probably for letting. In 1903 no. 3 and the cottage at the rear were then sold to Adelaide Ellen Kynaston, wife of John Kynaston, a furniture maker living at no. 3 (BRO: 20940).

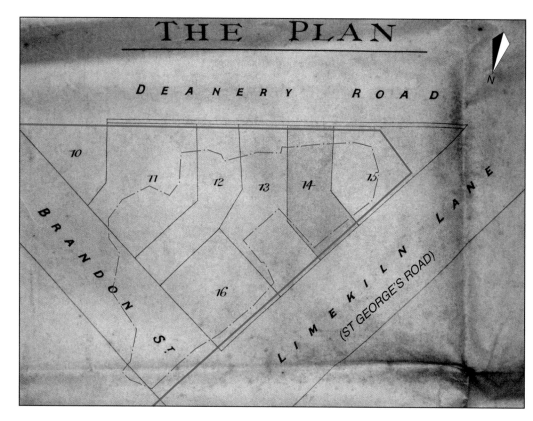

Fig. 6   *Extract from a plan of 1874 showing Deanery Road sale plots with the site and Area 1 outlines superimposed (BRO: 20940–1)*

The first occupants of no. 4 are not identified, but from 1897 and in 1904 it formed part of the slaughterhouse and stables of William Jocham in St George's Road (BRO: 20941).

Development of Area 2

Nos 38–42 College Street (originally nos 54–56)

Nos 55 and 56 College Street were renumbered nos 38 and 40 in 1888. No. 54 was demolished in 1865. Nos 38–42 were built as one row of three houses by Thomas Stocking, a tiler, whose lease from Samuel Worrall was dated 24 December 1784, for 84 years at an annual rent of £14 5s (BRO: 05502). Stocking's lease was of a plot 'containing in front next College Street aforesaid sixty-two feet or thereabouts, be the same more or less, and extending from thence backward to a certain street commonly called Limekiln Lane [i.e. St George's Road] bounded on the north-eastward side by other part of the same close of ground [i.e. the Bishop's Park] lately granted by two several indentures of lease to Thomas Sims, carpenter, and on the south-westward side by other part of the said close of ground laid open as a Street and called Brandon Street, together with the walls bounding the said

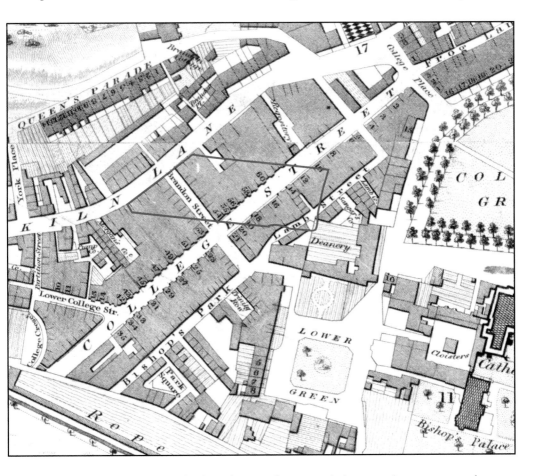

Fig. 7   Extract from Plumley and Ashmead's map of 1828, with the site outline superimposed

ground towards College Street, Brandon Street and Limekiln Lane'. The width of 62ft corresponds exactly to the width of the three plots nos 38–42 College Street, as numbered by 1888. The total width of College Street was to be 40ft, there being reserved for Stocking 3ft in which to place an area and/or bow windows, and 5ft within which Stocking was to provide a footway.

The lease to Stocking made stipulations concerning the houses to be built, that he should enclose the ground within six months and complete within three years 'one or more substantial messuage or tenement with proper offices' and expend £600 in the building of these, and 'that the front of each messuage or tenement...towards the said street shall be built in conformity to the plan hereinbefore mentioned for laying out the said ground and shall have no bow window or other projection above the ground floor thereof neither shall any bow window which may be made on the first [perhaps a mistake for 'ground'] floor nor any area [i.e. the railed in area in front of the house] extend further forward than three feet from the front of the said ground and that the said buildings towards College Street shall not be dessightly [i.e. disagreeable or unsightly] toward the said street but as much as can be consistent with such buildings ornamental to the said street and at least uniform'. Other conditions were that businesses dependent upon fire must be sited in 'some back building under a different and distinct roof which shall have no timber therein communicating direct with such front building'.

Thomas Stocking retained the ownership of at least no. 54 until 1820 when it was sold to a Mr Greenwood. Accompanying the deed of sale was a plan of the property showing the location of the dwelling house, the privy, the rear court and a passage to a pump, which lay behind no. 55 (later no. 40) (BRO: 05502) (Fig. 8). By 1853 the plot no. 20 as allocated in 1770, was subdivided as five plots (20ae), and was leased by the freehold owners William Tanner and Thomas Urch to Thomas Carlile, grocer (no. 54), to John Stratford esq. of Ross

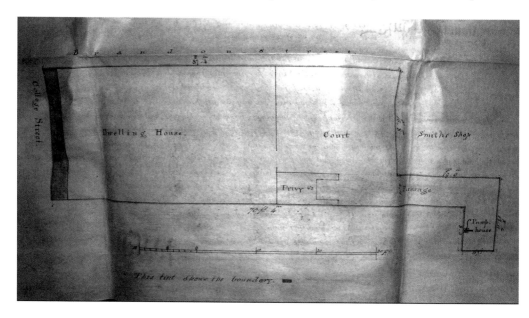

Fig. 8   Plan of no. 54 College Street, c. 1820 (BRO: 05502)

in Herefordshire (no. 55, later no. 40) and Henry Clarke of Bristol, baker (no. 56, later no. 38) (BRO: EP/E/3/1). It was Mr Carlile (the owner by 1837) who sold no. 54 to the Bristol Local Board of Health for the construction of Deanery Road in 1867 (BRO: 05502).

As renumbered in 1888, nos 38 and 40 remained part of the Tanner estate until sold at auction in 1950, and were then purchased in 1957 by the City of Bristol for the construction of Cabot House (BRO: 12054[18]; 11284).

Details of the College Street properties

The sources available for the study of the houses built in the Bishop's Park are the account by Ison (1952) and photographs, principally by Reece Winstone and Aerofilms. There is an absence of detailed plans, none being included in the plans deposited with the Urban Sanitary Authority.

Ison's account (1952, 210–11) reads as follows:

'College Street: An advertisement addressed to builders, published in Felix Farley on 29th September 1770, stated that the ground was 'to be laid out for building. The principal street to be 40 feet wide, of which the road level will be 6 feet higher than the level of the houses now in the occupation of Mr Vaughan and Mr Patty. A frontage also to Limekiln Lane, and proper sewers. Builders will be permitted to make cellars under the streets as in the new buildings in Bath'. On 17th November 1770 Sarah Farley was able to report that 'this week was finished the main Sewer in the Ground called Bishop's Park, lately laid out for Building'. The streets were planned, and the general lines of the design for the house-fronts were laid down by Thomas Paty and Sons, who were to be closely associated with Worrall's building promotions......

Apart from a few which are double-fronted, the houses are generally of moderate size. The original layout of their accommodation is described in a contemporary sale advertisement 'The Premises consist of Two Parlours, a China Pantry, Kitchen and arched Cellar, with a spacious Outlet or Garden Plot behind the whole; a Dining-Room, Bedchamber, and light Closet on the first Floor, and two Bedchambers in the Attic Story.' The fronts, which are three stories high and generally have two windows to each upper story, are built of red brick sparingly dressed with freestone. This is used for the pilasters that define the party-walls, generally plain but sometimes of channel-jointed stones; for the flat or segmental arches of stepped and projecting voussoirs to the upper story windows; and for the rather insignificant crowning cornice that forms a coping to the walls. Bay-windows of wooden construction, occasionally segmental but usually angular on plan, project boldly from the ground-story, and the doorways generally have surrounding architraves surmounted by triangular pediments resting on consoles.'

Nos 32–40 College Street are shown on photographs published by Reece Winstone (1969, plates 37–40), most clearly on plate 40 (Fig. 9), taken in January 1954. Nos 32–36 and 38–40 appear as two separate rows, with parapets and second-floor windows of equal and distinct height, all with entrance doorways to one side of the front rooms, all of which had bay windows. The doorway positions for nos 38 and 40 correlate with the plans obtained from excavation, indicating that at cellar level the spaces below the ground floor entrance halls were separate rooms.

The same houses are shown on two photographs (NMR: Aerofilms P5447 and 52883),

Fig. 9   College Street in 1954, with pre- and post-1888 house numbers added above relevant properties, looking west (Winstone 1969) © Reece Winstone Archive

of 1921 and 1957 (Fig. 10). These show the roofs and overall structure, especially the projecting wings behind nos 38 and 40 lit by windows on the same levels as the principal floors. These could have been constructed originally for privies serving the rooms on the same floors, rather than projecting stair turrets which often had staggered windows to light the stairs as they ascended between floors.

Later history of nos 34-42 College Street

The occupancy of these houses can be traced through the use of the 1837 survey, the 1851 street directory and the census returns of 1851, 1871 and 1881. The houses could not be identified in the return for 1841 and the return for 1861 for College Street appears to have been misplaced. The occupants of nos 36, 38 and 40 College Street have also been traced through the 1911 census return.

No. 54 (would have been renumbered no. 42 if not demolished)

By 1837 the occupier was F. Virtue. By 1851 it was occupied by four separate households, a total of 20 persons, the largest family being that of the police constable Joseph Way, other families headed by a clockmaker, brightsmith (two related trades) and a lawyer. Way's household included an 80-year old visitor from Devon, perhaps his mother-in-law. By 1871 and in 1881 the house was evidently empty or demolished, pending the construction of the new Deanery Road.

Fig. 10   Aerial view of the rear of nos 34–40 College Street, 1957 (NMR: Aerofilms 52883) © English Heritage NMR Aerofilms Collection

No. 40 (previously no. 55)
By 1837 the occupier was W. Batchelor, the occupier in 1837 and in 1839 as listed in the schedule attached to the renewal of the lease (see above). By 1851 it was occupied by the household of John Wills (Willis in the street directory of the same year), the owner in 1837. Wills was a colonial broker, and in contrast to his neighbours was able to afford to use the entire house for his family, his wife, two adult daughters and their servant. By 1871 Wills's family had left and, like its neighbours, the house had been given over to multiple occupation now occupied by four separate households, a total of nine persons, the largest family that of James Norman, a coach trimmer. By 1881 the total had increased to 11 persons, with only the two lodgers from 1871 now remaining. By 1911 the three households at no. 40 totalled 17 persons. The households were headed by a greengrocer dealer, a coal dealer and Harriet Ranahan, 'wife', for whom no occupation is listed and who occupied the premises with four daughters and her mother.

No. 38 (previously no. 56)
By 1837 the occupier was Mr Henry Clark, also the owner. By 1851 it was occupied by five separate households, a total of 20 persons, the largest families being those headed by Richard Williams, a seaman, and Joseph Nock, a cooper. By 1871 there had been a total change of occupants, now 16 persons in all, the largest households being those of John Webb, possibly the proprietor of the lodging house, and of Henry Arnold, a carpenter. By 1881 the number of households had reduced to four, only Arnold's family remaining and now augmented by a further five children. The three other households were headed by a boatman, tailor and sailor. In 1911 a total of 18 persons, derived from four households,

occupied the premises. The largest household was headed by William Snooks, a labourer at the Gas Works who lived with his wife, two adult daughters employed in a paper bag manufactory, and seven further children.

No. 36 (previously no. 57)

By 1837 the occupier was Mr Cornish, also the owner. By 1851 it was occupied by six separate households, a total of 15 persons, the largest families being those headed by Thomas Shuborne, a coach trimmer, and Anne White, a seaman's wife looking after two children and a visitor, Joseph Cottle, from Yorkshire. The smallest household was that of Auguste Millien, a teacher of French and born in France. By 1871 there had been a total change of occupants, now four households and 12 persons in total, the largest household being that of George Duckham, an unemployed ship's carpenter, the other heads of households being an engineer, coachman and stableman. By 1881 the number of households had reduced to three, only Duckham's family now remaining, and he now a shipwright. The two other households were headed by a gardener and mason. The 1911 census lists four households, totalling 13 persons; the largest household headed by Edward Mortell, a blacksmith employed by the Gas Works and including a female boarder, Kate Mortell, single, aged 28, possibly a sister or niece to Edward, and employed in a printing works.

No. 34 (previously no. 58)

By 1837 the occupier was Henry Lawson, the owner Mr Cornish (see above). By 1851 it was occupied by five separate households, a total of 12 persons, the largest family being that of the tide waiter Edward Connelly, originally from the London Thames, other working adults including a piano tuner, two dressmakers and a laundress.

DISCUSSION
by Mary Alexander and Keith Wilkinson

Period 1

The radiocarbon result of 2870–2500 cal. BC (Wk 25622, 4100±31 BP) from the borehole sequence from Cabot House suggests sedimentation linked to rising sea levels commenced in the Middle/Late Neolithic period. Analysis of the pollen stratigraphy suggests a wetland environment dominated by freshwater alder carr and/or riparian (waterside) woodland, that later underwent a transition towards more open herb-rich and salt marsh communities in response to wetter conditions. These results are broadly consistent with the sequence of radiocarbon-dated strata in central Bristol at Cabot Circus (Wilkinson and Head 2008; Ridgeway and Watts [eds] [forthcoming]), the former Bryan Brothers' Garage (Wilkinson *et al.* 2002, Cox *et al.* 2006) and Harbourside (Wilkinson and Tinsley 2005; Alexander and Harward 2011 [this volume]).

The results of the radiocarbon dating at the former Bryan Brothers' Garage suggested that peat formation ceased around 3550–3050 cal. BC, a period between c. 200 and 1000 years prior to the commencement of sedimentation at Cabot House. Similarly, organic sedimentation is estimated to have ceased around 3750 cal. BC at Harbourside. The difference is probably because of the higher elevation of the Cabot House site, and together the three sites indicate a progressive rise in relative sea levels (RSL) with a dated sequence of environmental change.

The earlier sequences (c. 4200–3000 cal. BC) at the former Bryan Brothers' Garage and

Cabot Circus contain palynological and sedimentological evidence that indicates Early Neolithic human manipulation of woodland on the hills surrounding those parts of the Avon and Frome valleys now occupied by central Bristol. Human activity is indirectly indicated by elm declines at Cabot Circus and Harbourside, and directly by the decline of lime species at both the former Bryan Brothers' Garage and Harbourside, by the presence of weed taxa following a reduction in arboreal pollen at all three sites, and by magnetic susceptibility evidence for burning within the catchment at Cabot Circus and the former Bryan Brothers' Garage. However, there is only equivocal evidence for human use of the 'upland' areas from the Middle/Late Neolithic deposits at Cabot House. Indeed the palynological data from Cabot House suggest that broad-leaved lime was an even more important component of the dry woodland than before, while there is limited evidence for the ingress of weed taxa and none at all for burning. In other words, the main archaeological contribution of the new geoarchaeological and palaeoenvironmental data from Cabot House is to indicate the apparently limited nature of human activity in the catchment during the middle and later third millennium BC.

Evidence for Roman or medieval activity was not found at Cabot House; the single sherd of medieval pottery from a cellar backfill was clearly residual and could have derived from a number of sources. Up to 6m of 'made ground' was recorded in borehole samples, and the upper 2m of these deposits in trench excavation at the back of no. 36 College Street. Cartographic evidence (e.g. Millerd 1673; Rocque 1743) depicts the area as open ground within a dry valley, which largely remained as parkland until the sale of the Bishop's Park in 1770 for redevelopment. The excavated sequence at Cabot House suggests that the 'made ground', derived predominantly from building rubble, ash and soils, was deposited in the late 18th century to fill in and level the natural topography in advance of construction. A similar sequence was recorded at the former Bryan Brothers' Garage where part of a dovecote of a 14th-century style was excavated, overlain by dumped deposits dating to the 18th century, containing 12th to 14th-century residual pottery (Cox *et al.* 2006).

Period 2

The properties recorded in plan at St George's Road and Deanery Road were not subject to detailed excavation. Although the foundations were truncated by later activity and much of the cellar infills were not removed from the buildings, it was possible to see how the construction of Deanery Road in 1869 had affected the original plan of the buildings fronting St George's Road. Most notable was the use of the triangular yard space behind no. 48 St George's Road and no. 4 Deanery Road, which appeared to be accessed from both properties. These two properties were sold as a single plot (no. 14) on a sale document of *c.* 1874 (Fig. 6) and this arrangement may be connected with the identification of no. 4 Deanery Road as part of the slaughterhouse and stables of William Jocham in St George's Road (BRO: 20941), documented in 1897 and 1904.

Excavation of the earliest foundations at nos 38 and 40 College Street in Area 2 has shown that these structures were a single contemporary build, and thus consistent with the building stipulations within the lease of 1784. Sale plans of the property to the south-west (no. 54, demolished before 1869) show that this property occupied one third of the leased land and was identical to that excavated at no. 40. Excavation revealed internal details of the properties at cellar level; a sale advertisement for a College Street property would suggest that the cellar was occupied by a china pantry, kitchen and arched cellar, and this would conform to the layout at nos 38 and 40. Excavation also showed that the front and back rooms both accommodated a fireplace and bread oven, with provision for a water-heating copper in the front room. These features appear to be part of the original build, but were not fully dismantled during excavation. Bread ovens in both the front and back rooms would be unusual under single occupancy, but would be an asset when tenanted by multiple households as the 19th and 20th-century records record, although this feature was subsequently blocked off with brick in no. 38 College Street. In no. 40 the space for the water heater was reused to store coal. There was also evidence for the ingress of coal through a window at the back of the property, and both may point to the independent storage of fuel relating to the multiple occupancies of the building, which the census returns suggest began to the second half of the 19th century. The excavated sequence shows the addition of a privy at the back of each property, just visible in photographic evidence from the 1950s (Fig. 10). The excavated evidence could not date these additions and alterations, but it is interesting to note that the plan dated to 1820 of the demolished property (no. 54, in the old numbering system) shows the privy marked in the area where there is excavated evidence for a staircase in both nos 38 and 40 (Fig. 8). If it is assumed that nos 38 and 40 followed a similar layout, the stairs in this room in nos 38 and 40 must be a later alteration, post-dating 1820, and probably coincidental with the construction of a privy on the back of the original property.

The truncated remains of properties at nos 34 and 36 College Street suggest a similar pair of houses; no. 36 was built against no. 38, with which it shared a party wall. In no. 36 the slightly wider back room was later converted to accommodate a fireplace, and outside privies added to both properties required the blocking of the back door in these rooms. Photographic evidence (Fig. 10) shows that these back rooms were not overbuilt to a second storey and there is no evidence that they accommodated a staircase; in no. 36 this would appear to have been housed instead in the middle room, the equivalent area in no. 34 was truncated by the construction of Cabot House.

The Bishop's Park Development of the late 18th century was one of a number of speculative developments that formed part of a continuum of suburban expansion that began in the mid 17th century (Leech 2006, 67). The elegant bay-fronted four-storey buildings of College Street were originally constructed to house a single family and their servants, but mid 19th-century street directories and 19th and 20th-century census returns chart the rise of multiple occupancies, supported by the physical evidence for later additions and alterations at the back of these properties recorded in the archaeological investigations. The occupations listed in the 19th and 20th-century census returns reflect the low economic status of these households. Demolition of properties in advance of the construction of Deanery Road in 1869 may have added pressure to the existing housing stock, whilst slum clearance in the early part of the 20th century in the St Augustine's suburb, including streets surrounding College Street (BRO: 11172/3; 12054[23a]), is further evidence of the economic decline of the area, and may have escalated the overcrowding in the College Street properties.

ACKNOWLEDGEMENTS

Cotswold Archaeology is grateful to Westmark Developments for funding this project and to Wring Group Ltd for their close cooperation on site. Thanks are due to Bob Jones of Bristol City Council who monitored the site and commented on the post-excavation report.

Fieldwork was directed by Chris Pickard and Ray Holt, and surveying was undertaken by Andy Loader. The fieldwork was managed by Simon Cox and Mark Collard and the post-excavation work by Mary Alexander. Robin Latour and Pete Moore prepared the illustrations. The authors are grateful to Martin Watts for comments on an earlier draft of this article. CA thanks the Reece Winston Archive and the National Monuments Record for permission to reproduce their photographic images.

ARCA would like to thank Mary Alexander, Mark Collard and Jon Webster (Cotswold Archaeology) and Fiona Petchey (Waikato Radiocarbon Laboratory) for their help during the course of the geoarchaeological analysis. Claire Lorrain, Phil Marter, Myra Wilkinson and Keith Wilkinson drilled the boreholes at Cabot House in August 2008. Myra Wilkinson undertook the laboratory sedimentological analysis and Rob Batchelor and Dan Young carried out the palynological analytical work outlined in this report. The finds and archive will be deposited with Bristol City Museum and Art Gallery under accession number BRSMG 2008/33.

BIBLIOGRAPHY

Primary Sources

BRO (Bristol Record Office):

05492(1-26), Provisional Orders, mortgage agreement between Edward Rosser and William Lamb

05502, Provisional Orders, deeds for no. 54 College Street

06495(1), Provisional Orders index, Schedule of leases from Samuel Worrall to Roach, Marriott, Hobbs and Willis in BRO 05503 (now lost)

11172/3, report to the Bristol Housing Reform Committee 1907

11284, Estate title deeds, sale of nos 38–40 College Street to the City of Bristol

12054[18, 23a], Estate title deeds, deeds for plot no. 20 College Street, exchange to the City of Bristol

12149, deeds and papers of the Worrall family

20940-1, Estate title deeds for nos 3–5 Deanery Road 1874, 1880, 1897, 1903 and 1904

34631(6)a, Deeds and papers, 1719–1851, of various properties in Bristol, Gloucestershire, Somerset and Ireland mainly concerning the Henwood and Bowyer families, mortgage agreement between Benjamin Tucker and Thomas Blatchley 1788

EP/E/3/1, Register of leases 1820–57 for nos 54 College Street and 55–56 (later 40 and 38) College Street

EP/E/4/3, Rental 1821, fol.2, Bishop's lease of the park to Worrall, 1770

EP/E/4/3, Rental 1821, fol.21, lease by Samuel Worrall to John Crouch of Hanham 1772

EP/E/4/3, Rental 1821 onwards, with schedule of properties including those in Limekiln Lane 1839 fols.228–35

EP/E/5/1, lease of part of the Episcopal estate, 1772, Bishop's lease of the Bishop's Park to Samuel Worrall

HLL (House of Lords Library):

Private Act, 10 George III, c.5

NMR (National Monuments Record):
Aerofilms 52883
Aerofilms P5447

Secondary sources

Alexander, M. and Harward, C. 2011 'Harbourside, Bristol: investigations from 2003–2006', in M. Watts (ed.) 2011, *Medieval and post-medieval development within Bristol's inner suburbs* Bristol and Gloucestershire Archaeol. Rep. 7, Cirencester, Cotswold Archaeology, 79–119

BaRAS 2005 (Bristol and Region Archaeological Service) 'Archaeological evaluation of land at Cabot House, Bristol', BaRAS unpublished report **1567**

BGS (British Geological Survey) 1996 *1:50,000 Geological Survey of Great Britain (England and Wales), Solid and Drift, map sheet 264: Bristol* Keyworth, British Geological Survey

Cox, S., Barber, A. and Collard, M. 2006 'The Archaeology and History of the Former Bryan Brothers' Garage Site, Deanery Road, Bristol: the evolution of an urban landscape', *Trans. Bristol Gloucestershire Archaeol. Soc.* **124**, 55–71

Ison, W. 1952 *The Georgian Buildings of Bristol* London, Faber and Faber

Leech, R.H. 2006 'The Bishop's Park', in S. Cox, A. Barber and M. Collard 2006, 67–70

Millerd, J. 1673 *An Exact Delineation of the Famous City of Bristol and Suburbs Thereof* Bristol

OS (Ordnance Survey) 1951 *1:2500 series, map sheet 31/5872*

Plumley J. and Ashmead G.C. 1828 *Plan of the City of Bristol and its Suburbs* Bristol, G.C. Ashmead

Ponsford, M.W. 1988 'Pottery', in B. Williams 1988, 'The excavation of medieval and post-medieval tenements at 94–102 Temple Street, Bristol, 1975', *Trans. Bristol Gloucestershire Archaeol. Soc.* **106**, 107–68

Ponsford, M.W. 1998 'Pottery', in R. Price with M.W. Ponsford 1998, *St Bartholomew's Hospital, Bristol: the excavation of a medieval hospital 1976–8* CBA Res. Rep. **110**, York, Council for British Archaeology

Ridgeway, V. and Watts, M. (eds) (forthcoming) *Cabot Circus, Bristol: the archaeology of the Broadmead expansion project, 2005–8* CAPCA monograph **1**, London, Cotswold Archaeology/Pre-Construct Archaeology

Rocque, J. 1743 *A Plan of the City of Bristol Survey'd and drawn by John Rocque Engrav'd by John Pine. 1742* Bristol, Hickey

Wilkinson, K.N. 2006 'Cabot House, Bristol: a geoarchaeological study of borehole stratigraphy', ARCA unpublished report **0506-3** (Department of Archaeology, University of Winchester)

Wilkinson, K.N. and Head, K. 2008 'Broadmead Development, Bristol: Geoarchaeology and Bioarchaeology Analytical Report', ARCA unpublished report **0809-3** (Department of Archaeology, University of Winchester)

Wilkinson, K.N. and Tinsley, H. 2005 'Harbourside Development Area, Bristol: the geoarchaeology of borehole stratigraphy', Archaeostrat. unpublished report **05/06-3**

Wilkinson, K.N., Cameron, N., Kreiser, A., Jones, J. and Tinsley, H. 2002 'Stratigraphy and palaeoenvironment of the Deanery Road site, Bristol', ArchaeoStrat. unpublished report

Winstone, R. 1969 *Bristol as it was 1953-1956* Bristol, Reece Winstone